Colonies and Colonial Federations

THE ENGLISH CITIZEN

HIS RIGHTS AND RESPONSIBILITIES

	Area. Sq. miles.	Population	Revenue	Expenditure	Debt
			£	£	£
I. United Kingdom [2]	121,027	42,372,556	151,551,698	184,483,708	798,349,190
II. India—British [3] .	1,087,404	231,898,807	76,344,525	71,394,282	229,686,346
Native States, &c. .	679,393	62,461,549	—	—	—
Total India .	1,766,797	294,360,356	76,344,525	71,394,282	229,686,346
III. Colonies with self-govt.: Australian Common- wealth—					
N.S. Wales . . .	310,700	1,359,133	12,486,575	12,348,359	66,108,359
Victoria . . .	87,884	1,201,341	8,049,168	8,329,115	50,408,957
Queensland . . .	668,497	496,596	4,242,295	4,674,234	39,387,177
S. Australia. . .	903,690	362,604	2,829,839	3,110,188	26,448,045
Western Australia .	975,920	184,124	3,936,926	3,694,363	14,942,310
Tasmania . . .	26,215	172,475	896,593	1,011,223	9,111,649
Total Common- wealth [6] .	2,972,906	3,776,273	32,441,396	33,167,482	206,406,497
New Zealand . . .	104,471	772,719	6,506,752	6,331,607	55,899,019
Cape Colony . . .	276,995	2,433,000	9,050,371	8,617,626	36,970,929
Natal . . .	36.170	925,118	3,439,820	3,097,601	12,519,143
Canada [5] . . .	3,619,820	5,371,315	11,932,662	10,596,488	75,307,020
Newfoundland and Labrador [5] . . .	162,734	220,249	450,891	470,641	4,038,595
Total with self-govt.	7,173,096	13,498,674	63,821,892	62,281,445	391,141,203
IV. Colonies with partial self-govt.:					
Malta . . .	117	184,742	445,065	439,562	79,168
Cyprus [8] . . .	3,584	237,022	160,112	232,514	—
Mauritius and depend- encies [3] . . .	729	375,882	609,383	602,871	1,182,984
Bermuda . . .	19	17,535	56,666	50,308	46,600
British Guiana [7] . .	109,000	293,958	557,351	501,704	991,320
Bahamas . . .	4,404	53,735	72,442	74,613	104,926
Barbados . . .	166	195,588	161,585	194,346	428,600
Jamaica and Turks Is. .	4,373	771,853	1,016,711	953,185	3,902,664
Leeward Islands . .	700	127,336	128,355	136,751	285,021
Trinidad and Tobago .	1,868	273,899	745,117	705,180	1,104,033
Windward Islands .	500	160,869	167,926	166,467	391,320
Total with partial self-govt. . .	125,460	2,692,419	4,120,713	4,057,501	8,426,636
V. Colonies without self- govt.:					
Gibraltar . . .	2	20,355	80,399	58,241	—
Ceylon [3] . . .	25,365	3,565,954	1,813,204	1,869,474	4,976,842
Straits Settlements [4]	1,472	572,249	661,020	650,201	—
Hong Kong [4] . .	30	297,142	359,800	351,140	341,800
Labuan [4] . . .	30	8,411	3,950	5,450	—
British New Guinea	90,540	350,000	16,868	31,346	2,378
Fiji . . .	7,740	120,124	132,513	113,341	191,255
Seychelles [3] . .	148	19,237	29,165	33,159	27,037
Orange River Colony	50,000	208,000	271,999	235,170	15,000
Transvaal . . .	111,700	1,000,000	3,141,119	2,963,622	2,500,000

(continued on following pp.)

[1] Including bullion and specie. [2] For the United Kingdom the population is that of dollar at 1s. 8½d. [5] The dollar at 4s. 1½d. The registered shipping of Canada includes state trade amounted in 1902 to 40,678,239l. for imports, and 43,915,227l. for exports. stated is exclusive of grant-in-aid (33,000l.): the expenditure is inclusive of tribute to

EMPIRE, 1902–1903.

Total Imports [1]	Total Exports [1]	Imports from U.K. [1]	Exports to U.K. [1]	Registered Tonnage		Tonnage entered and cleared	Railways. Miles
				Sailing	Steam		
£	£	£	£				
581;874,048	399,680,556	—	—	1,950,675	8,104.095	99,872,719	22,152
74,091,655	92,702,825	47,585,580	24,174,443	19,955	47,681	10,926,560	22,689
—	—	—	—	—	—	—	3,242
74,091,655	92,702,825	47,585,580	24,174,443	19,955	47,681	10,926,560	25,931
25,974,210	23,544,051	8,572,370	7,102,596	57,772	71,953	8,728,144	3,107
18,270,245	18,210,523	6,935,040	3,432,800	37,545	72,805	6,739,040	3,294
7,352,538	9,171,023	2,496,851	2,736,632	10,243	15,001	2,067,611	2.974
6,181,000	7,890,072	1,907,907	1,932,869	19,775	33,330	4,131,276	1,882
7,218,352	9,051,358	3,350,644	4,364,910	6,811	5,708	3,358,074	1,989
2,442,745	3,244,508	585,750	654,174	8,979	9,246	1,767,215	620
67,439,090	71,111,535	23,848,562	20,223,981	141,128	208,043	26,791,360	13,866
11,326,723	13,644,977	6,851,452	9,450,648	42,806	62,027	2,137,949	2,404
34,220,500	17,456,131	22,304,990	15,972,517	331	7,134	12,511,691	2,648
15,656,052	3,653,790	8,470,619	2,221,072	365	1,453	3,833,611	643
43,633,310	43,503,836	10,160,136	24,115,823	469,499	183,836	14,731,488	18,714
1,610,874	1,963,574	461,303	432,680	109,205	9,728	1,774,372	659
173,886,549	151,333,843	72,097,062	72,416,721	763,331	472,221	61,780,471	38,934
—	—	—	—	4,819	1,529	7,060,314	8
434,458	327,756	61,265	85,845	—	—	689,427	—
2,076,235	2,425,942	547,895	291,023	5,384	99	746,517	104
801,189	111,135	410,723	6,328	6,930	64	708,417	—
1,371,388	1,757,053	728,526	765,654	1,732	1,230	729,531	95
306,098	207,601	62,651	16,978			1,044,588	—
872,679	592,465	381,447	51,233			1,419,335	28
2,061,787	2,324,888	1,032,018	439,034	50,086	7,023	2,622,728	185
397,652	343,310	165,958	78,292			1,885,548	—
2,672,087	2,472,181	983,216	626,194			1,593,597	89
644,555	428,154	211,870	305,947			2,637,476	—
11,638,128	10,990,485	4,585,569	2,666,528	68,951	9,945	21,137,478	509
—	—	—	—	1,389	1,522	8,686,774	—
7,297,884	6,626,859	2,179,823	3,576,217	14,792	1,328	9,955,256	369
30,022,550	25,750,889	2,909,506	5,321,262	43,741	29,775	15,831,279	—
—	—	—	—	6,191	28,129	16,275,998	—
194,000	100,000	—	—	—	—	340,826	—
70,817	68,300	—	—	—	—	52,116	—
552,375	535,171	103,952	—	177	97	349,655	—
62,921	82,493	18,065	26,463	—	—	237,987	—
1,663,103	110,030	—	—	—	—	—	
14,972,925	7,431,632	5,818,691	—	—	—	—	1,335

1903 ; the commerce that of 1903 ; the shipping that of 1902.   [3] The rupee at 1s. 4d.   [4] The inland navigation.   [6] The trade of the Commonwealth of Australia (exclusive of Inter-[7] The dollar at 4s. 2d.   [8] Cyprus is only under British administration. The revenue here Turkey (92,000l.).

	Area Sq. miles	Population	Revenue	Expenditure	Debt.
			£	£	£
V. Colonies without self-govt.—(continued):					
Lagos	3,420	41,847	275,022	235,495	1,187,675
Gold Coast	71,300	1,379,000	511,503	522,608	2,082,718
Sierra Leone	4,000	76,655	205,765	184,939	589,448
Gambia	69	13,461	51,016	51,536	—
St. Helena	47	3,342	23,095	18,614	2,000
Ascension	35	400	—	—	—
British Honduras [2]	7,562	37,479	53,362	51,850	34,736
Falkland Islands and S. Georgia	7,500	2,050	16,070	14,790	—
Total without self-govt.	380,566	7,715,706	7,645,870	7,390 976	11,959,889
VI. Administered under Charter:					
British North Borneo [3]	34,000	200,000	70,900	137,680	—
Rhodesia	580,000	1,000,000	586,144	933,217	—
Total under companies	614,000	1,200,000	655,044	1,170,897	—
VII. Protectorates and other Possessions :					
Federated Malay States	26,960	735,000	1,757,580	1,362,150	3,152,120
Hong Kong leased territory	376	102,250	—	—	—
Wei-hai-wei	285	124,000	2,600	16,000	—
Sarawak [3]	50,000	600,000	102,200	97,300	—
Tonga and Pacific Islands	800	30,000	—	—	—
Basutoland	10,293	330,000	101,400	76,300	—
Bechuanaland	380,000	130,000	30,931	78,590	—
Central African Protectorate	42,217	970,000	70,164	107,256	—
East African Protectorate	200,000	4,000,000	95,284	294,869	—
Uganda	86,000	4,000,000	54,711	217,297	—
Zanzibar Protectorate [4]	1,020	200,000	148,112	140,119	—
Northern Nigeria	323,000	20,000,000	—	300,000	—
Southern Nigeria	49,700	—	440,809	455,294	—
Lagos Protectorate	23,280	1,024,300	—	—	—
Gold Coast Protectorate	48,000	107,500	8,000	52,000	—
Sierra Leone Protectorate	30,000	—	37,743	27,734	—
Gambia Protectorate	3,550	90,350	—	—	—
Somaliland Protectorate	60,000	153,000	37,452	69,831	100,000
Total Protectorates, &c.	1,335,481	32,596,400	2,886,986	3,294,740	3,252,120
SUMMARY.					
I. United Kingdom	121,027	42,372,556	151,551,698	184,483,708	798,349,190
II. India	1,766,797	294,360,356	76,344,525	71,394,282	229,686,346
III Colonies with self-govt.	7,173,096	13,498,674	63,821,892	62,281,445	391,141,203
IV. Colonies with partial self-govt.	125,460	2,692,419	4,120,713	4,057,501	8,426,636
V. Colonies without self-govt.	380,960	7,715,706	7,645,870	7,390,976	11,959,889
VI. Ter. administered under Charter	614,000	1,200,000	655,044	1,170,897	—
VII. Protectorates, &c.	1,335,481	32,596,400	2,886,986	3,294,740	3,252,120
Total British Empire	11,516,821	394,436,111	307,026,728	334,073,549	1,442,815,384

1 Including bullion and specie.   2 The dollar at 4s. 1½d.

Total Imports [1]	Total Exports [1]	Imports from U.K.[1]	Exports to U.K [1]	Registered Tonnage		Tonnage entered and cleared	Railways Miles
				Sailing	Steam		
£	£	£	£				
930,745	1,259,683	572,350	285,711	⎱	⎱	⎧ 1,144,457	124
2,120,433	774,186	1,550,607	339,463			1,696,451	87
625,935	403,518	455,922	123,272	⎰ 1 538	⎰ 132	1,467,988	76
303,615	248,140	136,326	18,759	⎰		⎩ 286,878	—
100,478	1,755	93,920	1,168	—	—	234,443	—
—	—	—	—	—	—	—	—
252,382	280,010	69,334	85,771	4,686	1,326	416,420	—
63,851	90,838	56,852	90,838	198	—	202,546	—
59,234,014	43,763,504	13,956,348	9,868,924	72,712	62,309	57,179,074	1,991
326,370	313,540	—	—	—	—	218,240	100
1,443,053	679,600	—	—	—	—	—	586
1,769,423	993,140	—	—	—	—	218,240	686
3,661,130	6,094,100	—	—	—	—	1,390,867	300
—	—	—	—	—	—	—	—
—	—	—	—	—	—	—	—
413,600	580,430	—	—	—	—	111,976	—
—	—	—	—	—	—	—	—
—	259,000	—	—	—	—	—	—
—	—	—	—	—	—	—	—
153,990	34,765	125,698	28,097	—	—	—	—
443,032	165,060	126,050	59,509	—	—	—	584
62,537	32,179	27,974	—	—	—	—	—
1,106,247	1,080,277	156,503	90,852	—	—	705,500	—
59,048	68,442	—	—	—	—	—	—
1,246,481	1,254,696	1,004,959	820,058	—	—	584,500	—
—	—	—	—	—	—	—	—
—	—	—	—	—	—	—	—
—	—	—	—	—	—	—	—
355,175	348,920	—	—	—	—	84,180	—
7,501,240	9,917,869	1,441,184	988,516	—	—	2,877,023	884
581,874,040	399,680,556	—	—	1,950,675	8,104,095	99,872,719	22,152
74,091,655	92,702,825	47,585,580	24,174,443	19,955	47,681	10,926,560	25,931
173,886,549	151,333,843	72,097,062	72,416,721	763,331	472,221	61,780,471	38,934
11,638,128	10,990,485	4,585,569	2,666,528	68,951	9,945	21,137,478	509
59,234,014	43,763,504	13,956,348	9,868,924	72,712	62,309	57,179,074	1,991
1,769,423	993,140	—	—	—	—	218,240	686
7,501,240	9,917,869	1,441,184	988,516	—	—	2,877,023	834
909,995,049	709,382,222	139,665,743	110,115,132	2,875,624	8,695,251	253,991,565	91,087

[3] The dollar at 1s. 8½d.   [4] The rupee at 1s. 4d.

COLONIES

AND

COLONIAL FEDERATIONS

BY

E. J. PAYNE

FELLOW OF UNIVERSITY COLLEGE, OXFORD

London

MACMILLAN AND CO., LIMITED

NEW YORK : THE MACMILLAN COMPANY

1904

PREFACE

In the original issue of *The English Citizen* a single volume, entitled "Colonies and Dependencies," was devoted to Imperial relations, and most of the space was taken up by the Indian Empire, less than eighty pages being allotted to the Colonies and Colonial questions. Much of what was then written has by this time become obsolete, and in view of the greatly increased importance of the Colonies, the deeper interest which recent events have aroused in all that concerns them, and the gravity of the issues pending in connection with them, it has been decided to deal with them separately, and in a volume of larger compass. With the object of conveying a more vivid impression of the subject in its various aspects the writer has in each chapter approached it from a different point of view. It is hoped that by passing from one point of view to another the reader will be enabled to form a better idea of the Empire as a living and working whole, destined to cohesion and co-operation, and probably to a greater future than can be foreseen under the imperfect conditions of to-day.

London, *September* 1904.

CONTENTS

CHAPTER I

GEOGRAPHICAL

CHAPTER II

HISTORICAL

CHAPTER III

ECONOMIC

CHAPTER IV

POLITICAL

MAPS

* From *The Statesman's Year-Book*, 1904 (by J. Scott Keltie, LL.D.).

CHAPTER I

GEOGRAPHICAL

COMPILERS of geographical manuals assure us that the Britannic Empire, comprising the British Isles, British India, and the Colonies and Federations treated of in the present volume, has a larger area and population than either Russia or the United States of America—which two Powers rank in these respects next after it; that it includes nearly one quarter of the geographic land surface, more than one-sixth of the inhabitable surface, and a larger proportionate part of the inhabitants, of the globe,—facts capable of being stated in another form by saying that if the Empire, together with a marine area similarly proportionate to the total marine area of the globe, could be constituted as a separate planet, such a planet would be of size intermediate between Mercury and Mars, and would have a population comparatively denser than that of the earth; that Canada alone is nearly as large as Europe, and thirty times as large as the United Kingdom; that Australia and New Zealand together are larger than Canada; that the British Asiatic provinces are nearly half as large as Europe, and contain a population more

B

than three-fourths that of Europe; and much more to
the same effect.   Large allowances of various kinds must
be made before drawing any conclusions from any such
comparisons.   The distinctive eminence and character of
the Britannic Empire depend less on advantages capable
of expression in figures than on special circumstances of
position and distribution; on its traditions of a great
historic past, and anticipations, amounting to certainty,
of a greater future; on the singular energy with which
its economic resources have been and are being developed; on the varied individuality, in their social
and political aspects, of the members which compose it;
and on a pervading and sustaining sense of cohesion
among those members, inspired partly by common
interests, partly by participation in the blessings of
order and liberty derived from a common source, and
partly by consciousness of the weight which their
union gives them collectively in the affairs of the world
at large.   In the present volume we shall contemplate
it chiefly in these special aspects; and the first fact
which arrests attention is that its territory, unlike that
of the other Powers above mentioned, is distributed on
most of the world's great maritime highways, occupies
advantageous positions on those highways, and is
united by them into a continuous whole.

Besides many islands, parts of islands, groups of
islands, and most of that vast aggregate of island groups
called Polynesia, the Britannic Empire includes one
continent, and portions of all the others.   It includes
a small fraction of continental Europe, and a large part
of Asia; a larger holding in Africa, and a still larger
one in America; all Australia is Britannic soil.   Com-

pared with these dispersed and apparently disconnected territories, the vast and compact dominions of Russia, and of the United States, appear like results of geographical accident rather than conscious and voluntary enterprise. Given an aggressive nation established in Eastern Europe from Archangel to Moscow and the River Don, urged to aggrandisement under ambitious sovereigns, with unstable Powers on one side and Tartar hordes on the other—and the Russian Empire, stretching from the Baltic to the Pacific, follows almost as a matter of course. Given thirteen vigorous English colonies, newly stimulated by federal union and successful war, with the Atlantic on one side, wandering Indians on the other, diplomatists shrewd enough to seize every favourable opportunity for extension—whether by timely bargain, as in the case of "Louisiana" (meaning the vast tract between the Mississippi and the Rocky Mountains), or by secret intrigue and overt filibustering, as in that of Texas, or by forced sale after invasion, as in that of Utah, New Mexico, and California,—and the empire of the United States, stretching from the Atlantic to the Pacific, follows absolutely as a matter of course. Given the island of Britain, with a disaffected dependency on the west, an envious rival, sometimes ally, sometimes enemy, on the east, and two formidable foes, each, in its turn, the most powerful of European monarchies, on the south—and the Britannic Empire certainly does not follow as a matter of course. What might be expected to follow is that England's enemies would do their best to stifle her energy of enterprise, to cripple her commerce, to crush her naval power, and to undermine her independence; and would join hands for that purpose whenever opportunity served. And that is precisely what has happened. But for external pressure of this kind—continued from one quarter or another with little remission or intermission from the accession of Elizabeth to Waterloo, and the indomitable resistance, promptly transformed into an irresistible counterpressure, which it continuously provoked—there would certainly have been no Britannic Empire on anything like the present scale. Possibly by this time there might have been none at all, and Britain might have figured in history on no larger scale than the kingdoms of Scandinavia. Probably there would have been a colonial system of some kind, extending, like that of Holland, both to the East and the West, but of larger area, although not including Canada, Australia, or British Africa.

Owing to the insulation of Britain, her territorial extension could only be transoceanic ; and as her enemies were before her in the transoceanic field it was for her to follow them, and, so far as might be necessary for her protection, to expel them from it, or at least to prevent them from extending their positions, or from otherwise hampering her own transoceanic enterprises. Was England strong enough, at home and on sea, to accomplish such a task ? Spain in the sixteenth and seventeenth centuries, Holland and France in the seventeenth, France and Spain united in the eighteenth, found by experience that she was more than adequate to it ; and among her own sons there was never a doubt of this from the first. From the moment when hostile pressure was first felt from without, and resistance and counterpressure were provoked from within, the Britannic Empire began to take shape.

Only once—when her American colonists revolted and accepted the aid of her enemies—has its growth been arrested; and this momentary arrest did but direct an ever-increasing force into new channels of action. The loss of the United States at once produced the development of Canada, and the colonisation of Australia.

To explain that power of commanding the ocean which enabled Britain to found a Britannic Empire we must again seek light from physical geography. This power originated in the aggressive force of ocean itself. "Nowhere," says Tacitus, "does the sea dominate more extensively, forcing back and forth the waters of many rivers; nor does it merely swell upon and retreat from the shore—it invades and environs the land, plunging among the hills and mountains as if they were its own." When the Roman legions had been withdrawn this restless ocean, invading Britain through its estuaries, changed the destiny of the island. It bore on its tide swarms of "Jutes," "Angles," and "Saxons" from the opposite shore, already masters of its navigation through long practice on the most tempestuous of its arms. For centuries these tribes had infested the south and east coasts of Britain as marauders. The withdrawal of the legions brought them in greater numbers under a new guise; they posed as protectors of Romanised Britons against invaders by land from the north. In Britain, with its cattle, its corn, its timber, its minerals, its fisheries, its hundred ports, and its abundant supply of native labour, the newcomers found a richer economic basis, and an ampler and more advantageous field for the development of maritime enterprise, than they had enjoyed at home; and the new English nation, compounded of many elements, did more than merely hold its own against its continental neighbours. It claimed, as part of its dominion, the marine areas bordering on its shores ; and events proved it to be ripe and ready for transoceanic enterprise some years before Colombo's discovery of America.

Such power at sea no other people possessed except the Northmen, to whom the English were indebted for the first awakening of their energy of resistance on land and sea under Alfred. A compromise was made with the new invaders, authorising a partial settlement which brought a vigorous strain into the blood of the race, and added to English maritime skill and experience. The Northmen were the first European discoverers of America. Had they possessed in their homeland an ampler economic basis, a disposition to trade rather than to plunder, and a situation more favourable to distributive commerce, they might perhaps have been the founders of a colonial empire. The poverty of their homeland having driven them forth to seek new countries, they spent most of their energy of enterprise in other parts of Europe ; the commerce which they might have engrossed fell into the grasp of the Hanse Towns ; they must, in any case, have lacked the energy of resistance and counterpressure aroused in England by the pretensions and policy of Spain and France—an energy far more powerful than those of voluntary enterprise and deliberate aggression. England had been internally consolidated, had conquered Wales, and secured her hold on Ireland long before France and Spain took their places as consolidated Powers. They were still loose aggregates of small kingdoms and provinces under various families. So long as English kings held Normandy and Aquitaine, French enterprise on the ocean was confined to Breton fishermen. In Spain only the Gallegos and Biscayans navigated the Atlantic. Portugal, and the kingdoms and provinces on the Mediterranean coast of France and Spain, barely held their ground against the Moors. When Ferdinand and Isabella set about creating a navy, their shipbuilders, ships' officers, and, to a large extent, their ships' crews, were Genoese. Before Charles V. England commanded the ocean; the ambitious designs of his successor involved depriving her of a primacy which Englishmen in general regarded as a national right.

On the Netherlanders, the only other stock capable of maintaining itself on the Atlantic, the hand of Spain had fallen with crushing force when it was first raised in idle menace against England. England helped the Dutch with money and men; and when the independence of the Seven United Provinces was achieved the Dutch displayed great enterprise and ability as seamen and traders both in the East and the West. Until the Navigation Acts of 1651 and 1661 ousted them from the British carrying trade, of which they had almost obtained a monopoly, it seemed as if the world's commerce was destined to be theirs. From that time the prospects of Holland as a competitor with England and France for commercial and colonial supremacy became clouded; and when in 1780 the Republic practically threw in its lot with France and Spain, it had lost the power of independent action. In the period which followed it became a mere tool in the hands of France; and by the settlement made after

Waterloo, Holland was definitively deprived of the Cape
and Ceylon, and with them of its only chances of ever regaining its position in the colonial world.   Full value was
given by Britain, in that settlement, for these provinces ;
Java also, captured by Britain in 1811, and retained
under British government during seven years, was
restored to the Dutch, much to the chagrin and the
moral and economic disadvantage of its inhabitants.
The value of Java as a colonial possession dates from
its administration as a British dependency under Sir
Stamford Raffles.

Although the imperial career of Britain began after
England and Scotland had become vested in the same
crown, England had long been indicated, both at home
and abroad, as the imperial power of the future.   In
virtue of her primacy on the ocean, Bacon prophesied
that the Eastern and Western fields of enterprise,
temporarily grasped by Spain, must alike ultimately
fall to the English race.   Shakespeare more emphatically
expressed contemporary belief by the person of Cranmer,
who prophesies of new nations to be founded under the
first sovereign of united Britain.   British history has
been in the main a continuous fulfilment of these
prophecies.   Yet the Empire is not wholly the result of
piecemeal accretion by maritime effort.   In almost every
part it exhibits the same process of natural territorial
extension from a given basis which has expanded the
principality of Muscovy into the empire of Russia, and
the Thirteen Colonies on the Atlantic into the empire
of the United States.   British India, Canada, Australia,
and South Africa are the most prominent instances of
continental extension ; Western Africa and the Straits

Settlements illustrate it in a minor degree. Maritime by origin, and distributed, in early stages, on the world's maritime highways, the Empire has in later stages obeyed the same law of development as continental states; and this continental character, superinduced on an essentially maritime fabric, has been realised on a large scale in four distant continents. There are those who argue that the advantages of dispersion and distribution are outweighed by their disadvantages, and that Russia and the United States, with their vast unity and compactness of territory, are on the whole better off; and this objection is usually reinforced by auguries of the insecurity and transitoriness of maritime empire, drawn from the examples of Athens and Carthage, of Venice and Spain, of Portugal and Holland, and of Britain herself 125 years ago. Equally pertinent illustrations of the fate which impends over compact and self-contained continental empires, however vast and populous, might be drawn from history, and illustrated by the plight of modern China. Probably every large self-contained continental state tends to become, in the course of centuries, what China now is.[1] The sense of economic self-sufficiency and unchecked political power within wide limits, whether such power be vested in an emperor or in a federal government, especially if there be added a rooted conviction of some superiority inherent in themselves on the part of the people thus circumstanced, cannot but be fraught, for such a people, with insidious peril of a serious kind. The composite character of the Britannic Empire — both maritime

[1] Palmerston used to call a certain empire "European China."

and continental — secures it alike against this peril, and against that which threatens all merely maritime empires having no separate centres of vitality in their outlying possessions. That elastic energy which in past times carried the English along the world's highways, and secured them advantageous positions and enormous holdings in remote continents, everywhere persists as a circulating or commercial energy, an economic or resource-developing energy, and a political or dominating energy. It has gained in intensity as it has advanced by diffusion ; it has found new centres of action, created new forms of Britannic nationality, and accumulated reserves of economic and political force at many seats of commerce and government. It has swept less energetic races into its channels of activity, carried them with it, challenged them to earn the rewards of labour, conferred on them the blessings of ordered liberty, shown them a higher standard of life and duty, and taught them to respect themselves as Britannic citizens, scarcely less the children of Britain than Britons themselves. In all this, British enterprise has used pre-existing systems of maritime communication as bases, improved, extended, and completed them, found new points of departure on them, travelled far away from them, across and around ocean and continent alike, and by this means, at the same time, enlarged and consolidated the Empire. Australasia and British Polynesia on the ocean, the Dominion of Canada and British Africa on land, prominently illustrate these ultimate phases of colonial activity.

Of the world's maritime highways the most ancient, the most frequented, and the most important, measured by the economic rank of the nations which communicate by means of it, is the great central route of the Old World—the highway from the European West to the Far East by way of the Mediterranean, the Red Sea, the Indian Ocean, and the China Sea. A majority of the human race dwell on or close by this route. Commerce and colonisation, the twin agencies which have transformed the world, began their career by discovering this route, in its two sections, western and eastern. All other maritime routes are either tributary to it, substitutes for it, or extensions of it. Tributary to it are the route from Northern Europe by the North Sea, English Channel, and Bay of Biscay to Gibraltar; the Adriatic, which joined it with Venice; the Euxine and Ægean; the Persian Gulf, and the coast route of Eastern Africa. The route from Western Europe to India, round the Cape of Good Hope, was opened by the Portuguese in the fifteenth century as a substitute for it. The route from Europe to the New World was designed by Colombo, its first successful explorer, as an alternative substitute. This route was unexpectedly found to be an extension of it, in the direction of a continent hitherto unknown; and this extension, once effected, naturally produced a farther extension from the New World to the Far East of Asia, whereby for the first time human enterprise engirdled the globe.

Until 1869, when the Suez Canal was opened for traffic, the great central highway consisted of two separate sections. Maritime enterprise had been practised in each of these sections—the Mediterranean and its tributary seas in the west, and the Indian Ocean in the east, for at least 2500 years before the Portuguese, in 1500, made good their substituted route round the Cape of Good Hope.   In the eastern section, bordered by the ancient civilisations of Arabia, Babylonia, Persia, India, and China, maritime commerce and colonisation had their beginnings.   The movement was begun by the Semitic tribes of the Persian Gulf [1] and the Red Sea. By their voyages through the "Seven Seas" of Asia, [2] and their settlements in Eastern Africa, Western India, the Malay Peninsula, and the delta of Cochin-China, adventurers of these tribes founded an extensive system of commercial intercourse closely corresponding with the eastern front of the Britannic Empire of to-day. Emigrants of these tribes crossed the mainland to the Mediterranean, settled in Phœnicia and Cyprus, and carried commerce and colonisation along the western section of the great central highway as far as the Pillars of Hercules.   These two isolated fields of maritime activity were connected by several lines of overland traffic ; and the two sections of the great central tradeway, thus united, served the purposes of the world's commerce until the occupation of Syria and Egypt by Mohammadans.   This occupation produced the Crusades, and through the Crusades a development of the maritime power of Portugal at the expense of the Mohammadans of North-West Africa.   The last phase of this anti-Mohammadan movement was the daring and successful attempt of the Portuguese to establish an alternative route round the Cape of Good

[1] The earliest known seat of the "Phœnicians" was the Bahrein Islands.

[2] The "Seven Seas" were seven divisions of the Indian Ocean adjacent to the Asiatic coast, from the Persian Gulf to the China Sea. To each a distinctive name was given by the Arab geographers.

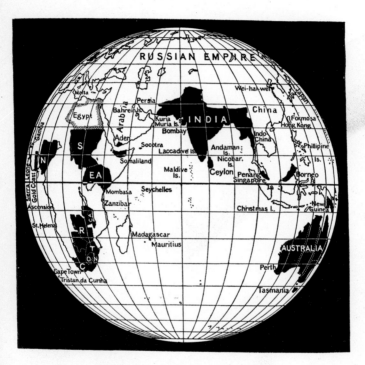

HEMISPHERE OF THE OLD WORLD.—P. 12.

Hope, and by this means to divert the commerce of the East for their own benefit.

During the first eighty years of the sixteenth century, while Spanish predominance in the American seas was openly challenged by France and England, Portugal enjoyed an undisturbed monopoly of so much of the Eastern trade as passed round the Cape. Spain, having annexed Portugal in 1580, succeeded to this monopoly, and quickly lost it; for during this period the Dutch, English, and French, taking advantage of the proved weakness of Spain on the Atlantic Ocean, forced their way into the eastern seas also, establishing factories and acquiring territory, partly at the expense of native sovereigns, partly of resident Arab traders, and partly of their Spanish and Portuguese rivals. The Eastern trade with Western Europe now rapidly increased in importance; and ultimately in the nineteenth century an immense development of steam navigation, the consolidation of the British Empire in India, the extinction of the East India Company's monopoly, the steady growth of the China trade, the successful colonisation of Australia and New Zealand, and the opening of Japan combined to make the construction of the Suez Canal a mere question of time. In 1869 the Canal was opened, and the world's central highway thereby completed as a water-way from end to end.

The route from Europe to the New World, designed by the seaman who was its first successful explorer as a second alternative to the central highway of the Old World, became an extension of the latter highway. During the Spanish ascendancy, when America, north of Mexico, was little known, and commerce was mainly concerned with the West Indian Islands, Mexico, and Peru, this route began at Seville, passing by the Canaries to St. Domingo and Cuba. Here it bifurcated, one branch leading to the Mexican port of Vera Cruz, the other to Puerto Bello on the Isthmus of Panama. From each of these marine termini a land route led to the Pacific. From Puerto Bello the isthmus road reached the port of Panama, whence a merely local maritime highway followed the western shore of South America, serving the commerce of Peru and Chile, and having an alternative homeward course still farther southward by the Strait of Magellan or Cape Horn, and the coast of Brazil. The land route from Vera Cruz passed through the city of Mexico to Acapulco on the Pacific ; and from this port a course across the world's greatest ocean, traversing about one-third of the earth's circumference in the vicinity of the northern tropic, terminated at the Philippine Islands, on the eastern margin of the China Sea. Thus was the circuit of the earth completed.

But for the vicissitudes of states and kingdoms the whole of this route—a modern one in its entire length from the European West to America, across America, and from America to Eastern Asia—would have been absolutely controlled by the Power which established it. But the misfortunes of Spain encouraged the French, English, and Dutch to dispute successfully her monopoly of the route across the Atlantic to the West Indian Islands, and to establish themselves permanently in those minor islands which the Spaniards had left unconquered. The Spanish conquests and settlements extended no farther north than the Gulf of Mexico. Beyond this point, North America lay at the disposal of Spain's competitors ;

and it was inferred from what was known of its configuration that a shorter and wholly maritime route from the European West to Eastern Asia might be found by rounding its northern shores. An Englishman began the quest of a North-West Passage (1576). Had a practicable passage existed in this direction England, France, and the Netherlands would have secured a much shorter route to the Far East than either of the routes traversing the Indian Ocean. During two and a half centuries the quest employed English seamen, only to be proved fruitless. Just as the impracticability of the Arctic passage as a North-Western route to the East was finally demonstrated, an English invention practically superseded it. When Parry in 1825 returned from his third and last expedition in search of it, the first railway for the carriage of goods and passengers by steam traction, designed by Stephenson, had just been opened. Nothing more convincingly illustrates the law that Imperial development depends on facility of movement than the transformation wrought throughout the Empire by the combined effect of the ocean steamer, the steam-railway, and the electric telegraph. In the old countries of Europe and Asia these inventions, influential as they have been, merely replaced, or supplemented and developed, facilities which had existed from remote times. New countries may be truly said to have been created by them. While the organic development of the Empire depends on ocean navigation, that of its great continental members depends on the extension of railways; but in British North America, by a marvellous coincidence, the great economic necessity of the Canadian Dominion is at a momentous

juncture the imperative necessity of the Empire. Without cheap and speedy railway carriage from the Atlantic
to the Pacific the Dominion could not be fully opened
to agriculture, nor could its superabundant produce be
brought to the best markets—those of the parent
country on the one hand, and of the Far East on the
other. Without such facilities, for want of a maritime
North-West Passage, the chain of connection which unifies
the Empire would remain incomplete. Without a railway
passing through the Dominion's middle zone, near the
south end of Hudson Bay and the north end of Lake
Winnipeg, and terminating opposite Dixon Entrance, the
strait separating the Queen Charlotte Islands, belonging
to Canada, from Prince of Wales's Island, belonging to
the States as the southernmost part of the Alaska purchase, the Imperial strategic base must remain, as it
remains at the present moment, conspicuously defective.
Such a railway alone could countervail the advantage
recently gained by Russia on the Pacific, in virtue of her
trans-Asiatic railway to Dalny and Port Arthur.[1]

The Dominion owes its existing transcontinental railway to the example of the States. The continent
immensely broadens northwards from the Gulf of
Mexico, and is bisected in the same direction by a
chain of lofty mountains; and although the development of California, the settlement of the vast vacant
tracts dividing it from the middle and eastern States,
and the force of economic consolidation, would doubtless
in time have led to transcontinental intercommunication
by railway, such a consummation must have been long

[1] Such a railway, it will presently appear, has been authorised and
commenced.

delayed, but for imperative demands of national policy and considerations of strategic necessity at a critical moment. In the latest stage of the Civil War, when there were doubts as to the loyalty of the Pacific states to the Union, the completion of railway communication from east to west was pushed forward as a measure of national safety; and in the same year (1869) which saw the opening of the Suez Canal a transcontinental service was opened from New York to San Francisco. Its economic success was the signal for other similar undertakings; and six transcontinental railways are now open in the States alone. The supreme importance of through communication in the development of the American interior having been demonstrated, public opinion and enterprise in Canada were stimulated to the provision of a transcontinental service for British North America as a condition necessary to the incorporation of its provinces in a single confederation. The Canadian Pacific Railway was opened in 1886 from Montreal to Vancouver. It afforded, by means of a line of steamships provided by the railway company, a passage shorter by 530 miles at the least from Liverpool to Eastern Asia than the shortest possible route through the States; and Great Britain now possessed for the first time a westward route to the Far East passing over nothing but the ocean and British soil.[1] This new railway, compensating for the want of a North-West Passage by sea, was in the nature of a North-West Passage by

[1] This "all-British" route, however, is only practicable during about two-thirds of the year. During four or five months, the Canadian-Pacific, if it carried its ordinary traffic, would have to send it across the State of Maine to St. John, New Brunswick. During these months, however, most of the Canadian traffic is diverted, being conveyed through Boston or New York.

land ; and a still closer approximation to the supposed
line of the North-West Passage was to follow. The
Canadian Pacific, running near the southern fringe of
British North America, having enormously contributed
to the settlement and development of the tract which
it traverses, it became apparent that another transcontinental route was needed farther to the north ; and
less than ten years from the opening of the Canadian
Pacific a second railway was authorised, having two
starting - points — one at Quebec, the other at the
port of Chicoutimi on the Saguenay River, passing
near the southern shore of Hudson Bay and the
northern shore of Lake Winnipeg, piercing the immense
and fertile agricultural tracts of North-West Canada,
and terminating at Port Simpson on the Pacific. This
railway, called the Trans-Canada, has been commenced
at the eastern end, but remains incomplete. The Grand
Trunk Company, also, has been empowered to extend
its line from Lake Superior to Port Simpson ; and in
any case, the time should not be distant when there will
be two transcontinental railways on British-American
soil, making, together with those traversing the States,
no less than eight through routes of communication
between the Atlantic and Pacific Oceans across the broad
expanse of the American continent. It is by no mere
figure of speech that these trans-American railways are
ranked as belonging to the system of the world's
maritime highways. Although brought into existence
by the internal needs of a continent, and taking their
direction from east to west by the force of geographical
necessity, the shipping trade of the harbours which they
unite is largely under the control of those who own

them, and from an economic point of view these harbours have altogether lost their terminal character.
Steamships controlled by the railway companies transport across the ocean the freights which the railways
transport across the land, and the maritime highways
to the New World practically form prolongations of the
New World's railways. The trans-Canadian railway
system thus constitutes a "North-West Passage by
Land," and completes that circuit of the globe, maritime
in the rest of its length, on which the Empire has
been developed. From the Imperial point of view this
system remains imperfect while the Trans-Canada railway remains unfinished. The Canadian Pacific, skirting
the southern fringe of the Dominion, and closely
implicated with the railway system of the States, has
other defects impairing its value as an Imperial route.
Crossing the Rockies by a pass 5400 ft. high, the cheap
food-products of the Dominion cannot be carried over
it, at remunerative rates, to what might be their best
markets—the populous nations of the Far East. As a
mail route, the Trans-Canada, crossing by a pass 2000 ft.
high, and terminating in a shorter passage across the
Pacific, will have an advantage over it of three days.
As a strategic route, men and munitions of war could be
carried from Britain over this route to Japan or Shanghai
a week earlier than by the Canadian Pacific. This railway
seems indispensable to the unification and commercial
development of the Empire. As no other scheme can
take the place which the Trans-Canada has been
designed to fill, it is an Imperial necessity that it should
be completed with all possible expedition.

From the termini of the trans-American railways the

world's principal highway sweeps by many converging
ocean routes across the Pacific to Japan, completing
the circuit of the globe by regaining the coast of
China. In this section, it passes no Britannic territory.
The Aleutian Islands, which any course from British
Columbia in the direction of the ports of Eastern Asia
necessarily passes at no great distance on the right, belong
to the States, as do the Sandwich Islands, lying far to
the left; the Kurile Islands, farther on the right,
belong to Japan. No part of the world's chief highway shows a greater vacant interval in the chain of
Britannic territory; but it is not the fact, as is sometimes alleged, that the islands passed on the route
between British Columbia and Japan offer no site worth
settling upon; and by arrangement with the States an
improvable harbour in one of them might probably be
obtained, and a coaling station, equally valuable to the
States, Japan, and Britain, be established. Such a
station, if leased to Britain, would complete the chain
of Britannic territory extending from British Columbia
in the west to Northern China in the east, along the
great highway of the habitable world — the Canadian
Dominion, Newfoundland, the British Isles, Gibraltar,
Malta, Cyprus, Aden, British Somaliland, British India
and Burmah, Ceylon, the Straits Settlements, British
Borneo, Hong-Kong, and Wei-hai-wei. It is noticeable
that the chief gaps in the chain are filled up by possessions belonging to nations in permanent alliance of a
more or less intimate kind with Britain,—to Portugal,
Egypt, Abyssinia, Siam, and Japan—and by the trans-
marine possessions of the States, notably the Philippines.
The members of the Empire adjacent to the great

encircling highway of the globe include about half of
the Empire's area, and four-fifths of its population.

Could a spectator be endowed with telescopic vision,
and enabled to ascend to some fixed point between earth
and sun sufficiently elevated to permit him to behold
the revolving globe, and thence to contemplate during
twenty-four hours the Empire's commerce moving in
its principal orbit along this encircling highway, he
would notice that during the first eight hours, from
Britain to Vancouver, the highway lies nearly beneath
his feet, traversing latitudes varying little from that
of Britain—that is, nearly parallel to the equator,
and about 50 degrees distant from it; that during the
next eight hours it takes a south-westward direction,
approaching the equator, moving farther and farther
from his ken, crossing the tropic off the coast of China,
and nearly touching the equator at Singapore; and
that during the remaining eight hours it returns north-
westwards, gradually regaining its original latitude,
recrossing the tropic in the Red Sea, and sharply turning to the north round south-west Europe. Its whole
course lies in the northern hemisphere, most of the
course outside the northern tropic, and not much of that
half of the Empire adjacent to it lies within the
equatorial zone.

The rest of the Empire lies south of this great encircling highway, for the most part south of the Tropic
of Cancer, and is approached by branches of the principal
highway. One of these is of immemorial antiquity;
the rest have been opened since the beginning of the
fifteenth century by Spanish, Portuguese, and Dutch seamen, and brought to completion by British exploration in

times comparatively modern. Excepting the West Indies, and the West African colonies formerly held for the purposes of the West Indian slave trade, this southern area represents a growth of British enterprise recent in its origin, hitherto extremely rapid in its development, and full of extraordinary possibilities in the near as well as the remote future. These possibilities, it must be admitted, are attended with some uncertainties. In contemplating the great continuous chain of the Britannic position throughout the northern hemisphere we are tolerably sure of our ground, and can make forecasts in the light of a large series of facts, events, and experiences. Looking at the adjoining United States on the one hand, and the more distant but not very remote parent country, on the other—both countries abounding in capital and labour, and equally interested in the welfare of the Dominion—we can have no doubt as to the future of Canada. We are tolerably sure of our position throughout Africa, and on the northern shores of the Indian Ocean. Can as much be said of Australasia? This question will be touched upon in our concluding chapter.

Hitherto the world's great maritime highway has been considered in its existing aspect—an aspect dating from the year 1869, and only likely to be maintained in times of peace between the European Powers. Prior to 1869 the maritime highway from the European West to the Far East crossed the equatorial zone, rounded the Cape of Good Hope, and again crossed the equator, in the reverse direction. By the "Overland" route, established in 1837, mails were carried across Egypt from Alexandria to Suez, and thence by ship to India and the Far East; and shortly afterwards the Peninsular and Oriental

Company began to carry mails and passengers from
England along the entire great central route. But
general commerce with the Far East took the Cape route.
At any moment it may be compelled to take it again;
for although the Suez Canal is open by treaty to men-
of-war of all Powers, alike in war and peace, it would
be liable to closure in time of war. The principal
strategic front of the Britannic Empire stretches from
South Africa in the south-west—where it has one of
its strongest and most important maritime bases—to
Japan in the north-east; and were Britain at war with
Powers having bases on the Mediterranean, the practical
closure of the Suez Canal, which bisects her strategic
front, and the restoration of the conditions existing
before 1869, must be considered an extremely probable
consequence. We have therefore to consider the
world's great maritime highway in this altered aspect—
immensely prolonged in linear extent by environing
the African continent from the Pillars of Hercules in
the west to Somaliland in the east. From our original
point of view, this prolongation may be considered as a
pair of supplementary routes branching southward from
the great highway, one commencing off the coast of
Morocco, the other off Somaliland—and converging on
the southern coast of Cape Colony.

The latter of these branch routes is the older and
the more important. Long before the Indian Ocean
was entered by Western navigators, much longer before
the islands flanking it on the east were delineated with
any approach to accuracy, and ages before the discovery
of Australia, Arab traders were familiar with the east
coast of Africa in most of its length. Giving continuous

access, as it does, from Aden and India to the south-
west part of the Empire's strategic front, and to the
richest part of Africa,—the eastern half in its whole
length from the Anglo-Egyptian Sudan to Cape Colony,
—having good harbours and roadsteads, to several of
which railways under the control of Britain or of her
ally, Portugal, have been made to the interior, the value
of this route, already great, increases with the growth
of British Africa. Of the western section little needs
be said. The route to the Cape soon quits the coast,
passing through mid-ocean by St. Helena. This is the
only route available for sailing ships to India and the
Far East on the one hand, and Australasia on the other.
In time of war it would also become one of the only
two routes from the imperial base in the northern hemisphere to the strategic front, the other being the route
from British Columbia to Japan. From this main West
African route another diverges eastwards along the
Guinea coast, giving access to the rising colonies of
British West Africa.

There remain the West Indian and Australasian routes.
The former diverge from the principal maritime highway
near the Azores, and thence (1) by Bermuda to the
western parts of the British West Indies and British
Honduras, or, (2) by courses more southward, to the
Leeward and Windward Islands, and to Trinidad and
British Guiana. Considered as Imperial routes these are
the shortest of all, and merely represent the maritime
portions of the old Spanish transcontinental routes—
one by Puerto Bello across the isthmus to the Pacific
and Peru, the other by Vera Cruz across Mexico to the
Pacific at Acapulco, and thence to the Philippines.

Gilbert and Drake, the founders of the colonial empire, appear to have contemplated the seizure of the Panama route to Peru. The higher genius of Raleigh perceived the loss of advantage in crossing the continent at its narrowest part. He proposed to utilise the waterway of the Orinoco, to seize for England this reputedly rich and undoubtedly populous valley, and from its western extremity to ascend the Andes and conquer Peru through New Granada. After the peace made with Spain at the accession of James I., England and France were tacitly permitted to occupy the derelict parts of the West Indies and North America, and all projects of conquest from the Spaniards were dropped ; to be theoretically revived, however, when a Spanish war seemed imminent, and to be practically revived by Cromwell, who sent a fleet and 10,000 soldiers to seize St. Domingo. Failing in their attempt, the English commanders, unwilling to return ingloriously, besieged and captured the capital of Jamaica, thereby winning for Britain this island and a dominant position in the western basin of the Caribbean Sea. St. Lucia in the eastern basin, and Bermuda in the Atlantic, form, with Jamaica, a valuable triad of naval stations, closely connected with the Imperial base on its Atlantic side, with the coaling station and fortified harbour of Freetown, Sierra Leone, and with the coaling and victualling station of Ascension, the latter being about mid-way between the West Indies and the south wing of the Imperial strategic front at the Cape of Good Hope. These West Indian bases thus lend support to the Imperial position on its western flank, and contribute materially to the security of the Empire.

Precisely the contrary is true of the Australasian and

Polynesian colonies. Removed by half the globe's circuit from the eastern half of the Imperial base—that comprising Britain, Newfoundland, and Eastern Canada—less remote, but still at an immense distance, from its western extremity in British Columbia, removed by the breadth of the Indian Ocean from the principal wing of the strategic front, and lying in isolated patches, varying in size from a continent to a coral-reef, in mid-ocean, they can be approached by friend or foe from the rest of the world in many opposite directions. The Australasian seas were first penetrated by Spanish adventurers sailing from Peru. The route taken by the Dutch explorers lay southward from the Java Sea, and hence into the Indian Ocean near the northern coast of Australia ; and this is still the route to the northern shores of Western and South Australia, Torres Straits, and Queensland. The route from Britain followed before 1869 diverged from the sea route to India at the Cape, pursued a course nearly in the same latitude to the south-western angle of Australia, thence continued to its south-eastern angle and New Zealand.[1] Though longer by some days than that through the Suez Canal, which strikes the Australian coast farther to the north, this route is adopted by some lines of steamships, and is the universal route for sailing vessels. Adding to these routes the eastern coast route of Australia, and those leading thence to New Zealand and the scattered colonies of British Polynesia, it will be seen that the numerous communications of this vast and isolated tract of the Empire, both with the rest of the world and among its own distant members, are of

[1] As to the route to New Zealand by the Falkland Islands, see p. 51.

enormous aggregate length, extremely complicated, and dangerously exposed in time of war.

We remarked that the Empire occupies advantageous positions. It includes units of every size, from mere footholds in the ocean like Tristan da Cunha and Pitcairn Island, solitary ocean settlements like Ascension or St. Helena, and small promontories like Gibraltar, to large continental areas, unbroken, as in Canada, or practically unbroken, as in India and South Africa; and in the case of Australia, an entire continent. To trace their distribution, we will scan the globe, first following its principal highway from west to east—from Canada to China — thence turning southward, crossing the equator, and returning the reverse way through the southern hemisphere by Australasia and British Africa, and ending with the British West Indies.

In North America, splendid and full of promise as was the heritage which Britain in 1783 relinquished in favour of her offended children, there was still something left for those who preferred to remain loyal to her; and this residuary endowment, in itself considerable, proved capable of a development not less astonishing than that of their neighbours. Even after the lapse of 120 years it cannot be quite safe to draw comparisons between the growth of the States and that of Canada; but it is certain that the independent republic began with advantages in most respects greater than the Dominion, and has enjoyed a better position in the race of development. It is also certain that the days when it was contemplated as a possibility that Canada would become absorbed in the States are ended. The days, moreover, when capital and labour filtered through the frontier, as through a sieve, into the wealthier and more attractive States, are not only ended, but a reaction has begun, and the tide of both capital and labour is over-flowing in the reverse direction. From a cosmic point of view no part of America could have better fitted into the scheme of the Britannic Empire than the Canadian Dominion. The farther to the north, the nearer to Britain, and the less the distance to be traversed by sea and rail, in passing from Britain to the Far East by an overland North-West Passage. Britain, moreover, needed, above all things, a colonial offshoot in the closest possible vicinity to her shores, capable of supplying her continuously with food-stuffs in unlimited quantities. Nature and the course of events provided her with precisely this in Canada. Nor are the advantages of position enjoyed by Canada as a producing country limited to her nearest neighbours—the United States, Mexico, and the West Indies on the one hand, and Britain on the other. From her Pacific ports she should in time compete with the States in pouring food-products into Japan and China.

Could any colony claim special advantages of position it is Newfoundland—the outpost of North America towards Europe, the seat of the richest fisheries in the world, discovered by Bristol seamen before any European eye since the days of the Northmen had beheld the American continent, and the scene of that memorable ceremony by which Sir Humfrey Gilbert, in 1583, took possession of North America on behalf of England—a possession, nevertheless, contested during nearly two centuries by France, who relinquished her claims to Newfoundland in 1713, reserving the right to

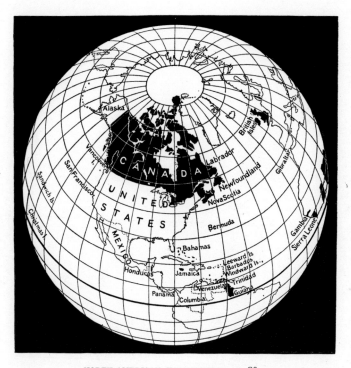

NORTH-AMERICAN HEMISPHERE.—P. 28.

land and cure fish on the northern shores. In 1763 the
islets of St. Pierre and Miquelon were ceded to her, and
in 1783 the landing rights were altered and extended.
The abolition of these greatly abused rights, or in any
case their reduction to their lawful basis, has been re-
peatedly demanded by the colonists; but the question
seems to be in course of solution by the gradual decay
of the French fishery, unable to hold its ground although
supported by heavy bounties.[1] Newfoundland, with the
adjacent Labrador coast, remains outside the Canadian
Dominion, and there are formidable, perhaps insurmount-
able, obstacles in the way of its incorporation with the
Dominion. Its very considerable resources in forests,
metals (copper), and coal are being rapidly developed,
although not so rapidly as could be wished, and its
hardy fishermen furnish excellent recruits to the British
Navy.

Having crossed the Atlantic, and touched the British
Isles—the centre of the globe's land surfaces—the great
highway traverses the Mediterranean Sea, of which
Gibraltar guards the western, and Malta the central
waters; while Cyprus, if need were, might be so fortified as to command the eastern extremity. Gibraltar,
though ranking as a colony, is a foreign possession
having a population largely of Italian descent, no local
resources, but of first-class importance as a naval base,
an impregnable fortress and arsenal, a commercial and
coaling station. The rock surmounting the town is one
of the two historic "Pillars of Hercules." "Gibraltar"
is properly Gebel-al-Tarik or Mountain of Tarik, the
Arab general who here invaded Spain and first fortified

---

[1] These rights have now been regulated by treaty (see p. 219).

the rock which bears his name. Recently Britain has awakened to the necessity of providing Gibraltar with the docks and harbours which its growing naval and commercial importance has long demanded. Four millions have been expended in improvements on the west side of the rock, the site of the old town; and it is in contemplation to construct an entirely new harbour and dock on the east side, with a breakwater having a frontage of two miles, at a probable cost of six millions and a half.

Malta, the ancient Melita (a name of Phœnician origin meaning "Refuge"), is not merely a first-class fortress, an important naval base and coaling-station, but, together with the neighbouring island of Gozo, a valuable colonial possession. The islands are densely populated, the natives being descendants of Oriental colonists who may have settled here 3500 years ago. They speak a Semitic language, apparently of Phœnician rather than Arabic origin. Their continual and rapid increase deserves consideration. Malta might probably furnish a comparatively small but steady supply of valuable emigrants to those African possessions where labour is in demand. The Maltese are industrious and intelligent, make good seamen and soldiers, and are loyal citizens of the Empire. Aided by excellent modern irrigation works they raise from an arid soil large quantities of vegetable produce, and are successful breeders of the useful animals.

Two days' sail from Malta the traveller enters on a wider field—the region of the states tributary to and in some loose way politically connected with the Ottoman Porte, throughout which events and circumstances have

compelled Britain to establish and maintain a predominant influence, and parts of which have been
either absolutely or conditionally incorporated with
the Britannic Empire. This region begins at the
western boundary of Egypt in the Libyan Desert, and
extends to the Persian Gulf, where it joins the western-
most shore under the influence of British India. From
the Libyan Desert in the west to the Chinese Sea in
the east, most of the continental shore, both in Africa
and Asia, is either British or under Britain's recognised
influence. In the western section, beginning with the
Libyan Desert and ending at the western frontier of
British India, the case is generally that of influence;
but in some districts British influence is of more
marked character, and it is here and there intensified
into direct dominion. Taking these shores in order
there are, in the Mediterranean, Egypt and Cyprus; on
the western shore of the Red Sea, Egypt and the Anglo-
Egyptian Sudan, and Abyssinia[1]; at the entrance to
the Red Sea, the British island of Perim; on the
Gulf of Aden, the British territory and port of Aden,
together with a protectorate, on the north, and the
British Protectorate of Somaliland on the south; on
the Indian Ocean, the island of Sokotra, under British
protection, on the south, and the continuous Arabian
coast, as far as and with the addition of the Kuria
Muria Islands, on the north; and the shores of the
Persian Gulf, with the Bahrein Islands, which are
subject to a sheikh established and protected by Britain.
Collectively, these colonies, possessions, protectorates,
and areas of influence, grouped around the Red Sea as

---

[1] Britain's position here is secured by treaty (p. 33).

their centre, form the vestibule of the Britannic Empire in India, the Far East, Australasia, Eastern Africa, and South Africa—a fact which constitutes the measure of their present and prospective importance. This vestibule of the Indian Empire, like British Africa, with which it is closely connected, affords great scope for new developments, and is likely to receive greater attention in the immediate future.

Cyprus, the first of this group in geographical order, stands for the present practically out of it. Acquired in 1878 as a "place-of-arms" by way of set-off in Britain's favour against Russian conquests in Armenia, and as a security for payment by the Porte of a former loan guaranteed by the British Treasury, events have made it hitherto unnecessary to use it as a military or naval station, though well adapted for both purposes. The economic development which is possible, and might have been anticipated as a consequence of good government, is yet to come; the fact being that Britain may resign Cyprus to its fate at any moment, and that capital avoids a country whose future destiny is uncertain. Money invested in irrigation, re-afforestation, wine-growing, and general agriculture might render this island an earthly paradise. Little has hitherto been done for it beyond the introduction of an effectual method of coping with a dreaded invader—the locust.[1]

The object intended to be secured by the acquisition of Cyprus was increased control of the Mediterranean Sea near the north end of the Suez Canal. Events in Egypt four years later rendered the acquisition

[1] See, however, p. 211.

apparently superfluous. Britain was compelled to intervene for the purpose of crushing a rebellion which had paralysed the progressive government established under the joint direction of herself and France; and as France declined to co-operate the burden of intervention fell on Britain alone. It became imperative not only to reorganise the government and army of Egypt under British direction, but to secure public order by a permanent British army of occupation. Egypt proper having been rescued from anarchy, it remained to do the like for the Egyptian province of the Sudan. A costly and difficult campaign with this object was jointly undertaken by the Egyptian and British governments, and was completely successful; and the Egyptian Sudan, with the exception of Massowah, already appropriated by Italy as the capital of an Italian possession called Eritrea, and of some other outlying portions now annexed to Abyssinia and British Somaliland, is now a joint possession of Egypt and Britain. Here an important development is already taking place, based partly on internal economic resources, partly on an increasing traffic with Uganda and British East Africa. Britain's position on the Red Sea, already assured by her practical partnership with Egypt, both in Egypt proper, which includes the region traversed by the Suez Canal, and the north-west shore of the Red Sea, and in the Sudan, which has its outlet to the Red Sea at the port of Suakin, has been strengthened by her recently concluded alliance with the Empire of Ethiopia (Abyssinia); an alliance likely to be permanent, and to do much for the consolidation of Britannic interests throughout Eastern Africa. By this treaty the Emperor has agreed to allow Britain to carry the Central-African Railway through his dominions, and not to obstruct the flow of water from Lake Tzana and the Blue or Abyssinian Nile into the Egyptian Nile.

One of the world's critical positions is the south end of the Red Sea, where the East African route and those to Bombay, Karachi, and the Persian Gulf diverge on either hand from the great central highway. Here Britain holds the fortified port and coaling-station of Aden[1] in the Arabian province of Yemen. Together with the island of Perim and a considerable portion of the Arabian mainland, Aden is British soil. Eastward of Aden the greatest panorama of the Empire comes into view as we advance into the open Indian Ocean. The Indian Ocean would be more properly named the Britannic Ocean. It gives access to three out of the four main divisions of the Empire—India, Australasia, and British East, Central, and South Africa. These include the whole of two out of its three continental shores—the Asiatic and the Australian—together with the best parts of the African shore, and nearly all that is valuable in the back districts where the shore is held by other Powers. All its larger islands, except Madagascar and Réunion, are British soil. No ocean is dominated in so large a measure by a single Power. On its coasts we encounter for the first time Imperial dependencies and possessions which have been acquired not for the purpose of securing access to what lies beyond them, but by reason of their intrinsic value, and colonies created by the attractions of their sites. The central maritime highway lies along its northern shores, touching,

[1] Arabic, '*Adan* = Place of Delight (ironical).

besides the coast of British India, the British colony of
Ceylon, the Federated Malay States, and the Straits
Settlements.   After passing the extremity of Asia at
Singapore, another of the world's critical positions, the
route enters and crosses the China Sea, leaving British
Borneo, the Philippines, belonging to the United States,
and Formosa, belonging to Japan, on the right; thence
to the British colony of Hong-Kong,[1] the centre of the
world's trade with China and Japan, and the principal
European military and naval station in the Far East.
Hong-Kong, with its commodious harbour, four miles
of docks, naval yard, immense local and transit trade,
vast Chinese population, and growing educated Anglo-
Chinese community is an unique monument of colonial
commercial enterprise, due, of course, to exceptionally
favourable circumstances.   Beyond Hong-Kong, at 1300
miles distance, is the British port of Wei-hai-wei, in the
Gulf of Pechili, obtained from China to countervail the
Russian acquisition of Port Arthur, on the opposite
shore.   Wei-hai-wei is at present only a military
station, Britain's recently concluded alliance with Japan
having enabled her to postpone the work of completely
fortifying and equipping it as a naval base.

While the great central waterway of the world
connects Britain with her possessions and colonies on
the Indian and Pacific Oceans, and links these in one
system, it also divides them into two classes.   To
the north of it Britain has built up her Empire
on a basis of pre-existing civilisations.   To the south
of it civilisation is mainly or wholly of recent
introduction.   Yet the branching waterways by which

---

[1] Chinese, *Hiang-Kiang* = Place of Sweet Streams.

these southern possessions and colonies are approached were known to Britain's predecessors, the Arabs and Portuguese, and were prolonged as lines of exploration, though not of exploration leading to settlement, by her rivals the Dutch.   Britain's conspicuously successful development of the countries adjoining to and beyond the Indian Ocean has mainly been due to the fact that it began with the nineteenth century, when steam navigation was coming into use, and enjoyed the advantages of the railway and telegraph, and of improved methods and means of land exploration, at a time when the capabilities of Canada were as yet unknown, and the stream of enterprise, which once poured over the now independent colonies of North America, was diverted to Australasia and South Africa.

Although the actual development of the southern colonies on the Indian Ocean began from the south, and was extended thence northwards,—the natural maritime access to the basin of this ocean being then from the south by way of the Cape,—the approach by way of the Suez Canal has come to be the principal one, and it is by this route that the traveller most commonly reaches them.   Following the main highway as it traverses the entire length of Asia, and then, instead of entering the China Sea, turning southward into the Java Sea, leaving the Java ports on the right, British New Guinea appears on the left, and Torres Straits are reached, where the route has on the right Thursday Island, the northernmost part of the State of Queensland.   Passing the Straits, it enters the Pacific Ocean, and turning southward, reaches the mainland of Australia.

Australia — the last continent added to the map,

because at once the most isolated and the most
remote from Europe—stands forth among the members
of the Empire with many distinctions of its own.   The
only continent which at its discovery and in the course
of its exploration exhibited no trace of even the lowest
forms of human advancement, it is the only one which
European civilisation has almost simultaneously attacked
and conquered from every side.   This unique feat has
been accomplished by a single European nation, seated
a few degrees from its antipodes.   Portuguese sailors,
who probably discovered it, seem to have shrewdly con-
jectured its size and configuration.   Spanish adventurers
sighted it, and decided that hereabouts no continent
could exist.   Dutchmen touched at its western shores,
placed them on the map, named them "New Holland,"
and left them alone.   Frenchmen supposed them to be
part of an immense continent lying round the South
Pole, named the aborigines of this imaginary continent
"Australians,"[1] and about 1756 simultaneously prepared
to drive the British from North America, and to annex
the "Austral Lands" to France.   A few years later,
Englishmen circumnavigated it, and founded colonies on
its more attractive sites.   Others explored it from sea to
sea, and in all directions discovered and developed its
unique resources.   The parent country poured into it
population and capital, conceded the right of its people
to the same full measure of political liberty as is enjoyed
by their brethren at home, and pointed the way to a
confederation of its five colonies into a single Britannic
commonwealth.   The recent accomplishment of this

[1] The name "les Australiens" is found in a French book pub-
lished in 1756.   Reversing the usual order, the name of the country,
Australia, was derived from the name thus given to the people.

design has made Australia, with the adjacent colony of
Tasmania, a single nation dominating an entire continent.
When it is added that Australia, situated half within
and half without the tropic, has a correspondingly varied
economic basis, unusually rich in every known element
of wealth; that its reproductive industries have been
rapidly extended ; that its people, taken in the mass, are
prosperous to a degree which leaves the average standard
of well-being in Europe far behind ; that it is the most
democratic country in the world ; and that it has taken
drastic, if unwise, precautions against industrial invasion
by lower races, it will be seen that its claim to distinction
among the Britannic nations is fully justified.   None of
these is better entitled to be called a Greater Britain, for
none more nearly reproduces, and on a gigantic scale,
the situation and social condition of the United Kingdom, than this great offshoot at the antipodes. Australia's
transcontinental railways are yet to be made. A North
to South railway, in the State of South Australia, following the line of an existing telegraph, has been authorised,
and will be finished in a few years.   A complete East to
West railway is projected, from Perth on the west coast
to Adelaide, and thence by existing lines to Melbourne
and Sydney.

The name Australasia (l'Australasie) was given by
French writers to the entire island region off the
south-east shores of Asia, from the Philippines and
Borneo in the north-west to New Zealand in the south-
east.   Besides Australia, the Empire includes large
portions of the islands of Borneo and New Guinea, and
all New Zealand. The contrast of climate found in
Australia becomes intensified when the whole of Aus-

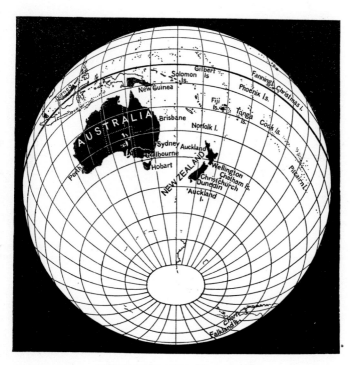

AUSTRALASIAN HEMISPHERE.—P. 38.

tralasia is regarded. Borneo lies under the equator, the north-west end (Dutch) of New Guinea nearly touches the equator, and both islands are among the hottest countries in the world. British Borneo includes the northern part of the island, abutting on the China Sea, not far on the right from that section of the great central route which lies between Singapore and Hong-Kong. British New Guinea forms the eastern part of the southern section of the island, and lies on the northernmost of the Australian routes, separated from Queensland by Torres Straits.

Twelve hundred miles east of Australia, and nearly at Britain's antipodes, lies New Zealand, often described as a counterpart of the parent country. Climate, soil, and capacities of production are somewhat analogous to those of Britain; the three islands are nearly the size of England and Ireland together. Industrially, socially, and politically, New Zealand resembles the extra-tropical colonies of Australia; but is not affected by those unfavourable physical conditions—lack of water, burning winds, disastrous droughts—which have greatly impeded Australia's economic development; and New Zealand's finance, necessarily framed on a more modest scale than that of the Commonwealth, is less subject to economic disturbance. Special features of interest in New Zealand are her fine native race, reclaimed from savagery and converted into a prosperous and loyal section of the community; her scenery, of extraordinary beauty and variety, attracting annually thousands of visitors, especially from Australia in the hot season; and her original system of local colonisation, which strove to reproduce in distant districts the features of different sections of society in the parent country. Provision was made for the incorporation of New Zealand in the Australian Commonwealth; but such a change is not viewed with favour, nor is it likely to be effected. The New Zealanders yield to none in loyalty to the Empire, and wish their existing position within it to be maintained.

Eastward—mainly north-eastward—from New Zealand, Australia, and New Guinea the "Milky Way of the terrestrial globe" stretches towards the New World, covering more than half the distance from Australasia to South America, and a quarter of the area of the Pacific Ocean. The Polynesian archipelago, with its myriad islands, marks the site of a continent long submerged, and ever sinking more and more beneath the ocean. Over two portions of it, at each extremity, one in the north-west, the other in the east, protectorates have been assumed by other Powers; the residue, forming the greatest part, belongs to Britain. German Polynesia, stretching north-eastwards from the northern part of New Guinea, also a German possession, faces Japan. French Polynesia faces Peru, but it throws out two lines westwards through British Polynesia, from Tahiti to the Wallis and Fotuna Islands, and thence to New Caledonia, a large island only 800 miles distant from the coast of Queensland. With the exception of these islands, and of the Samoa Islands, which are divided between Germany and the United States, Polynesia is British. The principal groups are the Fiji Islands, the most important,—the Governor here being also High Commissioner of the Western Pacific,—the British Solomon Islands, the Gilbert and Ellice Islands, near the equator, and the Tonga Islands. Over Fanning Island, half-way between the coasts of British Columbia and Australia, passes the " All British " telegraph, spanning the Pacific and connecting the Dominion and the Common-wealth.

From the easternmost margin of the Empire we glance backwards, recrossing the Indian Ocean, and passing the thriving island colonies of Mauritius and the Seychelles. Henceforward to the close of our survey we are in a homogeneous field—once the field of African slavery and the slave-trade. Here Britain has displayed most conspicuously her highest qualities—her humanity, jus-tice, and generosity. Elsewhere she has been conspicuous for her energy and skill of enterprise. In Canada she has created a nation rivalling the adjoining States, and having, like herself, that variety, favourable to cohesion, which comes of the union, under a common constitution, of provinces of different origin. In Asia she has ended centuries of bloodshed, and induced or compelled peoples more various in race, language, and religion, than those of Europe to dwell together in the harmony of the Pax Britannica. In Australia she has occupied a continent, and planted in it a Britannic nationality. In Africa, the West Indies, and British Tropical America she has vindicated the common rights of humanity for a race which all her predecessors in colonial enterprise treated as cattle, to be bought and sold, coerced to labour, and doomed to degradation and misery from generation to generation. For a time Britain was content to share the shame of slavery and the slave-trade with the Arabs, Portuguese, Spaniards, and French, and to justify her-self by the universal practice of the strong towards the

weak.   Arab discovery and colonisation in the East, and
in Africa, had been largely based on slave-raiding and
slave-trading.   On the West African coast the Portuguese
did but follow Arab precedents in both branches.   The
Spaniards during the first thirty years or so of colonial
history needed no African slaves, the American coasts
furnishing them with an adequate supply of native
slave-labour.   Subsequently they bought African slaves
of the Portuguese—for the latter a profitable trade, afterwards transferred as a monopoly to Britain.   Yet long
before the treaty of 1713 secured English merchants the
benefit of this monopoly, English consciences had been
stirred by the wrongs of the West Indian negro.   The
colony of Eleuthera in the Bahamas (1647) was
probably the earliest attempt at colonial enterprise
in hot countries without slavery.   In 1671 George
Fox prevailed on some Barbados planters to liberate
their slaves ; in 1684 the first anti-slavery association
was formed at Philadelphia.   This movement anticipated a corresponding change in political philosophy.
Aristotle, the most enlightened of the Greeks, thought
slavery necessary to society.   In More's *Utopia* slavery
still flourishes.   Francis Bacon, while nobly asserting
"a supreme and indissoluble consanguinity and society"
between man and his fellow-man, divides the species in
the same breath into two classes, and seems to admit
that something may be said for the practice of enslaving
the lower, and for the right of superior races to levy war
"against such routs and shoals of people as have utterly
degenerated from the laws of nature, have in their very
body and frame of estate a monstrosity, and may be
truly accounted disgraces and reproaches to human

nature."[1]   Slavery was recognised in the constitution
framed by Locke for Carolina, and that colony became
notorious, not merely for introducing and maintaining
negro slavery, but for Indian slave-raiding and slave-
trading.   Only when French and English economists, in
the eighteenth century, had cast doubts on the profit-
ableness of slave as compared with free labour was a
substantial beginning made in the movement which
ultimately abolished slavery and the slave-trade.

Britain's task was only begun when she abolished the
colonial slave-trade, and compensated wealthy colonists
for the compulsory emancipation of their slaves out of
public funds.   She turned to the African continent,
where slavery universally existed as an endemic plague
and prescriptive iniquity.   Fortune had given her a
foothold in South Africa at the Cape, and long before
this she had founded Sierra Leone as a refuge for
destitute African freedmen.   To suppress the Arab slave
trade on the east coast, which had received a new
impulse by the suppression of the trade on the west
coast, was a difficult task ; and when British explorers
dispelled the ignorance of ages, disclosed the resources
of the Dark Continent, and demonstrated its value as
a field for European enterprise, it was easy for Britain
to obtain from other Powers, who hastened to divide
it with her, assurances that the enslavement of the
natives should in no form be permitted—assurances
like those which she strictly exacted from the slave-
holding Boers whom she permitted to establish themselves on the borders of her southern colony, and

[1] Bacon assigns these words to a Roman Catholic zealot who is
justifying the crimes committed by the Spaniards in America in the
name of Christianity.

to spread over large tracts of the interior. How such assurances have been kept is matter of history. In no cases save those of Britain and France has the confidence of the natives been gained and retained ; a fact not without its bearing on the vast extension of the commerce, and through commerce of the territorial holdings, of these two Powers in various parts of Africa.

Apart from slavery and native questions generally, the part played by Britain in the development of Africa is less exclusive, less free from complication, and less advanced in progress towards completion than the part she has sustained elsewhere ; but these very facts lend it a higher degree of interest, and other circumstances render it even more remarkable. When Britain took possession of Australia, she possessed nothing in Africa but some parts of the west coast used as depôts for the slave-trade. She is now the predominant power in Africa ; and her predominance is most marked in the most valuable section of the continent—that facing Australia, and lying east of a line drawn parallel with the east coast, from the Egyptian boundary in the Libyan Desert, on the Mediterranean, to the eastern boundary of the Kalahari Desert and the mouth of the Orange River, on the Atlantic. Under the name of the " Cape-to-Cairo " route, British enterprise has long been building up through communication overland throughout Eastern Africa, ultimately, perhaps, to be wholly by railway, but for the present partly by road, partly by railway, and partly by lake and river—as an alternative for and supplement to the maritime highway along the east coast from the Red Sea southwards. We begin with this land route, destined to be a unique monument of British

engineering enterprise, traversing the heart of the continent, and giving direct access by land to vast tracts of
British territory which are separated from the sea by
the possessions of other Powers.

Through half the length of the continent from north
to south the route lies up the Nile, in Egypt and the
Anglo-Egyptian Sudan. Near Gondokoro it enters the
Nile Province of the British protectorate of Uganda,
which includes the northern and part of the western and
eastern shores of the Victoria Nyanza. East of this,
crossed by the railway from the lake to the sea at
Mombasa, lies the protectorate of British East Africa,
once under the nominal control of the Sultan of
Zanzibar. South of Uganda and British East Africa the
continuity of British territory is interrupted. A large
expanse of territory between Lake Tanganyika and the
Indian Ocean is under a German protectorate ; and west
of Lake Tanganyika stretches far westward to the
mouth of the Congo the territory of the Congo State,
administered under the presidency of the King of the
Belgians. Such communication as at present takes
place between Uganda on the north and British Central
and South Africa on the south chiefly passes through
German territory. But the most convenient route for
traffic is understood to lie west of Lake Tanganyika
over the upper levels of the Congo basin. At the
southern end of the lake British South Africa begins,
and from this point onwards all is British soil. The
route now traverses Northern Rhodesia, and the Zambesi
having been crossed below the Victoria Falls, the present
terminus of the railway is reached, and three-fourths of
the distance between the Mediterranean and the south

coast has been covered.   From Buluwayo, 200 miles
from the river, the railway passes through Mafeking, in
Bechuanaland, leaving the Transvaal colony at a short
distance on the left, and so through Cape Colony to Cape
Town and Port Elizabeth, with alternative routes either
through the Transvaal to the Indian Ocean at Delagoa
Bay, or through the Orange Colony and Natal to
Durban, the port of Natal.   About one-fourth—the
southernmost section—it will be seen, of the "Cape-to-
Cairo" railway is already made; and by means of a
branch railway, also already constructed, from Buluwayo
by way of Salisbury in Southern Rhodesia to the ocean
at Beira in Portuguese territory the sea passage from
the Red Sea to Cape Town can be reduced by a third.
Similar communication on the Atlantic side will shortly
be provided by a corresponding railway, from Lobito
Bay in Portuguese West Africa, through Barotseland to
the Zambesi; and the richest districts in British South
Africa—Rhodesia and the Transvaal colony—will thus
have two additional routes to Europe, neither passing
through the Cape.   Viewed from the coast, the Britannic
Empire is less in evidence.   North of British East Africa
a protectorate has been assumed by Italy, and south of
it by Germany; but the exceedingly important island of
Zanzibar, from the beginning of commerce the centre
of the coasting trade, and of Africa's commerce with
the Far East, is now a British protectorate.   From
Cape Delgado to Delagoa Bay, the coast tract corresponding to British East Africa, Rhodesia, and the
Transvaal in the interior, and forming the west coast of
the Mozambique Channel, is Portuguese; while Madagascar, of nearly equal length on the east side of the

Channel, is under the protection of France. Only when the Zululand coast is reached does British territory recommence; and from this point the entire circuit of South Africa, as far as the mouth of the Orange River on the west coast, comprising the entire seaboards of Natal and Cape Colony, is British. Throughout Eastern Africa, excepting German East Africa and the eastern margin of the Congo State, effective administration, whether British or Anglo-Egyptian, has been established, but it cannot be said that slavery has been wholly abolished. It is a matter of satisfaction that at the present moment, when the cruelties of the Congo administration have recently been exposed, and German colonial authorities are discussing the best mode of exacting forced native labour in German East Africa, no responsible voice has been raised in favour of any semblance of such a measure in the British colonies, where the natives are less numerous, and the need for labour more pressing.[1]

From the Orange River northward the west coast of Africa presents few attractions. It is held by Germany (except the British port of Walfish Bay, the coast immediately adjoining, and some small islands near this coast), Portugal, and France. British West Africa commences where the coast becomes better worth occupation, in the angle of the Gulf of Guinea, and lies in four separate sections, progressively diminishing in area. The largest is composed of the adjacent colonies of Nigeria and Lagos. Nigeria consists of two separate colonies—Southern Nigeria, formerly the Oil Rivers

[1] The question of labour for the Transvaal mines has now been solved by the introduction of Chinese contract labourers.

Protectorate, and Northern Nigeria, of much larger extent, established, and until 1900 governed by the Royal Niger Company. Northern Nigeria, now in course of organisation by a British Governor through the medium of native chiefs, has a reputed population equal to that of the United Kingdom, and is more than twice as large. Adjacent to Southern Nigeria is the colony of Lagos, with a protectorate comprising several native states. After an interval, occupied by German Togoland, comes the valuable Gold Coast Colony, to which the kingdom of Ashanti, where a native prince rules under the supervision of a British Resident, is now appendant as a protectorate. On the west coast lie Sierra Leone, and the old slave-trade colony of the Gambia River; the distant islands of St. Helena and Ascension, south of the equator, are halting-places in the ocean on the route to and from the Cape.

Crossing the Atlantic, we reach Bermuda and British Tropical America, comprising the West Indian islands, British Honduras, and British Guiana. Excepting the last, we are now in the field of the old Colonial Empire, and in what was once deemed its most valuable section. Possession had been taken of the Bermudas when Shakespeare described them in *The Tempest* as the "still-vexed (ever-vexed) Bermoothes." Ireland Island, often called the Gibraltar of the West Indies, is a first-class dockyard and naval station; and the islands are famous as a health resort. Most of the Bahama Islands lie without the Tropic line, which passes near Watling Island. Crossing this line, and entering the Caribbean Sea by the Windward Channel, the British West Indies lie before us in two groups 500 miles apart. The western group consists of Jamaica, the Bahamas, and British Honduras ; the eastern of the Leeward Islands, with the Virgin Islands, the Windward Islands, Barbados, and Trinidad with Tobago. Beyond Trinidad, and stretching at its southernmost point in the head-waters of the Essequibo nearly to the equator, lies British Guiana, having an area, little explored, considerably larger than the island of Great Britain. Of the two groups the eastern is the more important, both geographically and economically. The colonies included in it lie on the Atlantic, scattered over 15 degrees of latitude, while Jamaica and British Honduras lie in isolation far within the Caribbean Sea.

People are too prone to think of the West Indian islands together as forming a single group, and to consider them as subject to the same economic conditions. There are, in fact, from the economic point of view, two groups not identical with the two above indicated, and widely differing in their industrial prospects. The smaller, and the only one in the Empire whose economic future has given any cause for apprehension, consists of the essentially English islands of Barbados, Antigua, St. Kitts, and Nevis—all thickly populated, all hitherto dependent for existence on the cultivation of the sugar-cane, all capable of producing sugar, under equal conditions of competition, more cheaply than any other country in the world, and all, say their inhabitants, incapable of producing any other crop to any extent economically appreciable. They must, it is argued, grow sugar or become depopulated and derelict. The physical features of these islands, and the fixed industrial habits and ideas of their unusually dense population, no doubt render it more difficult to change the current of enterprise than elsewhere in the West Indian colonies ; and it is anticipated that permanent relief will be afforded to the sugar industry by recent European arrangements counteracting the effect of the continental sugar bounties.   But in any case too gloomy a view has been taken of the situation, for cotton has recently been planted in Barbados with good results, and this plant, ever in increasing demand, may possibly become an auxiliary means of restoring the old English sugar islands to prosperity.

The other West Indian islands, while holding their own in sugar production so far as sugar is found profitable, have many other resources only partially explored, and share with the rest of the Empire the prospect of great development in the immediate future.   What these resources are will appear in our third chapter. There is at length a prospect that the West Indian route, now isolated among the maritime routes of the world, will by the construction of the Panama Canal at the cost of the United States cease to end in a *cul-de-sac*, and have a threefold prolongation along the west of America; northwards to British Columbia, southwards along the western shores of the Spanish republics of Colombia, Ecuador, Peru, and Chile, and westwards towards British Polynesia, New Zealand, and Australia. Experts in the economics of distributive commerce are convinced that the tonnage passing through any Central American ship canal can never suffice to make such a canal commercially successful ; but this consideration is not likely to have any weight with the wealthy Power which announces its intention of con-

structing it. The object in making the canal is fundamentally a strategic one, and it cannot fail, when constructed, to have an influence for the better on the
prospects of the British West Indies.

The only colony remaining to be mentioned, the
Falkland Islands, off the coast of Patagonia, could have
no share in this beneficial result. These islands were
occupied by Britain in 1833 as a protection to and
source of provision for the whale fishery in the Southern
Seas, the decline of which had not been foreseen. They
include for administrative purposes the distant island
of South Georgia, forming together with it a colony
having an area larger than Wales. Though bleak and
gloomy of aspect, they are well adapted for sheep farm-
ing, and export increasing quantities of wool, sheepskins,
and tallow. Stanley, the capital, is a port of call for
vessels sailing round South America. The only route
which touches them, that along the coast of Brazil and
round Cape Horn to New Zealand, stands alone among
the highways of the world; and they are the only
Britannic colony, except New Zealand, approached by
this route. Should the Panama Canal be made, and
the trade of Chile with Europe, and of Argentina with
the Pacific coast of North America, pass through it, the
severance of these islands from the rest of the world
will to some extent be intensified Although ranking
among the poorer colonies, they are conspicuous for
advantages of position, and are coveted accordingly.
Both Argentina and Germany covet them, and a
German line of steamers calls regularly at Stanley on
the voyage to New Zealand.

CHAPTER II

To satisfy that historical instinct which grows with the
growth of civilisation and civic life, the colonial citizen
will scarcely be content with the annals of his own
colony. He will turn to those of the parent country, rich
in interest of every kind, from the days when it lay
under the shadow of a vanishing empire which stamped
civilisation on Europe, to the days, a thousand years
later, when it began to stamp its own civilisation on
other continents. The Canadian, Australian, and British
South African reckons the history of his country from
the beginnings of English history. The Canadian of
Quebec Province blends the historic glories of France
with those of England, and points to the matchless city
of Quebec as the symbol of a nationality descended from
the two greatest of European peoples. Some parts of
the Empire begin the reckoning in remoter times. The
Adenese and Zanzibari may claim descent from those
who quitted the ports of Sheba to discover the coasts
of Southern Asia and Eastern Africa, trade for spices
to the Malay Archipelago, and pursue the quest of
gold in the double Ophir of India and Rhodesia. The

Maltese speaks a dialect founded on the language of the Phœnicians—that memorable race whose only extant monuments are the ruined temples of Malta, Gozo, and Cyprus; the Sinhalese possesses written chronicles of his country from the immigration of his Rajput ancestors in 543 B.C., dates his religion from three centuries later, when Prince Mahinda introduced from Patna the faith of Gautama Buddha, and points to many ancient cities rich in palaces, temples, and shrines, as his national monuments. South Africa can show the ruined cities built by Arabian immigrants in Mashonaland. Canada has a unique historical monument in the Indian tribes of British Columbia, which represent the parent stocks of the Mexicans, the most advanced among the American aborigines, and perhaps of the Iroquois of the Great Lake Valley in the east. But if history is considered as merging in ethnology, every part of the Empire is rich in historic interest, nor does any aggregate of peoples present so extraordinary a variety of human stocks and degrees of advancement.

Beginning anew with the Age of Discovery, we find the principal historic sites associated with that famous age within the limits of the Empire. On the Portuguese line of African exploration there are the Gambia River, Sierra Leone, the Gold Coast with Elmina, Lagos, the Cape of Good Hope, Algoa Bay, and Natal. The islands first reached by Colombo in each of his four voyages—(1) Watling Island, (2) Dominica, (3) Trinidad, (4) St. Lucia—have long been British soil. The British islands of Jamaica, Antigua, Montserrat, St. Christopher, and Nevis, were also discovered by Colombo. The Labrador coast, the first part of the American continent

discovered by European seamen—reached by the Northmen in the tenth century, and rediscovered, together
with Newfoundland, by John Cabot in 1496 or 1497,
was the first place on the American continent where the
flag of a European power was hoisted, and the flag was
that of England, which still flies over it.   As if to mark
the transition from the old to the new, Cabot hoisted by
its side the flag of Venice.   The Italian population of
Gibraltar, mainly of Genoese descent, is a living monument of Cabot, Colombo, and the Age of Discovery.

Britain, we will admit, has largely reaped where
other nations and races have sown.   The labours of many
peoples, many bold adventurers, and many ages, have
been expended to make foundations for parts of the
superstructure of her Empire.   Yet she has not simply
played the part of the austere man in the parable.   The
motive which has principally inspired her is the same
which has inspired most states which have acquired extensive and lasting Empire, including ancient Rome—
the determination not to fall under the domination of
inferior states.   This motive has doubtless co-operated
with a generous ardour of enterprise, and a deep sense of
an imperial mission ; but, had it been wanting, these must
have fallen short of their full effect.   The real makers,
as the phrase goes, of the British Empire as it exists,
were Philip II. of Spain, Louis XIV. of France, and their
successors in title or policy.   But for those ambitious
sovereigns, although Great Britain might have acquired
colonial possessions, those possessions would have occupied scanty spaces on the map.   Possibly they might
only have extended, like the present colonial possessions
of the Dutch, to a few small islands in the West Indies,

some small part of the Guiana coast in South America,
and a few trading posts and islands in the East Indies,
with the addition of a few settlements in North America
made for the purpose of securing a share of the fishery
and the fur trade.   Availing themselves, in each case, of
the alleged right of a Catholic pretender to the English
crown, these eminent politicians compelled England to
exert in defensive wars a strength which they under-
estimated, and to take security for the future by cur-
tailing and circumscribing the colonial development of
the countries whose affairs they misguided.   The policy
of Philip was dropped by his successor, partly through
changed circumstances, partly from sheer inability to
pursue it with any hope of ultimate success.   The policy
of Louis was pursued with greater persistency and more
definite results, under his two immediate successors ;
but to effectuate those results to the fullest extent was
reserved for the genius of Bonaparte.   Louis XIV. lost
France her chances in Hudson Bay and Newfoundland,
lost her the colony of Nova Scotia, and compelled
Britain to occupy Gibraltar.   The ministers of Louis
XV. lost her Cape Breton and Canada, her chances in
India, all prospect of effective occupation in the
American West, and some of her colonies in the West
Indies.   Bonaparte sold Louisiana for a trifle, and compelled Britain temporarily to deprive France of every
colony that she possessed.   Incidentally he compelled
her to take and to retain the Spanish island of Trinidad,
the Dutch possessions of the Cape of Good Hope and
Ceylon, and the greater part of Dutch Guiana.   The
most brilliant result of French policy was to come after
Waterloo.   Had not the advisers of Louis XVI. insisted

on a definitive separation from Britain as the price of
their support to the United States, Britain might long
have postponed, perhaps never undertaken, the colonisation of Australia and New Zealand ; possibly the dream
which haunted Frenchmen in 1756 might have been
realised, and a French empire have been founded in
Australasia.

No sketch of the Empire's history could be in-
telligible without going back to the explorations of the
fifteenth century, in the course of which the Portuguese
made the surprising discovery that Africa, previously
supposed to terminate near the equator, extended as far
to the southward of the equator as to the northward of
it.   The profits of the Guinea slave trade enabled them
to execute a design, gradually formulated as they
advanced along the coast, for establishing communication
between Portugal on the one hand and India, the Far
East, and the Spice Islands on the other.   The distance
by sea round Africa having proved much greater than
had been anticipated, the Genoese sailor Colombo
proposed to reach the Far East by taking what he
believed to be a shorter course, and sailing westward
across the Atlantic.   This project having been rejected
by the king of Portugal, Colombo carried it to the
court of Castile, where it was accepted.   Provided with
the means of testing his theory, Colombo discovered
the West Indian islands in 1492, and the continent of
South America in 1498.   The king of Portugal in 1493
claimed the new islands as being within a vast field of
enterprise long previously confirmed to his predecessors as an exclusive possession by Papal authority.
This claim was disallowed at Rome ; a bull was issued

confirming the West Indies to Spain, and fixing a
meridian as the boundary of the prospective acquisitions
of the two crowns. This line was by treaty removed
farther to the westward; and when the outline of
America came to be traced it appeared that a large
section of South America—that part since called Brazil
—fell to the lot of Portugal. All the rest of America
fell to Castile; all Africa and Asia, together with most
of the Eastern Archipelago, were secured by the treaty
to Portugal. The lucky sovereigns who thus divided
the globe between them were not slack to take
advantage of their new opportunities. Spanish adventurers quickly overran those parts of America which
yielded the precious metals, secured the existing mines,
opened others, and reduced the native inhabitants to
slavery for the purpose of procuring a supply of labour.
From some of the American pueblos large accumulations
of gold and silver were taken; and the produce of the
mines, one-fifth of which was reserved to the Spanish
crown, became a continuous and ever-increasing source
of wealth. By the annual remittances from America
to Spain this fortunate country was flooded with
treasure, and its sovereign became the wealthiest of
European monarchs. Spanish America contributed
little to the markets of Europe beyond small quantities
of cocoa, chilli pepper, and tobacco, which had been
reduced to cultivation by the aboriginal Mexicans; of
cochineal, indigo, and the coarse spice called pimento,
which required no cultivation; and of hides and tallow
of horned cattle, introduced from Europe, and allowed
to breed and run wild in the vast vacant spaces of the
Spanish main and islands. Gold and silver, so long as

the supplies last, leave little energy to spare for those
forms of enterprise which create a nation ; and in Spanish
America, although tropical agriculture was not wholly
neglected, the quest of these metals long remained the
paramount object. In Brazil, where they were not unknown but less abundant, Portuguese emigrants were
industriously developing the reproductive capacities of
the soil. The Portuguese planters in Brazil were the
real pioneers of modern colonial enterprise.

The staple of Brazilian agriculture, so far as it
was carried on for purposes of export, was sugar.
Introduced to Europe from the East by the Arabs,
and cultivated successively in Sicily, southern Spain,
Madeira, and Santo Domingo, the sugar-cane proved a
most valuable economic plant ; for sugar had been for
two centuries and more in demand throughout Europe,
though hitherto a costly luxury. Next to the Spanish
treasure-ships, the cane plantations which sprang up along
the Brazilian coast chiefly aroused the envy of English
and French mariners ; and the advocates of colonisation
in England pointed to them as proofs of what might be
achieved in those parts of the New World which the
Spaniards, mainly intent on the quest of gold, had left
unoccupied. Out of Brazil, from an economic point of
view, grew the settlement of the English and French
West Indies. In the East the success of Portuguese enterprise was yet more conspicuous, though the commerce
of India and the Spice Islands, considerable as was the
wealth derived from it, proved less immediately profitable than the mines of Mexico and Peru. Thus during
nearly a century Spain and Portugal shared the field of
colonial enterprise between them. In 1580 Philip II.

of Spain decided the disputed succession to the
Portuguese crown by seizing it for himself, and with it
the Portuguese moiety of the globe; and during sixty
years the world outside Europe was claimed as a
curtilage of the Escurial. During those sixty years
events happened which had the effect of destroying
Spain's predominance in the colonial world, and trans-
ferring large sections of her heritage to three hostile
Powers—to France, her rival for predominance in
Europe; to England, of which Philip II. had been joint
sovereign, but which his policy turned into a stubbornly
aggressive enemy; and to the United Netherlands, a
portion of his dominions which that policy drove to
declare itself independent.

France had been the first to dispute Spain's
pretensions. No sooner had America's wealth in the
precious metals been demonstrated by the plunder of
Mexico than Francis I., then at war with Charles V.,
despatched an expedition to take possession, in his own
name, of America from Florida northwards. Henceforth this part of America was commonly called New
France; a name of evil omen, bestowed three centuries
before on the shortlived Latin empire of Constantinople.
Charles continued at war with France, with short inter-
missions, until his abdication in 1556. The war was
renewed by Philip, but terminated by the peace of
Cateau Cambrésis (1559). While it lasted, the French
plundered the Spanish vessels in West Indian waters,
captured the ports, held the inhabitants to ransom,
and proved the Spaniards incapable of excluding other
nations from the Spanish main and islands. During
intervals of peace they made fruitless attempts to

establish a colony in Canada. The experience gained
by them was not lost on the English, who watched them
with all the interest of prospective rivalry. England had
twice supported Spain in the contest with France, and
paid the penalty of her mistake in the loss of Calais, the
last remnant of her continental possessions. When
Elizabeth came to the throne she found her people
prepared to recoup themselves for this loss by forestall-
ing the French in their proposed occupation of North
America. Events moved slowly in the early years of
her reign ; and nearly twenty years passed before such
a policy was recommended by her responsible advisers.

The year 1577 marked a turning-point in English
policy. Philip was employing the treasure of America
in crushing the Reformation and overcoming the armed
resistance of the Netherlanders. After prolonged
vacillation Elizabeth was compelled, by the force of
events, to embrace their cause. Philip was known to be
meditating an invasion of England, the deposition of
Elizabeth, and the substitution of the Queen of Scots in
her place ; and Elizabeth's counsellors advised assuming
the offensive, attacking him in America, and cutting off
his resources at the fountain-head. The plan of attack
was a comprehensive one. The Spanish treasure-ships
were to be captured in the West Indies on their homeward voyage ; for this purpose suitable stations in Cuba
and St. Domingo were to be seized and held by English
garrisons. Settlements were to be established on the
coast of Florida, partly for the same purpose—for the
homeward route from the West Indies lay here—
partly by way of beginning a territorial conquest
intended to extend to the Appalachian mountains,

generally understood to be rich in gold and silver. New-foundland, with its fishery, hitherto common to all western Europe, was to be seized and held, together with the adjacent coasts, as an exclusive possession of England. Formulated by Sir Humfrey Gilbert, one of Elizabeth's most distinguished soldiers, whose draft of it, preserved in the Public Record Office, is dated November 6, 1577 the plan probably represents current military opinion ; and it embodies the whole of the policy which created the original English colonial empire. Forced on by the threatening attitude of Spain, it struck at pretensions long cherished by France ; and from the terms of Gilbert's proposals it is clear that he expected, in executing it, to have to reckon with both the Catholic Powers.

Gilbert was intrusted with the execution of his scheme, and led in person two expeditions to America. The first, aimed at the West Indies, met with disaster, and Gilbert returned with only a remnant of his arma-ment. Four years later (1583) he reached and took formal possession of Newfoundland for the English crown, received the submission of the foreign fishing captains, explored the adjacent shores, and perished on the homeward voyage, his little vessel, overladen with guns and fighting gear, having foundered in foul weather at midnight in the longitude of the Azores. Gilbert's patent was renewed in favour of his half-brother Sir Walter Raleigh, who had from the first been associated with his project. Raleigh spent large sums in an un-successful attempt to found a colony on the North Amer-ican coast, within the limits of the present State of North Carolina. Thus far, and for twenty years more, there was substantially no competition in the colonial field on

the part of France.   Down to the accession of Henry IV.
in 1589 France had been continuously torn by internal
dissensions ; the accession of Henry was followed by
war with Spain.   England's war with Spain, waged
with keen animosity, stimulated rather than checked
her colonial designs ; and in the midst of it Raleigh led
an expedition to Guiana with the object of establishing
an alliance with a reported aboriginal empire between
the Orinoco and the Amazon rivers, as the first step to
invading New Granada and Peru.   Nothing came of it ;
and the report proves to have been founded on a misunderstood description found on an old map of South
America.   When the sixteenth century, the reign of
Philip, and that of Elizabeth, alike terminated, the
world-wide colonial field still remained outwardly vested
in the Spanish crown.   Only in one quarter had the
monopoly been successfully attacked.   The Dutch,
excluded by Philip from trading with Lisbon, found
their way round the Cape of Good Hope, and
established commercial relations with Java.   A Dutch
East India Company having been formed, an English
East India Company followed ; and the two companies
were soon engaged in a fierce rivalry for the trade of
the East.   Here the form of enterprise was commercial
rather than colonial.   Although the struggle turned on
territorial possession, the countries of the East were for
the most part densely populated, and there was no
question of European immigration, or of the foundation
of new settlements.   The scene of the colonial struggle
was North America, and it included, besides the
continent, Newfoundland and such of the West Indian
islands as had not been occupied by the Spaniards.

Although both France and England claimed general rights over the entire field of North American colonial enterprise, the continent was at first divided between them by something amounting to a tacit understanding. Frenchmen had set their hearts on the occupation of the valley of the St. Lawrence, which led straight to the interior. Englishmen, familiarised with Raleigh's conception of a great English dominion on the coast, already named Virginia, strove steadily to realise it. Newfoundland, with its fisheries, and the West Indian islands, with their opportunities for piracy and contraband trade with Spanish America, were common to French and English. Between the Gulf of St. Lawrence and New England the peninsula of Nova Scotia formed a debatable ground. The French were the first to occupy it. The English dispossessed them; but the peninsula was restored to the French in 1632. It was again annexed by the New Englanders in 1654, but was restored in 1668. In 1690 it was again conquered by the English of Boston, but was restored in 1697. In 1710 it was once more captured by the English, to whom it was finally confirmed by the Treaty of Utrecht in 1713. To Nova Scotia now belongs the distinction of being Britain's oldest possession on the continent of America; and by the treaty which ceded it the island of Newfoundland, after being treated for two hundred years as common ground, was finally declared to belong as of right to Britain. Newfoundland is sometimes described as our oldest colony; but this is only true in a qualified sense. In the mere record of historical incidents Newfoundland must be admitted to take precedence of the rest of the Empire. In 1496 or

1497 John Cabot hoisted the English flag on the
Labrador coast, which forms part of the existing colony
of Newfoundland; and nearly a century later Gilbert
set up the arms of England on a pillar in St. John's Bay.
But for his untimely death Newfoundland might have
been the seat of the oldest English colony. But in
neither case was the act of occupation followed by
actual settlement. The earliest attempt at settlement
was made in 1624 by George Calvert, Lord Baltimore,
who abandoned the island in 1629 for the more genial
climate of Maryland; and the first permanent settlements were established by the French, who chiefly
frequented the western shore of the island. The policy
of England long forbade colonisation, as likely to prove
detrimental to English interests in the fishery; nor was
this policy abandoned until a few years before the entire
island was relinquished to Britain. Newfoundland can,
therefore, have no title to the designation of our oldest
colony, having substantially come into the English
colonial system at the same time with Nova Scotia.

The distinction of being our oldest colony really
belongs to the "still-vexed Bermoothes" of Shakespeare,
marked on a Spanish map of 1511, and visited in 1538
by a Spanish captain, who described its forests of palm
and cedar, its store of fish and pearls, and recommended
it for colonisation. English colonists established themselves on St. George's Island in 1612 under a grant from
the Virginia Company. Fresh relays of colonists arrived,
and after the settlement of a large body in 1619 the
administration became vested in a governor, council,
and elective assembly. The second place among the
existing members of the Empire belongs to the little

island of St. Christopher (St. Kitts), first settled in
1623. The French are said to have landed on the
island on the same day. However this may be, it
continued partly in English and partly in French
occupation until 1666, when the whole island was
conquered by the French. After being twice taken
by the French, and twice restored to the English,
St. Kitts became finally an English colony in 1713
by the same treaty which decided the fate of Newfoundland and Nova Scotia. The rest of the British Leeward
Islands were colonised from St. Kitts shortly after the
occupation of that island, and have always remained
unquestioned British possessions.

Scarcely had the English settled on St. Kitts when
an English nobleman procured from James I. a grant of
the island of Barbados, discovered by English seamen a
few years previously. Colonists flocked thither in such
numbers that in 1650 the population was estimated at
20,000, being more than that of Virginia, and almost
equal to that of New England. The enormous profits
of sugar cultivation quickly made Barbados the most
prosperous part of the British dominions, and its
populousness and wealth procured it the name of
"Little England." This conspicuous colonial success
determined Cromwell to revive the scheme of Gilbert,
and to strike a decisive blow at Spain in the heart
of the Spanish West Indies. In 1655 he despatched
Penn and Venables with instructions to capture the
island of St. Domingo. The attack on St. Domingo
failed; but the English admiral, nothing daunted, sailed
westwards, and captured the practically vacant island of
Jamaica. This island speedily became the resort of

F

emigrants, and rose to the position of the principal English colony. The colonial centre of gravity was shifted from Virginia to the West Indies; and in the reign of Charles II. a shrewd observer prophesied that

> New England shall trouble New Spain,
> And Jamaica be lady of the isles and the main.

Cromwell had formed the project, happily never executed, of removing the colonists of New England to Jamaica. The effect of this would have been to abandon all the American continent north of the Hudson to the French, at a moment when England had obtained a decided predominance both on the mainland and in the islands. When the events which preceded the fall of the Stuart dynasty forced England into a long struggle with France—a struggle which was in fact a struggle for her independence in the world of nations—she entered on it, so far as regarded the colonial field, with everything in her favour. In the eastern part of the West Indies she possessed Barbados, the Leeward Islands, including St. Kitts, Nevis, Montserrat, Antigua, Barbuda, and Anguilla, and the adjacent Virgin Islands. In the western part, to southward of Cuba, she held the great island of Jamaica; to the north of it, the Bahamas. The French had in the east nothing but Martinique, Guadaloupe with its dependencies, and Grenada; in the west, nothing but the western end of St. Domingo. On the continent England held the advantage in an equal degree. While the French were confined to the valley of the St. Lawrence and parts of Newfoundland and Nova Scotia, the English settlements now stretched in an unbroken line from the Bay of Fundy to South Carolina.

During half a century a colony founded by the Dutch on
the Hudson River and another founded by the Swedes
on the Delaware had threatened to deprive England of
a valuable section of the coast, and to cut the English
settlements in two.   But the Dutch had conquered the
Swedish colony in 1656; the English annexed the
Dutch possessions in 1664, and they retained them at the
treaty of Breda in 1667, in exchange for some English
settlements in Guiana which had fallen into the hands
of the Dutch.   The acquisition of the Dutch possessions
marks the turning-point in Anglo-American history;
for it was quickly followed by the grant of a charter to
the Hudson's Bay Company, and the settlement of Carolina (1670) and of the vast interior tract granted to
William Penn in 1680 by the name of Pennsylvania.
The English possessions were now divided only by a
margin of Indian territory from those of the French on
the St. Lawrence and Lakes Ontario and Erie; and
beyond the French colonies the Hudson's Bay Company
were in possession of a vast and valuable commercial
field.   In population, wealth, and prospects English
America was far in advance of New France.

This rapid growth of the English settlements in
North America was scarcely to be endured by France: a
country which the decline of Spain had left the first
Power in Europe, which held the English crown in
a species of tutelage, and was fully resolved to become
predominant in the New World also.   The ideas of the
two nations with regard to colonisation still exhibited
the contrast noticed above as marking the inception
of each.   The English aimed at the occupation of the
seaboard, the creation of new English maritime states,

and the development of commerce with the parent country. The French, intent on building up a territorial empire, aimed at the occupation of the interior, and the conversion and ultimate civilisation of the Indians. As a suitable base for such an empire they had very sensibly fixed on the valley of the St. Lawrence and the region of the great lakes; and from this base they had recently made an important advance. In 1682 La Salle had descended the Mississippi, and taken possession, in the name of the French king, of the great central valley of North America. The new province comprised all the district south of the Illinois River, and was named Louisiana.

Eager as were the English in America to save themselves from being hemmed in by the French, there was nothing to be done unless an outbreak of war in Europe should send an English fleet to their assistance. The desired opportunity came with the great War of the Spanish Succession (1702), waged for ten years with the object of excluding a French prince from the Spanish throne, and then abandoned. During this war Nova Scotia was again taken, and the Newfoundland fleet of England sailed up the St. Lawrence and attacked Quebec, but without success. The attempt was about to be repeated when the negotiations were opened which ended in the Peace of Utrecht (1713). By the treaty then made France renounced her pretensions to Hudson's Bay, Newfoundland, with Labrador, Nova Scotia, and the island of St. Kitts. On the Atlantic she now retained only the islands of Cape Breton and St. John's (now Prince Edward Island). Canada and Louisiana, both interior districts, were still French.

Compared with the immense tracts represented by these names, the territorial losses of France were inconsiderable; and she quickly set about making the most of what was left to her. In the south she founded New Orleans; in the north she fortified the fine harbour of Louisbourg, in Cape Breton Island, to be at once a protection to Canada and a base for future operations against the British settlements. For the ministers of Louis supposed their grandiose design to have only sustained a temporary check; and they were convinced that North America, minus the British colonies, was a field altogether too narrow for French ambition. But for this conviction on their part, most of that continent would probably by this time have been the seat of a French nation.

Thirty years passed before Britain was again at war with France. The parent country had, during this period, done nothing to extend its colonial possessions except to found the colony of Georgia (1732). Seven years later Walpole was driven by popular clamour to declare war against Spain. Again the design of Gilbert and Cromwell was revived; the Spaniards were attacked in Cuba and on the mainland, but with no success. England engaged in the European war of the Austrian Succession (1742), and hence found herself again at war with France (1744). The New England colonists, menaced by the recently built fortress of Louisbourg, attacked and captured it (1745); but it was restored at the peace of 1748 in exchange for Madras, which had been taken by the French, and was now restored to England. As some set-off to this abandonment of an important fortress, the British government sent 4000 settlers to Nova Scotia, and founded the city of Halifax. Slowly the grasp of England was tightening on those parts of North America which lay to the north of her own colonies, and commanded the supposed Northern Passage to the Far East. The peace of 1748, brought about by the exhaustion of the belligerents in Europe, produced no change in the conditions which forced the British and French colonists into collision in America. The boundaries even of Acadia, specifically ceded to Britain by France, were unsettled; the great valley of the Ohio, between Lake Erie and the mountains of Pennsylvania, Maryland, and Virginia, remained debatable ground, and the command of the interior beyond it evidently rested with whichever Power secured possession of it. English traders had pushed across the Alleghany mountains and established themselves in the Indian villages on the Ohio; and where the trader set foot, the farmer was sure to follow. Nine months after the treaty of Aix-la-Chapelle a French military expedition traversed the district, and haughtily warned the English off as trespassers. Three years later the French began to build a chain of forts, and to pour men and supplies into the district. The British colonists, encouraged by the home government, did the like, and a collision ensued in which the British were worsted, and troops were sent from Britain to support them. A much larger force was despatched from France to Canada; and the rival nations were now definitely engaged in a struggle which proved to be the most momentous in colonial history.

During two years fortune seemed to favour France; but the tide changed with the capture of Louisbourg

(1758). One by one the French forts were taken ; Quebec fell in 1759, and by the capitulation of Montreal, September 9, 1760, all French North America, except Louisiana, with the town of New Orleans, passed into the hands of England. Spain declared war in 1762, with the result that the English fleets captured Havana, Trinidad, and Manila. In the East Indies the English arms were equally successful. Here, as in North America, a determined attempt on the part of France to expel the British met with resolute resistance ; and, as in North America, the question of French or British supremacy was brought to an issue, decided in favour of England, and settled by the Treaty of Paris, 1763.

Britain now stood forth the predominant power of the colonial world. France, her only dangerous rival, was confined in North America to New Orleans and an undefined and unoccupied region west of the Mississippi ; in the West Indies to Martinique and Guadeloupe ; and in the East to a few commercial stations in India where she renounced the right of maintaining troops, and the island of Mauritius. Both in North America and in India, Britain had very largely increased her possessions, and had secured them against future aggression. Englishmen now beheld the model of the terrestrial globe in a new light. It was surprising to notice how little had been done in the course of two centuries to extend geographical knowledge. Two-thirds at least of the globe's surface were practically unexplored. Britain had proved herself capable of holding the ocean against the united fleets of France and Spain ; and the future of its unoccupied coasts manifestly rested with her.

The greater part of the unknown surface of the globe

lay in the southern hemisphere, beyond a line drawn from Cape Horn and South Africa in the west to Java, the Spice Islands, and the Philippines in the east. Farther northward the known world terminated with the sea which washes the eastern coast of Japan. In northern latitudes a few islands and island groups had been discovered by the Spanish vessels annually plying between the Philippines and Mexico. Southward of the route taken by these vessels trustworthy information was lacking. Those navigators who had occasionally crossed or penetrated these little-known latitudes reported the existence of many islands and island groups in the south Pacific, some of these islands being of great extent. Dutch captains had sailed past the northern and western coasts of Australia, and named it New Holland; had reached Tasmania, and named it Van Diemen's Land; and had given New Zealand the name by which it is still known. But the real configuration of these widely distributed coasts was unknown; and for practical purposes the ocean east and south of the Spice Islands was an unexplored region. And these discoveries in the southern seas were accepted by geographers as confirmations of a speculative theory which had naturally arisen after the southern extremity of Africa had been reached by the Portuguese. The Cape of Good Hope, the southernmost promontory of the Old World, lay only 35 deg. south of the equator; beyond it, so far as was known, there was nothing but ocean. But the whole of Europe, the greater part of Asia, and, as shortly afterwards appeared, the greater part of North America, lay beyond a line drawn in the corresponding latitude in the northern hemisphere.

Corresponding to this immense continental land-area in the northern latitudes of the northern hemisphere, there would probably be found, it was argued, a vast continental land-area in the southern latitudes of the southern hemisphere. This imaginary continent was named Terra Australis. When Magellan sailed for the first time between South America and Tierra del Fuego, the latter island was surmised to be a promontory of this great imaginary southern continent; and all lands discovered south of a line drawn from the Cape of Good Hope to the Spice Islands, and produced into the Pacific Ocean, were still supposed to be either parts of this continent, or islands lying at no great distance from its coasts.

The approach of a rarely recurring astronomical phenomenon furnished a reason for an exploring expedition to the southern seas. On June 3, 1769, the planet Venus was to cross the sun's disk; the phenomenon would be best observed at some point in the Pacific south of the equator, midway between the Spice Islands and South America. In the interests of science it behoved the English government to despatch an expedition for the purpose of observing the transit, and nothing could be more natural than some incidental investigation of the geography and resources of these little-known regions. The command was given to James Cook, a sailor who had rendered signal service as a nautical surveyor in the late war in America. The island of Otaheite, recently discovered by Wallis, was chosen as the place of observation; and, the work of the astronomers being completed, Cook visited the rest of the Society Islands, and sailed southward for New

Zealand, then generally believed to be a part of the great Terra Australis. Cook proved this belief to be false. Having circumnavigated, in succession, the North Island and South Island, accurately surveying their coasts, a task which occupied six months, he resolved to sail westward, and return by way of the eastern shore of New Holland, the contour of which was as yet unknown. Cook surveyed this coast from south to north, gave it the name of New South Wales, took possession of it in the name of Britain, noted Botany Bay, near Sydney, as a suitable place for a colony, and returned to England. He had found no Terra Australis, but he had prepared the way for the establishment of new branches of the British colonial empire in the southern ocean. In 1772-75 Cook made a second voyage in search of Terra Australis, in the course of which he revisited New Zealand, and discovered New Caledonia, the next in size of the Pacific islands, Norfolk Island, and South Georgia. By an exhaustive exploration he proved that there were no habitable lands south of those now made known, and that the south-polar continent, if it existed, could be nothing but an icy waste.

From the Antarctic Ocean Cook's attention was now turned to the Arctic. The acquisition of Canada by Britain had revived the idea of reaching the Far East and India by sailing westwards along the northern shores of the American continent; and Cook, now recognised as the first navigator of the age, undertook once more the Discovery of the North-West Passage. He determined to approach his task from the west instead of the east. Hitherto the north-west coasts of America had been only known through imperfect accounts of the voyages of Russian sailors. Having touched at the Sandwich Islands, Cook started from California, followed the coast line for some 3500 miles, passed Behring Strait, and entered the Arctic Ocean. Returning to winter in the Sandwich Islands, with the intention of prosecuting his task in the spring, Cook was murdered while regaining his boat after an affray with the islanders, February 14, 1779, having in ten years done more for geographical science than any man that ever lived.

At the time when Cook was laying down on the map new fields for British colonial enterprise in Australia, New Zealand, and British Columbia, trouble was gathering in the Thirteen Colonies on the Atlantic coast of North America. These now constituted the largest part of the British colonial empire. Under various forms of government, and in varying degrees of completeness, the people of both continental and island colonies in the New World had always enjoyed that political liberty which was the inheritance of all Englishmen. They elected their representative assemblies, and voted their own taxes; subject, as in England, to the concurrence of the Crown, they made and amended their own provincial laws. But the regulation of their commerce rested with the British Parliament; and the policy of Britain confined it, so far as it was to her interest, to her own ports. Only by her leave, and on conditions which she imposed, could the colonies trade with any foreign country. The complicated system of trade regulation which existed was felt as a grievance by the colonists; but they had prospered under it, and were content to endure it. But when the British government, compelled to impose new taxation after a costly war primarily waged for the protection of the colonies against French aggression, claimed and exercised the right of levying some contribution to this taxation in America, the colonists refused to submit. Coercive measures, unfortunately resorted to by the parent country, provoked armed resistance, and the British troops met with signal reverses; finally the colonists, to the amazement of Englishmen at home, accepted the support of France, insidiously offered on condition of their renouncing allegiance to their parent country for ever. France having declared war, Spain and Holland, both anxious to take a hand in the prospective humiliation of England, followed at France's heels. Britain made peace with her revolted colonies in 1782, on the footing of recognising their independence; and in 1783 she was fain to conclude a treaty with their European allies which deprived her in several points of the advantageous position she had secured in the colonial world twenty years previously. Yet neither the situation of France nor that of Spain was substantially improved, while that of Holland was changed for the worse; and thirty years later, at the close of the convulsions which followed the French Revolution, Britain emerged from a prolonged struggle, in which France, Spain, and Holland were once more arrayed against her, with her position effectually secured against almost every danger which had menaced it, and with the foundations of her Colonial Empire extended more widely than ever.

Britain is often depicted as an ambitious Power inspired by an insatiable greed of territory, and ever

scheming to prevent her European neighbours from
reaping the fruits of their own colonial enterprises.
The fact is, that although her colonial growth has at
every stage been guided by the necessities of self-defence,
at none of the international settlements by which her
position has been reassured after successive attacks
upon it has she taken unfair advantage of a defeated
assailant, or pushed her claims for compensation and
future security beyond the limits of moderation. By
the Treaty of Ryswick, 1697, Britain obtained no
extension of her colonial system. The Treaty of Utrecht,
1713, which secured Hudson's Bay, Newfoundland, and
Nova Scotia to Britain, merely had the effect of shifting
the French attack to a more vulnerable line of defence ;
and the French scheme for the conquest of the North
American continent was prosecuted from the St.
Lawrence and the great lakes as a base with scarcely
any intermission. "In 1713," said a Frenchman to an
English statesman a few years later, "you might have
crushed us outright. Why did you refrain?" The
peace of 1748 was but a truce dictated by the necessities
of the belligerents in Europe, and when Britain was
once more at war with France in 1756 the weakness of
her position in America was sufficiently proved by her
losses in the first stage of the conflict. These losses
amply proved the necessity of annexing Canada. But
Canada was annexed in the interests of the North
American colonies, rather than in those of Britain
herself ; and from the merely British point of view the
terms of the Treaty of 1763 were so favourable to
France that bribery of the British ministry in the
French interest was freely charged and generally

credited.   The chief interests of Britain, it was argued, lay in the West Indies.   Britain, in the course of the war, had not only captured the principal French islands—Martinique, Guadeloupe, and Grenada—but had taken possession of St. Lucia, Dominica, and St. Vincent, neutral islands on which French colonists had imprudently established themselves.   From the Spaniards she had captured Havana, and might without difficulty have seized the other ports of Cuba.   Had Britain demanded that to which her successes fairly entitled her, she might have annexed the most cherished West Indian possessions of France and Spain.   Of the islands to which France had a recognised title Britain annexed only Grenada with the Grenadines.   The four neutral islands, St. Lucia, Dominica, St. Vincent, and Tobago, might justly have been claimed as a trophy of the struggle.   Britain contented herself with a partition of these islands, which gave St. Lucia, in every respect the most valuable, to France.   Martinique and Guadeloupe she restored ; and the extent of her liberality in taking this course may be measured by the general opinion that Guadeloupe alone would have been a more valuable acquisition to the Empire than Canada.   Spain was treated with equal consideration.   Puerto Rico was named as the very least that ought to be demanded from Spain as the price of the restitution of Havana— the richest among the many prizes which had fallen to the British arms.   Britain left the Spanish West Indian possessions intact, taking in exchange for Havana only the deserted coast of Florida.

While France in 1763 retained her original West Indian possessions scarcely impaired, her rights in the

Newfoundland fishery under the Treaty of 1713 were confirmed and extended ; and no part of the terms of settlement became the subject of more adverse criticism. Not only was the liberty of fishing extended to the islands and coasts of the Gulf of St. Lawrence, but the islands of St. Pierre and Miquelon were ceded to France as places of shelter for the French fishermen.   Had the British ministry insisted, as they might, on the relinquishment of all French rights in the fishery, they would certainly have abolished what long proved to be a permanent source of irritation to the people of Newfoundland, and incidentally have dealt a severe blow at the maritime power of France.   The British ministry preferred to adhere to a bargain of fifty years' standing, in the maintenance of which British honour was thought to be involved, and abstained from bringing unmerited ruin on a great French industry. Nor was France precluded, by the terms arranged with Britain, from fulfilling her cherished aspiration of creating a new French nation in North America.   Together with New Orleans, she retained all that vast middle section of North America which lay between the Mississippi on the east and Spanish America in the west; and the navigation of the Mississippi was declared open to both France and Britain.   But France was in no mood for new colonial enterprises.   Mortified by the loss of Canada, she privately agreed, by an arrangement which took effect in 1769, to cede what remained of Louisiana to Spain in compensation for the loss of Florida ; and Spain now possessed a territory in North America stretching from the Pacific to the Mississippi, and rivalling in extent her possessions in South America.

In the same year (1769) Spain laid the foundation of
an extensive system of missionary settlements among
the Indians of California.   It seemed as though neither
France nor England, but Spain, was destined to be the
dominant power in North America.   Nothing seemed
more unlikely than that this immense territory would
fall to the Thirteen British Colonies on the Atlantic,
which it henceforth became the policy of France and
Spain in the first place to detach from the parent country,
and in the second place to confine within the narrowest
possible geographical limits.

That such was the aim of France and Spain was
demonstrated during the negotiations which preceded
the peace of 1783; nor is it surprising to find that the
two Powers which had so long opposed the colonial
expansion of Britain should prove themselves equally
hostile to the expansion of the new nation which they
had assisted, for their own purposes, in establishing its
independence.   If the States were allowed to retain the
eastern half of Louisiana, between the Appalachian
mountains and the Mississippi, Spain would have on her
eastern flank a republic of British origin, inheriting
British colonial traditions, and flushed with recent
military successes.   Spain had now reconquered Florida,
which had been British for twenty years; and it was
suggested that by virtue of this reconquest Spain was
entitled to all that lay to the north of Florida and west
of the Appalachian mountains.   To maintain so ex-
travagant a claim was out of the question; but it was
seriously proposed, on the part of Spain and France, that
Britain should retain as part of Canada all that lay
between the Mississippi and the Ohio, including the

present States of Ohio, Illinois, Indiana, Michigan, Wisconsin, and part of Minnesota; and that all south of the Ohio as far as the parallel of 31°—the northern boundary of Florida—should be neutralised as "Indian territory." Such a proposition could find no favour with British statesmen, and the territory in question was secured for the new American nation. Had the scheme of France and Spain succeeded, the 40,000 loyalists who migrated from the States to Canada would doubtless have peopled by preference the great middle valley of North America; Britain, retaining the navigation of the Mississippi, would have become once more predominant on the American continent, and Chicago have become the centre of a British dominion exceeding in extent and importance the thirteen federated colonies on the Atlantic.

Had British statesmen chosen to prolong the war they might probably have concluded peace with France and Spain on terms not substantially different from those of the treaty of 1763. But the main object of the contest was gone; and France was content with a change in the partition of the "neutral" islands in the West Indies by which she obtained the island of Tobago in addition to St. Lucia, with the restitution of the Senegal colonies in Africa, where Britain already possessed stations on the Gambia river, and with some concessions in India. Again Britain recognised the rights of France in the Newfoundland fisheries, and granted French fishermen the right of drying their fish on a more convenient part of the shore of Newfoundland, including part of the north and the whole of the western coast of the island. Spain had confidently expected to recover Gibraltar and the Bahamas, in addition to Minorca, which Britain had held between 1708 and 1782, when it was recaptured by the united forces of France and Spain. All that she obtained, besides the restitution of Minorca, was her old territory of Florida. This had been in British hands for twenty years, during which more had been done to develop its resources than had been done by Spaniards in the two hundred years preceding. The British colonists, 25,000 in number, now migrated to the adjacent States. In the East, Britain's position was greatly strengthened. Holland ceded to her the Indian port of Negapatam, and purchased the restitution of other Dutch possessions captured by Britain by granting her the right of free commerce with the whole of the Dutch Indies. The separation of the Thirteen Colonies was scarcely felt as a loss, for their trade with Britain steadily increased ; and a commercial treaty with France, concluded in 1786, seemed likely to herald a long period of friendly intercourse between Britain and her only considerable colonial rival.

The events of the ten years which elapsed between the Treaty of Versailles and the outbreak, in 1793, of a long war with revolutionary and imperial France foreshadowed the outline of the British Empire as it exists to-day. Canada, no longer an isolated French community, began to stretch forth westwards as a British dominion. During and after the war of independence thousands of loyalists quitted the States, many of whom sought new homes in Nova Scotia and the valley of the St. Lawrence. Many others, availing themselves of free grants of land offered by government, settled on the more attractive shores of Lakes Ontario and Erie, especially the pen-

insula of Niagara. Here a new and distinctively British
group of settlements came into existence. With the
original colony of Canada, which remained French in
language and social organisation, and Catholic in religion,
these new settlements had little in common, and
communication between the two districts was difficult.
The country above Montreal was therefore constituted
in 1791 as a separate province by the name of Upper
Canada. The original French colony was at the same
time reconstituted by the name of Lower Canada; and
governments were framed on the model of the
constitutions given to Nova Scotia in 1758, and to New
Brunswick in 1785. Each province had its Governor,
representing the Crown, assisted by a nominated
Legislative Council, and its Assembly of representatives
elected by the people. The colonial government was
only responsible to the Crown, the functions of the
Assembly being limited to granting supplies and passing
such legislative measures as were approved by the
Governor and Council. Small as was the measure of
political liberty thus granted, it sufficed for the needs
of the time; and after the proclamation of the new
constitutions British immigrants resorted to Canada in
increasing numbers.

While the Empire was thus vigorously throwing out
a new offshoot on the northern shore of the great lakes
of North America, facing the old colonies on the southern
shore, enterprises of not less importance were being
prosecuted on the opposite side of the globe. Two
years after the Treaty of Paris the East India Company
laid the foundation of the present thriving colonies on
the Straits of Malacca by acquiring from a native prince

the island of Penang (1785).   The colony of Malacca
was still in the hands of the Dutch, and so remained
for ten years longer.   Far away to the south-east, the
remotest shore of a vacant continent became the scene
of a bolder venture.   No such task had ever been
attempted as that undertaken by Britain in the settlement of Australia.   Compared with it, the English
settlement of North America had been an easy and
natural process.   Australia was five times farther from
Britain, and could only be reached by a tedious and
difficult navigation ; Bencoolen, the nearest British
outpost, was 4000 miles distant.   Wherever colonisation had hitherto been undertaken, some of the
elements of civilised life had been found ready to hand.
Everywhere there had been an aboriginal population
raised above the level of mere savagery, subsisting in
some measure by agriculture, and storing the means
of subsistence for future consumption ; in most places
there had been some native commodity worth exporting.
In case the settlement proved a failure, it was generally
possible for the emigrants to make their way back to
Europe.   The aborigines of Australia were few in
numbers, and lived from hand to mouth.   There was
no cultivated native food-plant ; game and fish were
said to be scarce, and the substantial means of subsistence must be imported ; should these fail, there was
little chance of relief from passing vessels.   There was
no native product capable of furnishing a basis for trade.
Every circumstance, in short, that had proved favourable to colonial enterprise in America was wanting in
Australia.   French writers had pointed out, thirty years
previously, that while such facts as these were un-

favourable to ordinary settlements in this remote quarter
of the globe none of them weighed strongly against a
penal colony, and some were positively favourable to it.
Such a settlement was accordingly resolved on by the
British government; and in 1788 the first Australian
colony, consisting of about a thousand persons, one-
fourth of whom were officials and soldiers, the residue
convicts destined to supply labour for the community,
was established on the harbour of Sydney. Another
colony of the same description, formed on Norfolk Island,
was, after some years' experience, removed to Tasmania;
both places in time became the resort of voluntary immigrants. The climate and soil proved eminently suitable
to agriculture and stock-raising; and before long it was
discovered that Australia was the finest wool-growing
country in the world. As if to prove the vitality of
British colonial enterprise in every continent, the settlement of Sierra Leone, destined for the reception of
emancipated negro slaves, was founded in the same
year (1787) in which the first colonising expedition was
despatched to Australia.

Six years later Britain's energy of resistance and
counterpressure was suddenly aroused in the great war
with revolutionary France, and maintained with little
intermission for more than twenty years. After bringing this unprecedented struggle to a successful conclusion, Britain might in other circumstances have
exacted substantial concessions from the nation which
had so long disturbed the peace of the world. But
the struggle had been maintained by Britain and her
allies as much for the benefit of the French people
as for their own. It was the interest of Europe that

France should be liberated once for all from the aggressive despotism of which she had become the helpless instrument. It was not the interest of Europe that she should be permanently weakened; and by the terms of peace in 1814 France was deprived of none of her ancient colonial possessions. All the "neutral" West Indian islands which by the Treaty of 1783 had been equally divided between Britain and France— Britain retaining Dominica and St. Vincent, and France obtaining Tobago in addition to St. Lucia—were now assigned to Britain; and the British position was strengthened by the acquisition of St. Lucia, strategically important on account of the fine harbour of Castries. Britain's only other acquisition at the expense of France was Mauritius, which had been occupied by the French after its abandonment by the Dutch. The situation of this island had enabled French men-of-war and privateers to inflict serious damage on the trading vessels of the East India Company. It was captured by the direction of the British ministry in 1810; and the same necessity which compelled its capture dictated its retention by Britain at the Peace of 1814.

As between Britain and France, the Powers mainly concerned, the adjustment of colonial gains and losses after the great European war represented little more than the final settlement of an old dispute over the "neutral" West Indian islands. As between Britain and the weaker Powers which the French Republic had held in compulsory alliance the settlement assumed a different character. Most of what Britain had taken from them was essential to her security. Even before the war Spain's hold over her American possessions was manifestly relaxing. The islands, it seemed, must fall either to Britain or to France; the continental districts must become independent, and their commerce be thrown open to Europe. By the infamous Peace of 1795 Spain ceded to France the Spanish part of St. Domingo; and the dismemberment of Spanish America was thus begun. Britain retorted by the capture of Trinidad, long the resort of French settlers, and rapidly becoming ripe for French annexation. In the hands of Britain, it was anticipated, Port-of-Spain, the capital, would become the Liverpool of South America; in any case it would be invaluable for the protection of British trade with the new South American nations. Simultaneously Britain acquired one of the most valuable sections of South America—the western part of Dutch Guiana. British Guiana, as it was henceforth named, was surrendered to the fleet by the Dutch inhabitants, who preferred British rule to annexation by France and incorporation in the French colony of Cayenne.

In the Old World as well as the New, Britain was more and more turning her attention southwards. She was definitely committed to the colonisation of Australia. British interests in India, already immense, were expanding, and the forces of the East India Company were encountering native enemies raised up by French intrigue and maintained by French subsidies. France openly threatened an overland invasion of India, and the Cape of Good Hope, the key of the maritime route, was held by one of France's allies. The occupation of the Cape, in such circumstances, was a necessity; nor was it possible to leave an enemy in possession of Ceylon. Malacca and Java, the principal of the Dutch oriental

possessions, fell to the British arms, as did the Dutch
West Indian islands.   These were restored, and of
her conquests from the Dutch, Britain retained only
the Cape and Ceylon ; like Mauritius, these were
indispensable to the security of the route to India.
One more possession, which the French had seized in
1798 without a shadow of right, was added to the
British Empire.   This was Malta, the island stronghold,
since 1530, of the Knights of St. John of Jerusalem,
and once the maritime bulwark of western Europe
against the Turk.   Britain expelled the French, and by
the treaty of Amiens (1802) agreed to restore Malta to
its owners, Bonaparte having already twice undertaken
to evacuate Holland.   The treaty was a disadvantageous
one for Britain ; but Bonaparte was resolved to break it
and renew the war, as a means of obtaining for himself
the imperial dignity ; he therefore refused to move the
French garrisons from Utrecht and Flushing.   The result
was that Britain permanently secured this dominant
position in the Mediterranean.   Britain refused to
evacuate Malta, and the war was renewed.   At the settlement of 1815 Britain retained it.   The seven "Ionian "
islands near the western coast of Greece, once among
the possessions of the dissolved Venetian republic, had
been captured by France early in the war.   They were
recaptured by the British fleet, were placed in 1815
under British protection, and were deemed part of the
Colonial Empire until 1863, when they were transferred
to the kingdom of Greece. The result of a fundamentally defensive struggle, maintained by Britain during
more than a century, had been to extend the Empire to
its existing geographical outline ; but when what this

outline embraced in the whole is compared with the actual
losses sustained by other Powers, the extent of these
losses appears disproportionately small.   French Canada
consisted of little more than the banks of the St.
Lawrence below Montreal, with at most 60,000 inhabitants.   The Dutch population of Cape Colony was
about 35,000.   But Britain in each case secured the
same advantage which she had secured in Australia—an
opportunity of continental extension, such as she had
secured for the new Anglo-American nation created by
her sons in the middle latitudes of North America.
Instead of a single base for the development of
Britannic nationality, she now possessed three.   In
Australia there was nothing to obstruct the process.
The aboriginal inhabitants, low in advancement and
incapable of organisation, retired before the settlers
towards the interior, and gave no serious trouble.   In
Canada the Indians, reconciled for the most part to the
presence of the white man by commercial intercourse
and missionary effort, accepted reserved lands and
government allowances; while the French colonists
rarely crossed the limits of their own province unless to
migrate to the States.   In South Africa these fortunate
conditions were reversed; and the very fact that it
offered every facility for the rapid extension of settlements condemned it for nearly a century to a condition
of unrest fatal to continuous development.   The names
of its various districts, which represent either immi-
grations by warlike African tribes from the north-east,
or counter-settlements from the south by Dutch fugitives
from British rule, bear witness to a state of things
involving difficulties without a parallel elsewhere.

Of the new fields thus opened to British enterprise, the virgin soil of Australasia offered the best facilities for speedy development. Like the eastern coast of North America, the south-eastern shores of Australia and all the coasts of New Zealand offered attractive sites for large colonies without penetrating far into the interior. In New South Wales and Tasmania the convict system provided labour for road-making and bridge-building; many convicts in time attained their freedom, and received grants of land. Immigrants came in large numbers as the colonies prospered. Agriculture and sheep-farming were extended, and in 1824 New South Wales began to export corn and wool. In the same year a settlement formed on the Brisbane river became the nucleus of the present State of Queensland. Van Diemen's Land, now Tasmania, became a separate colony in 1825. Western Australia was settled in 1826, and constituted a colony in 1829. Port Phillip, now Victoria, and South Australia were colonised in 1836, and New Zealand in 1840. Meanwhile the Straits Settlements, begun by the occupation of Penang simultaneously with the earliest Australian colony, had grown into an important group of dependencies. Province Wellesley, on the mainland opposite Penang, was purchased in 1798. Malacca had been captured from the Dutch in 1795, but was restored, together with Java, in 1818, when Sir Stamford Raffles selected the island of Singapore as the future seat of British trade with the Far East. It was settled in 1819, and became a colony in 1824. In the same year Malacca was ceded by the Dutch in exchange for Bencoolen and other possessions of the East India Company on the west coast of Sumatra,

thus finally becoming a British possession.   The extinction of the monopoly of the East India Company in
1834 led to a great increase of trade with China.
Oppressive treatment of British merchants in Canton
led to a Chinese war ; and China, besides agreeing
to pay an indemnity, ceded to Britain the island of
Hong-Kong as a commercial station (1840).   In 1846
the island of Labuan was secured as a similar station
for the trade of Borneo, on the north-west coast of
which James Brooke, having succeeded in putting down
piracy at sea and establishing order on land, had been
recognised by the native Sultan as Rajah of the province
of Sarawak.   Thus, throughout Australasia and eastern
Asia colonial extension and economic development pro-
ceeded with little hindrance and no complication.

British North America, meanwhile, had advanced in a
different way.   While the Australasian colonies were as
yet in their infancy, the two Canadas and the Maritime
Provinces were fast approaching maturity.   In the two
generations which followed the war of American
independence the Canadian population had increased
tenfold, although little progress had been made in
filling up with new settlements the vast area which
awaited them.   Growing in wealth and numbers, with
the democratic United States hard by, and receiving
a constant stream of British immigrants, it was impossible for either Lower or Upper Canada to remain
content with representative assemblies having no substantial control over the colonial governments ; but it
was not until Parliamentary reform had triumphed in
Britain that Canadian discontent passed the point of
refusing to vote supplies, and reached that of open

rebellion. Lord Durham's mission of 1838 led to the
union of the two provinces, and the establishment of a
government responsible to the Assembly; and the year
1841, in which this change took effect, began a new era
in imperial history. Australia followed quickly in the
wake of Canada. There were now 80,000 colonists in
New South Wales, which as yet included Victoria and
Queensland. To these it was impossible to refuse what
had been granted in Canada fifty years before; and
representative government was established in 1842.
One-fourth of the representation was assigned to the
district of Port Phillip. The rapid growth of this
district, and the concentration of a large commerce at
Melbourne, pointed to its separation from New South
Wales, and in 1851 it was constituted an independent
colony by the name of Victoria. A more important step
was taken at the same moment. The complete political
freedom which Canada had obtained only after twenty
years of agitation was conceded with less reluctance to
Australia. The four colonies of New South Wales,
South Australia, Van Diemen's Land, and Victoria,
were empowered to frame constitutions for themselves.
Five years later (1856) government by ministries
responsible to the assemblies had been established in
each, and the name of Van Diemen's Land was changed
to Tasmania.

Very different was the course of events in South
Africa. No natural difficulty stood in the way of opening
this fine country, equally rich, in its way, with Canada
and Australia in the elements of wealth, to civilisation.
Although broken by arid bush and bare mountains,
the vast spaces of the interior, fertilised by periodical

rains, swarmed with large game, and afforded unlimited
facilities for raising sheep and cattle. Besides the low
savages called "Bushmen," the more advanced, but in-
dolent and thriftless, Hottentots wandered over the
land with their flocks and herds, and the Dutch, following in their tracks, found the exploration and occupation
of the country a singularly easy task. The aboriginal
Bushmen gave as little trouble as the blacks of Australia.
The Hottentots frequented the settlements of the newcomers for purposes of petty trade and plunder; and
the Dutch, spreading from Cape Town in the south-
west along the south coast and far into the interior,
easily dispossessed them, and largely reduced them to
slavery. Advancing still eastwards, the Dutch found
themselves in contact with a very different race—the
warlike Kaffirs, who poured in by thousands from the
populous tracts of the north-east. A border warfare
on the eastern frontier of Cape Colony had become
chronic when Britain took possession. With the
object of interposing between the Kaffirs and Dutch
a barrier of peaceful colonists, the Eastern Province,
with a separate port on Algoa Bay, was settled by the
British government in 1820. The device proved ineffectual; the Kaffir clans of the coast continued their
raids, and punitive expeditions from the colony only
provoked fresh attacks. In 1834, 30,000 Kaffirs
suddenly assailed the British frontier in every part,
from the mountains of the interior to the sea. Meanwhile trouble arose in the western or Dutch part of
the colony. The Dutch were slave-holders, and in the
Cape Town district depended for labour on imported
negroes. When Britain annexed the colony the slaves

outnumbered the white population. Britain had abolished the maritime slave-trade, and the last ship-load of imported slaves was landed at Cape Town in 1807. The Dutch continued to enslave the Hottentots of the interior, and in 1815 an attempted rebellion against Britain ensued on some prosecutions for maltreating them. A new cause of irritation on the part of the Dutch arose after 1815, when British missionaries settled in the country, converting the native races to Christianity, and teaching them the elements of European civilisation. What completed the exasperation of the Dutch population was the abolition of slavery throughout the British dominions in 1834, and the recognition of the natives as human beings entitled in some degree to civic rights. Refusing, in many cases, the compensation awarded them for the loss of their slaves, and accusing the government of encouraging Kaffir invasions in order to exterminate them, many thousands of Boers sold or abandoned their farms, and passed over the Orange River in search of a country where the arm of the law could not reach them, and missionaries were unknown. North of the Orange River were the Griquas, mainly half-breeds derived from the association of the Dutch with their female Hottentot slaves. Farther north, beyond the Vaal River, were the Matabele, a powerful body of Kaffir warriors who had recently invaded the district, and were spreading southward, driving the Griquas before them. The Boers offered the Griquas help against the intruders, defeated and expelled them, and settled down in the country. Many followed the retreating Matabele into the country beyond the Vaal, and ultimately cleared the land of them as far as the

Limpopo. Others crossed the Drakenberg, descended into Natal, and proclaimed the republic of "Natalia."

There was already a British settlement at Port Durban, and the immigrant Boers, after suffering severely in a struggle with a large body of immigrant Zulus, were compelled to recognise British authority. Many upon this recrossed the Drakenberg, and rejoined those of their number who had remained on the other side. The reunited settlers elected a popular assembly, or Volksraad, which exercised little control over its constituents, and was never recognised by the British government. The continual encroachments of the Boers on the Griquas and Basutos made it necessary to take these tribes under British protection ; and Britain unwillingly assumed the sovereignty of the Boer district also. In 1845 a British resident was established at Bloemfontein ; and in 1848 the country between the Orange and Vaal rivers was proclaimed British territory by the name of the "Orange River Sovereignty." Mortified at finding themselves once more under British authority, a considerable body of the Boers now rose in arms, but were defeated and dispersed. The insurgents crossed the Vaal River, where they subsequently proclaimed the "South African Republic," better known as the "Transvaal." Under British government the Orange River Sovereignty gave promise of prosperity and peaceful development ; Dutch and British immigrants came from the Cape Colony, and the inhabitants obtained a nominal representation on the Legislative Council (1849). But this hopeful prospect was clouded. A fresh war with the Kaffirs on the eastern frontier of Cape Colony (1850-1853) was followed by native troubles in the Sovereignty, where the protected native tribes were assailed by the warlike Basutos. The Dutch of the Sovereignty were unwilling to give military service in the interest of the natives, and found sympathisers among their kinsmen beyond the Vaal. The misconduct of the latter, who maltreated the natives, and obstructed traders and missionaries passing in the direction of Central Africa, called loudly for intervention. The British ministry decided that this was out of the question. Weary of pursuing these recalcitrants into the remote interior of Africa, and dreading their interference in the affairs of the Sovereignty, Britain agreed to a convention recognising the independence of the Boers beyond the Vaal, subject to an acknowledgment of British suzerainty, and to provisions intended to secure the liberty of the natives (1852). The troubles of the Sovereignty were not ended. The Basutos maintained a threatening attitude, a vigorous attack by the British arms led to no decisive result, and the Sovereignty could only be permanently held by maintaining there a large British garrison. The colonists were dissatisfied, and clamoured for representative government; many of the Dutch aspired to that independence which had been formally conceded to their kinsmen beyond the Vaal. In these circumstances, contrary to a strong current of opinion in the Cape Colony and in the Sovereignty itself, the home government resolved to withdraw. In 1854 British authority was declared to be at an end in the Orange River Territory, and its inhabitants organised themselves as a "Free State" or republic.

This disposition to evade imperial responsibilities in South Africa was only one among many signs of a

widespread but not universal indifference to colonial
interests which had recently been gaining ground.
Colonies, it was plausibly said, were troublesome to
govern, costly to defend, and of little value as append-
ages to a kingdom which had almost a monopoly of the
world's maritime commerce.   The original colonies of
North America, now the United States, had claimed and
received their independence.   The Spanish and Portuguese colonies had followed.   Canada and Australia,
having obtained self-government, were on the same road.
It was natural for colonial communities, having outgrown
the period of youth, to separate from the parent stock
and set up in the world of nations for themselves.   Since
the abolition of slavery, the West Indies had lost much
of their prosperity and commercial importance.   The old
system, under which the trade of the colonies was regulated for the exclusive benefit of themselves and the parent
country, had been terminated.   The timber of Canada, the
sugar of the West Indies, and the wines of the Cape no
longer had a preferential position in the British market;
and the colonies made no distinction in favour of the
parent country in levying the import duties which
furnished the greater part of their public revenue.
The large and growing trade of Britain with the United
States was pointed to as evidence that both the parent
country and its offshoots would gain by separation.
Meanwhile the colonies must learn to bear their own
burdens.   Imperial troops should be withdrawn, except
in the case of the garrisons of a few naval stations
necessary to secure the command of the sea and the
security of commercial routes.   Of the application of
these doctrines South Africa was the most obvious

H

instance.   The Cape had been acquired solely as a naval post to secure the route to India.   Yet Britain had been led by its acquisition to spend millions on the government and defence of a vast continental territory.   It was time that the Cape colonists should manage their own affairs, as their kinsmen of the Orange and Transvaal States were able to do.   The possession of Cape Town was not necessary for imperial purposes.   As a naval station Simon's Bay, on the other side of the promontory, was amply sufficient.

But the way was being prepared for a larger conception of South Africa.   The credit of the change is mainly due to two Scottish missionaries.   Thwarted in his efforts by the Dutch, Robert Moffat conceived the idea of passing beyond the limits of their settlements, and planting Christianity and civilisation among tribes where no animosity against the European as yet existed. For fifty years he toiled among the Bechuanas, and made many journeys among the Matabele of what is now Southern Rhodesia.   Moffat's work was continued by his son-in-law, David Livingstone.   In the intervals of missionary labour this intrepid explorer crossed the Kalahari desert, reached Lake Ngami, discovered the Zambesi, with its famous " Victoria " falls—the largest in the world,—and made his way both to the eastern and western shores of the continent.   In later years Livingstone explored the Shiré river, discovered Lake Nyassa, and traversed the region between that lake and Lake Tanganyika.

Until the publication of Livingstone's Travels in 1857 most English people probably knew more about the Esquimaux and the Polynesians than about the Kaffir, the

Hottentot, and the Boer who shared with a few recently introduced British colonists one of the most promising bases for colonial expansion, and one of the most important strategic positions, in the Empire. British ministries were better informed ; they knew that the establishment of the Eastern Province had proved a failure so far as it had been intended as a measure of defence against Kaffir invasion. They saw in the two Boer republics two barriers between the Kaffir clans and Cape Colony ; and the convention of 1852 practically encouraged the Boers to extend their area of domination as far northwards as they pleased. Livingstone was the first to point out what this meant for the native races ; and with the publication of his journal a new era began for Africa south of the equator. In the course of the next thirty years, largely in consequence of the interest excited by his adventures, British travellers explored Africa from the Zambesi to the Egyptian Sudan. The problem of the sources of the Nile was solved. Burton and Speke (1857-1858) reached Lake Tanganyika, and the latter discovered the southern shore of the Victoria Nyanza. Speke and Grant (1860-1863) ascertained the Victoria Nyanza to be the reservoir in which the waters of the great river were gathered before rolling northwards. The last years of Livingstone, who died in 1873, were spent in endeavouring to trace the Nile to its source above the Nyanza ; and his gravestone in Westminster Abbey is appropriately inscribed with two verses of a Roman poem, recording a similar aspiration of Julius Cæsar.[1]

---

[1] Tantus amor veri, nihil est quod noscere malim
Quam fluvii causas per sæcula tanta latentes.

Lucan, *Pharsalia*, x. 189.

It was Cæsar's ambition to mark the culmination of an empire embracing three continents by reaching the fountains of the Nile; and what was denied to Rome was at length achieved by Britain.

While the African continent was thus assuming an aspect which suggested a great extension of colonisation, the work of Imperial consolidation was begun in British North America. Something resembling consolidation had been effected by the union of the two Canadas under responsible government in 1841, but the experiment had not proved entirely successful. The possession of power oscillated between a British and a French party, each contending for its own interests; and there were many who advocated incorporation with the United States, where the hope of annexing Canada to the Union had always been vaguely entertained. Whatever there may have been to justify such a hope, so long as the Canadians were denied full political liberty, had been removed by the grant of responsible government. To the soil of Canada the United States had no shadow of claim. Lower Canada and the Maritime Provinces had been fairly won by the British arms from the Power which had begun by seeking to dominate all North America, and ended by forcing the Thirteen Colonies into permanent separation from the parent country. Upper Canada was the refuge of those loyalists whom the United States had expelled. Little could those have known of Britain who imagined that she would abandon her faithful sons; as little could those have known of Canada who imagined that Canadians would voluntarily renounce their allegiance. But their aversion to annexation, it was thought, might be removed by appealing to their material interests; and after the withdrawal of mutual preferences between themselves and the parent country, it was natural for the Canadians to accept the offer of the States to abolish restrictions on the importation of unmanufactured produce on each side of the common frontier. During the eleven years' existence of the Reciprocity Treaty, Canadian produce was more and more largely sent over the frontier to the ports of the States for shipment to Europe, and Canada seemed to be fast becoming a commercial dependency of the States. Yet there were no signs whatever of a desire for political union; on the contrary, the British North American provinces determined on forming a separate federation under the British flag. Like the two Canadas, Nova Scotia, New Brunswick, and Prince Edward Island had obtained responsible government; on the Pacific the new colony of British Columbia came into existence in 1858. Three years later the American Union was plunged into a civil war which had the effect of embittering feeling in the Northern States against Britain; and in 1864 the victorious North, having crushed the rebellion, made a final effort to force Canada into the Union by terminating the Reciprocity Treaty, and raising a tariff wall between the two countries. Under the Treaty, Canada had so signally prospered that its abolition was believed to be more than she could bear. Exactly the contrary effect was produced. Parties laid their differences aside, the parent country passed an enabling Act in 1867, and the British Provinces became a united nation. The difficulties which had attended the union of Upper and Lower Canada vanished when each took its place as

a self-governed unit in a self-governed Dominion. Nova
Scotia and New Brunswick joined the federation at once;
British Columbia and Prince Edward Island speedily
followed. The completion of the Inter-Colonial Railway,
connecting Lower Canada, now the Province of Quebec,
with the harbours of St. John and Halifax, and the
commencement of the Canadian Pacific Railway, were
visible signs of the unification of Canada; and the
occasion, if not the actual cause, of this first step in the
consolidation of the Empire was the same which had in
earlier stages contributed so materially to its extension
—the pressure of unfriendly force from without. We
shall next trace the contributory effect of causes of
the same kind on the extension of the Empire in
South Africa.

While the hitherto unknown and uncolonised interior
of South Africa was being brought within European
knowledge, those districts which had been occupied by
Europeans were steadily advancing. The immense development of wool-production in Australia, and the
stimulus thereby given to the British woollen manufacture, led to an increased production of wool for
export in the Cape Colony. A representative constitution was granted in 1853, and the first Cape
Parliament assembled in 1854; in 1856 Natal was
constituted a separate colony. Natal, which had become
thoroughly British, proved capable of producing other
things beside wool. Coolies were introduced from
India, sugar culture was successfully established, and
other tropical products were added. In 1865 the
pacified native district of British Kaffraria was incorporated in Cape Colony. Additional prospective

value was given to South Africa by the discovery, in
1867, of diamonds in Griqualand West, and of gold
in the Transvaal in 1868. Griqualand West, hitherto
reputed part of the Orange River State, was also
annexed to Cape Colony; the diamond industry produced an increased prosperity which justified the grant
of responsible government in 1872. The same year saw
the establishment of Britain's principal West African
possession on an enlarged basis. In 1871 the original
British possessions on the Gold Coast had been
augmented by the acquisition of the Dutch forts,
including Elmina, to which the King of Ashanti made
a claim which he sought to enforce by invasion. After
a costly war, the invasion was repelled, the British
protectorate recognised, and the district organised as
the Gold Coast Colony (1874). Britain now possessed
settlements in four different parts of the West African
Coast, the island of Lagos, where the native kings
refused to join in suppressing the slave-trade, having
been practically subject to British control since 1851;
in each district there was a growing export of native
produce to European markets, and attention was more
and more directed to the undeveloped resources of the
little-known tracts of the interior.

The natural effect of these events, which foreshadowed the universal colonisation of a continent
hitherto, for the most part, abandoned to native races,
was to introduce yet another element of disturbance.
Other European Powers aspired to take part in it.
Almost simultaneously aspirations of this kind were
awakened in the two combatant nations when the
Franco-German war of 1870-1871 was ended. France,

curtailed in her European territory, sought to extend her colonial possessions, especially in Africa, where she held Algeria in the north, the Senegal and parts of the Gold Coast in the west, and some islands in the Indian Ocean in the neighbourhood of Madagascar. The new French colonial movement dates from the ministry of Ferry in 1880. The first advance was made from the old French colony of Senegambia. Military expeditions were sent in the direction of Timbuctu; and the region of the Upper Senegal, Gambia, and Niger rivers was reduced under military rule. As a result of this movement, most of the interior of North-West Africa, including the Sahara with its oases to the south of Constantine and the Niger basin above Gando, either became French or fell under French influence. French North-West Africa includes also large tracts of the Atlantic coast, in Senegambia, French Guinea, the Ivory Coast, and Dahomey. On the Mediterranean a protectorate over Tunis was assumed in 1881. Another extension was made on the west coast of equatorial Africa, where some settlements on the bay of the Gaboon, acquired in 1839 and subsequent years, had been abandoned. These were reoccupied, and became a basis for the acquisition of the territory of the French Congo, which was extended so far to the north-east as to reach the border of the Bahr-el-Ghazal province of the Egyptian Sudan.

Stanley's exploration of the Congo basin (1877), the result of an expedition designed to complete the discoveries of Livingstone in the Lake region, marks the turning-point in the movement for the European occupation of Africa. Had this expedition taken place ten years later the fortunes of the Congo State might have been widely different. The discovery ought to have been taken up by Britain, the only Power capable of adequately dealing with the immense tract now added to the map of Africa. But public opinion was not as yet ripe for any extension of Britain's already grave responsibilities in this continent. Serious peril threatened the colony of Natal, largely in consequence of the liberty which had been given to the Transvaal Boers. Something in the nature of a settled government had been established, loans were raised in Europe, and in 1876 the Boers thought themselves strong enough to declare war against the native chief Secocoeni to recover a disputed piece of territory. The Boers were defeated, and after sustaining heavy losses returned to their homes, refusing either to fight any longer or to pay taxes. The Boer government was bankrupt. Meanwhile Cetewayo, a more formidable foe than Secocoeni, threatened the Transvaal from another quarter. Anticipating a rising among the Natal Zulus in case of a successful attack on the Transvaal by Cetewayo, the British had no alternative but to assume the conduct of affairs in the Transvaal (1877). The task of breaking Cetewayo's power fell on Britain, and was accomplished at a cost of £5,000,000 to the British taxpayer; Secocoeni's fortress was taken and his forces disbanded. With scarcely an exception the Boers stood aloof, and allowed Britain to maintain, single-handed, and at her own expense, a contest which rescued them from imminent destruction.

Immediately after the annexation of the Transvaal the British Parliament had passed an Act authorising a confederation of all the South African provinces; and it was urged on the Boers that their acceptance of unification under the British flag would lead to a grant of self-government in as ample a measure as was enjoyed by their kinsmen of the Cape; while the economic development of their country would be secured by a closer connection with the colonies to the south and east, and by the final pacification of the natives on their frontiers. These advantages they were not prepared to appreciate; but in all probability they would have settled down quietly as British citizens but for the duplicity of those prominent men among them, who, having accepted paid posts under the new government, sedulously fomented their disaffection to it—and but for the encouragement their disaffection received from utterances by British politicians in opposition to the ministry under which the annexation had taken place. Regarding these utterances as a pledge that another ministry would reverse the policy of annexation, and finding themselves disappointed, they refused payment of taxes, and broke out in open rebellion. A small British force despatched in haste from the Cape sustained severe disasters before reinforcements could arrive; and a misguided ministry, under colour of generous treatment to an ill-used and misunderstood people, restored the Transvaal to semi-independence, restoring thereby an inveterate obstacle to the opening of the African interior, and inspiring the Boers with the belief that they were more than a match for any force which Britain could put in the field against them.

The hopes of those who sought to create a united South Africa under the British flag thus received a check; and events elsewhere indicated an unwillingness on the part of Britain to increase her responsibilities in

Africa. Already the explorer of the Congo had found that the results of his labours evoked no practical interest among his own countrymen. Britain, it was commonly said, had black subjects enough. The development of the vast region opened by Stanley's explorations fell to the lot of Belgium; France established her authority over the immense district to the north called the French Congo. After the retrocession of the Transvaal it seemed to the purblind quidnuncs of Europe that the star of Britain, as an African power, was on the decline; and Germany, which had recently obtained a predominant position in Europe, prepared to secure a footing, intended to lead to a predominant position in Africa. An obvious step in this direction was to assume an attitude of patronage to the Transvaal Boers. It had been plausibly suggested that the new German Empire was destined to absorb the Netherlands, and by this means to succeed to the Dutch heritage in the colonial world. Of this heritage the Transvaal, it was assumed, formed part. To secure an informal protectorate over the Boers, to acquire in the Transvaal an economic ascendancy to the exclusion of Britain, and to obtain for Germany territorial bases in the neighbourhood on the Atlantic and Indian oceans, became henceforth objects of German policy. As it happened, Britain was now engaged in a task of unusual difficulty and magnitude in another part of Africa. In Egypt, where the Khedive's government had long been too weak to stand alone, Britain and France had formerly exercised a joint control; but British interests preponderated, and Britain increased her stake in the country by the purchase of the Khedive's shares in the

Suez Canal (1875). For the further security of British interests in the eastern Mediterranean, Cyprus had been acquired in 1878. In 1882 a formidable rebellion under Arabi Pasha necessitated a military occupation of Egypt in which France declined to take part; and Britain, left to suppress the rebellion single-handed, accomplished the task in a campaign terminating with the battle of Tel-el-Kebir (1882). Britain being now paramount in Egypt by the force of events, the dual control in which France had been associated was abolished in 1883. Somaliland, on the south coast of the Gulf of Aden, had been held as part of Egypt by the Khedive's forces; the Egyptian garrisons having been withdrawn, Britain was compelled to occupy the country, and it became a British protectorate (1884). A more difficult task confronted Britain in the Egyptian Sudan—an immense region stretching on either side of the Nile from the Nubian desert in the north to the Equatorial Province in the south. An Egyptian force under Hicks Pasha having taken the field and been defeated, the Sudan fell into the hands of a fanatic styled the Mahdi, or Mohammadan Messiah, whose followers ruined and depopulated it; it seemed impossible to rescue the Egyptian garrisons, and the country was abandoned. Meanwhile the Transvaal Boers, in defiance of conventions, were invading Bechuanaland.

At this juncture, Britain being apparently embarrassed in every quarter of the African continent—in West Africa by the rapid advance of France, on the side of Egypt by the Mahdists in the Sudan, on the Cape frontier by the Boers—extensive annexations by Germany in four different parts of Africa were almost

simultaneously announced to the world. The districts
annexed had evidently been selected in accordance with
a carefully concerted plan. Between Bechuanaland and
the Atlantic lay Great Namaqualand and Damaraland,
with a long and generally barren coastline, on which
Britain had, in 1878, taken possession of Walfish
Bay, the only spot considered worth occupation. A
German trader obtained from native chiefs a concession
on the bay of Angra Pequeña; and on the strength of
this acquisition the whole coast, with the exception of
Walfish Bay, was now proclaimed German territory
(1884). In the same year German emissaries reached
Togoland, on the eastern border of the British Gold
Coast Colony, and concluded with the native king a
treaty placing this country under German protection.
The Cameroons district, where British influence had long
predominated, and the native chiefs had petitioned for
a British protectorate, was annexed by Germans a few
days later. Before the end of the year another party
of adventurers arrived on the opposite side of the
continent, and obtained from the native chiefs concessions of the coast now known as German East Africa,
nominally under the sovereignty of the Sultan of
Zanzibar; an acquisition intended to include not only the
interior country as far as the Victoria Nyanza, but the
fertile kingdom of Uganda, on the border of the Egyptian Equatorial Province. It was understood amongst
the promoters of these enterprises that their ultimate
object was the creation of a "Greater Germany,"
embracing as much as possible of the African continent,
and that this object would be facilitated by securing the
co-operation of the Transvaal Boers. Little attention

was paid to the fact that these were British subjects at the time of their emigration, that they had emigrated into the back country of a British colony, that they acknowledged British suzerainty, and that they were, under the conventions authorising their semi-independent government, expressly debarred from entering into treaties with foreign nations, save with the consent of the paramount Power.   Encouraged by the easy attitude of Britain, the Boers were already clamouring for the abolition of the suzerainty, and the recognition of the Transvaal as a "sovereign international State"; and they did in fact obtain from Britain in the same year (1884) a modification of the convention which, according to their own interpretation of it, gave them in substance all, or nearly all, that they wanted.   From the German point of view it was now the obvious policy of the Boers to ally themselves with Germany, which could offer them an outlet on the Atlantic, and perhaps secure them another on the Indian Ocean ; and in the end they might probably be induced to throw in their lot altogether with the "Greater Germany" about to come into existence in Africa and elsewhere.

With such ideas the Boers were as little in accord as with the British policy of confederating South Africa, and opening the continent northwards to commerce and civilisation.   The mineral wealth of the Transvaal was known to be very great, and the Boers resolved to secure its advantages for themselves, to govern the country in their own fashion, and by all possible means to keep down and deprive of political rights the British settlers who flocked into the country as the mining districts came to be taken up and developed.   Monopolies, covering most of the field of internal trade, were granted to favoured individuals; the sole right to make railways was vested in Hollander and German capitalists. The external policy of the Transvaalers was to discourage communication with the Cape Colony, to secure by some means an outlet to the Indian Ocean, and to prevent the advance of Britain on their western flank by throwing themselves across the trade route leading to the heart of the continent,—the "Suez Canal," as it has been called, "of South Africa,"—on the maintenance or closure of which the future of the continent now mainly turned. The question was an old one; Livingstone had formulated it in a previous generation. Early in his career the Boers, in the course of a raid on the natives, destroyed his little mission-station in Bechuanaland, and burned all his possessions. This outrage, he wrote, only set him entirely free to pursue the greater object on which he had set his mind. "The Boers resolved to shut up the interior, and I determined to open up the country. We shall see who have been most successful in resolution, they or I."

The retrocession of the Transvaal in 1881 encouraged the Boers to adopt a bolder policy than that of mere raiding. Entering Bechuanaland in force, they established two new Boer states—"Stellaland," having its capital at Vryburg, and "Goshen" farther to the northward, in the country of the Baralong. Others crossed the eastern frontier of the Transvaal into Zululand, embraced the cause of Dinizulu, Cetewayo's son, against a rival chief, and obtained from him extensive concessions of land. In virtue of these they proclaimed a third new state called the "New Republic," designed to extend to the Indian Ocean, and to have a port on St. Lucia Bay. In the alternative it was suggested that the seaboard of Zululand, together with St. Lucia Bay, should be annexed by Germany. Incredible as it may seem, it was expected that Britain would stand by while Boers and Germans not merely snatched the benefit of the costly war by which she had crushed the Zulu power, but established themselves in a strong position on the Indian Ocean within 150 miles of Port Durban—a position, moreover, which had been formally ceded to Britain forty years previously. These expectations were quickly dispelled. In December 1884 the British flag was hoisted on St. Lucia Bay. In the same month Sir Charles Warren landed at Cape Town, marched with a strong force into Bechuanaland, cleared the country of the Boers, and broke up the republics of Stellaland and Goshen. In the next year (1885) Bechuanaland, as far north as the northern limit of the Transvaal, was organised as a British colony. The timely occupation of St. Lucia Bay, and the organisation of British Bechuanaland, proved the vitality in South Africa of the policy which in 1842 added Natal to the Empire, in 1848 established the Orange River Sovereignty as a British province, in 1871 brought Griqualand West, and in 1877 the Transvaal under British Government. The retrocession of the Transvaal in 1881, and the modified convention of 1884, had been rashly misinterpreted as indicating that this policy was a thing of the past; and by those who counted on the decline of British influence these signal proofs to the contrary were received with surprise mingled with keen disappointment. There was little room for surprise on the part of those who had watched

the course of events elsewhere in the Empire during
previous years. Everywhere there were signs of extension. In 1874 the Gold Coast Colony had been re-
organised on an enlarged basis. In the same year
the connection between the Straits Settlements and
some native states of the Malay Peninsula was placed
on a new footing by the establishment of a protectorate over Perak and Selangor; and the Fiji Islands,
for many years the scene of British missionary
labour and the resort of settlers from Australia and
New Zealand, were ceded to Britain by the native
chiefs, and constituted a British colony. A British
company formed for the purpose of developing the
resources of North Borneo had received its charter in
1881. In the following year Britain had undertaken the
formidable task of restoring civilisation and order in
Egypt; and when the British flag was hoisted at St.
Lucia Bay a British force was traversing the Sudan to
relieve the heroic Gordon in Khartûm. Ill supported
by statesmen at home, the efforts of British soldiers to
rescue the Sudan were for the time ineffectual; and
after the fall of Khartûm and the death of Gordon in
1885 this province remained during ten years abandoned
to barbarism. During these ten years events happened
elsewhere which opened the eyes of those who counted
on Britain's abandonment of her Imperial mission.
Nigeria, from the Gulf of Guinea to the Sahara, was
constituted a British protectorate; the most valuable
section of the sultanate of Zanzibar was organised as a
British protectorate, and the island of Zanzibar itself
secured as a British possession; the middle region of
South Africa, from Bechuanaland in the south to Lake

I

Tanganyika in the north, became the British territory
now so well known as Rhodesia; to the north-east of
Rhodesia, British settlements of long standing on the
Shiré River and the shores of Lake Nyassa were organised
as British Central Africa. Rapidly succeeding these
acquisitions came the establishment of a protectorate
in Uganda, the recovery of the Sudan, and its recon-
stitution as an Anglo-Egyptian province. Lastly, a long
preconcerted invasion of British South Africa by the
Boers of the Transvaal and the Orange River republics
decided the fate of these provinces by leading inevitably
to their reincorporation with the British Empire. Never
has the march of events in any continent been more
rapid than in Africa during the twenty years following
the retrocession of the Transvaal in 1881.

This recent stage of the Empire's development
furnishes new illustrations of the principle which
moulded its earliest growth—the principle of resistance
and counterpressure consequent on pressure from without. It cannot be said that but for the action of France
in absorbing vast districts in the rear of the British
West African colonies, of Germany in laying hands on
large sections of the coast in other parts of the continent,
and of the Transvaalers in invading Bechuanaland
and Zululand, the acquisition of Nigeria, British East
Africa, Uganda, and Rhodesia would not have taken
place. In each of these districts, all opened by British
explorers, British missionaries and traders had long
been busy as pioneers of civilisation. The appearance
of hostile or rival elements on the scene precipitated
changes to which the natural course of things was slowly
leading up; and events which might otherwise have

been spread over a century came to be crowded within the space of a generation. The German occupation of Togoland and Cameroons, following on the conquests of France on the upper Niger, forced on the British protectorate of Nigeria. British interests had long predominated in the lower valley of the Niger when the principal company engaged in its commerce, ably directed by Sir George Goldie, bought up the rights of rival French companies between 1882 and 1884, and in 1886 obtained a new charter under the name of the Royal Niger Company; and by a system of treaties with native chiefs the whole valley of the lower Niger from the Sahara to the Gulf of Guinea became qualified to enter the British Empire as a new colonial province by the name of Nigeria. By the acquisition of this large and populous territory, counterbalancing the very much larger acquisitions of France in the western Sudan in the rear of the other British colonies of Western Africa, the most advanced peoples of the central Sudan, including the native states of Sokoto and Gando, with many large towns each numbering many thousands of inhabitants engaged in agriculture, manufacture, and commerce, were brought under British protection. The administration of Nigeria passed from the hands of the Niger Company into the direct control of the British government in 1900. Since that date the consolidation of the protectorate has made rapid strides, under the direction of Sir Frederick Lugard, and it promises to become one of the most flourishing and important provinces of the Empire.

The charter granted to the Royal Niger Company was followed in 1888 by that of the Imperial British

East Africa Company, constituted somewhat tardily
to secure British interests on what had once been the
most important section of the African shore.   Occupying the space between the western shore of the Mozambique channel, which was claimed by Portugal, and the
desolate coast of eastern Somaliland (since nominally
annexed by Italy), the Suaheli or Zanzibar coast had,
after the decay of Portuguese commerce, been subject to
the Arab sultans who ruled in the island of Zanzibar,
the ancient emporium of African commerce with Arabia
and India.   Britain had long been engaged in endeavouring to repress the slave-trade, which entered largely into
this commerce, when the Sultan of Zanzibar in 1877
offered a lease of his dominion to Mr. Mackinnon, the
principal representative of local British interests.   In
reliance on British influence over the Sultan, this opportunity was neglected until German agents, treating
directly with native chiefs, had secured the southern
half of the coast for Germany (1880 to 1885).   In 1887
Mr. Mackinnon secured the. northern section, including
the ancient Arab ports of Mombasa and Melindi, for
the commercial association which in 1888 was chartered
as the Imperial British East Africa Company.   By
arrangement with Germany in 1890 the island of
Zanzibar was included in the British protectorate, and
the kingdom of Uganda, on the northern shore of the
Victoria Nyanza, was admitted to be within the British
area of influence.   Under the Company's rule an efficient
administration was established, and progress was made
in the exploration and development of the interior ;
but difficulties were encountered which the Company
were unable to surmount, and in 1896 their interests

were purchased by the nation. Considered merely from the maritime point of view, the situation of British East Africa, midway between the Suez Canal and the Cape of Good Hope, and also midway between the Cape and India, renders its possession a matter of imperial moment. From the continental point of view it is equally important as the district lying between Uganda and the head-waters of the Nile on the west, and the ocean on the east. For its development in this respect a railway was necessary from the port of Mombasa to the shore of the Victoria Nyanza: an enterprise too great for the resources of the Company, which the nation has undertaken and completed.

The next step in securing the British position in Africa was to take up the interior north of the Transvaal, including Matabeleland and Mashonaland; west of the Transvaal access to the north had been secured in 1885 by the establishment of the southern part of Bechuanaland as a British colony. In 1888 Sir Sidney Shippard, the administrator of British Bechuanaland, concluded a preliminary treaty with the Matabele king Lobengula, and in 1889 the British South Africa Company received a charter by which the interior districts from British Bechuanaland in the south-west to Lake Tanganyika in the north-east—a distance of 1200 miles—passed under its administration. The protectorate of northern Bechuanaland, originally included in the charter, was annexed to the colony of British Bechuanaland in 1890. At the other extremity of the Company's territory was the large district called British Central Africa, first opened to British exploration and missionary labour by Livingstone, and subsequently entered as a commercial field by the African Lakes Trading Corporation, which had during several years maintained, with the assistance of the natives, an indecisive struggle against Arab intruders, established there for the purpose of slave-trading, and held in check the Portuguese, who were advancing inland from Mozambique. The agents of the British South Africa Company established their authority over the north-western parts of British Central Africa—the district of Lake Mwero and Lake Bangueolo—extending the territory of the Company to the frontier of the Congo State, Lake Tanganyika, and the frontier of German East Africa; and in 1891 the eastern part of British Central Africa, lying west and south of Lake Nyassa, was organised as a separate British protectorate. From the enterprising speculator who formed the South Africa Company, its vast territory obtained the name of Rhodesia.

From Rhodesia the consolidation of British interests in Africa was pushed steadily northwards. The northern limit of Rhodesia is the southern end of Lake Tanganyika—a broad water-way stretching northward for 400 miles, having the territory of the Congo State on the north and west and German East Africa on the east. Distant only 150 miles from its northern end, across Congo State territory, lies Uganda, the next district to be organised as a British protectorate. Discovered by Speke in 1862, the ancient kingdom of Uganda, on the shore of Victoria Nyanza, had been invaded by Egypt from the north, penetrated by Arab traders from the south, and made the scene of missionary efforts in which French Catholics and British Protestants competed with zealous Mohammadans for the conversion of its prosperous population. The crisis of its fortunes came with the competition of Britain and Germany for predominance on the neighbouring Zanzibar coast, and in 1890 it was admitted to be within the British area of influence. Uganda fell naturally within the operations of the British East Africa Company, who took possession of it, but failed to hold it, and in 1894 it was declared a British protectorate.

Northward of Uganda, beginning at Gondokoro, the head of the Nile navigation, was the Equatorial Province of Egypt, where Emin Pasha still maintained Egyptian authority after the Sudan had been abandoned at the instance of the British government in 1885 to the misrule of the "Khalifa" or "successor" of the Mahdi, and the fanatical dervishes who supported him. The rapid recovery of the finances, and the efficiency of the army, of Egypt under British control justified its government in undertaking the rescue of the Sudan from the barbarism which desolated it; and in 1896 events occurred which made British intervention imperative. Italy, with Britain's assent, had occupied the Red Sea coast land of Abyssinia, formerly under the protection of Egypt, designating it the Colony of Eritrea; and by arrangement with Britain the Sudanese fortress of Kassala, near the Eritrean frontier, had been garrisoned by Italian troops. In 1896, Italy having sustained a severe defeat in a campaign against Abyssinia, Kassala was besieged by the dervishes; and an Anglo-Egyptian expedition despatched for its relief was the first step in the recovery of the Sudan. The battle of Omdurman (1898) annihilated the dervish army, and established Anglo-Egyptian authority in the northern Sudan; in the following year the Khalifa was finally defeated and slain in Khordofan, and the course of the Nile from the Victoria Nyanza to the Mediterranean came under British control; and the whole country from Wady Halfa in the north to Gondokoro in the south, has since been jointly administered by the Egyptian and British governments.

Throughout the Empire, South Africa excepted, the nineteenth century promised to close peacefully on a record of unbroken achievement; here, too, the record of achievement was maintained, but only by force of arms. The politicians who restored the Transvaal to semi-independence in 1881 supposed themselves to be putting an end to South African troubles : events now proved that they had prepared the way for disorder in a more dangerous form, and on a greater scale. The checks imposed by Britain on the advance of the Boers into Bechuanaland and Zululand, and the extension of British colonisation northwards, embittered them anew against the paramount Power, and aroused in them a determination to shake off the British suzerainty. When after 1886 the mineral wealth of the western Transvaal was rapidly developed, and Johannesburg became the largest city in South Africa, it seemed as if the means of doing so had been providentially placed in their hands. The events of 1881 seemed to prove that they were a match for the forces of Britain; and they now imagined that by means of the wealth exacted by taxation of the gold region, and with the aid of their kinsmen in the Orange River State and the Cape Colony, they might free themselves from British authority, and perhaps expel Britain altogether from South Africa. Their policy in the mining districts proved that they had little intention of observing the conditions on which they had obtained their semi-independence. One of these conditions pledged them to grant equal rights to all settlers. The mines were being developed and could only be developed by capital, labour, and skill from outside the Transvaal. Obviously, if political rights were granted to the industrial and commercial element thus introduced into the population, the Boer vote would in time be swamped, and that exclusive control of the government which must be maintained, if an anti-British policy was to take effect, would be at an end. Thousands of British citizens were therefore persistently excluded from ordinary civil rights, and treated with gross injustice by an administrative service chiefly composed of Hollanders and Germans; and the situation thus produced became intensified after an abortive attempt at revolution in Johannesburg in 1895. Meanwhile the Transvaal government accumulated arms and ammunition, secured the prospective co-operation of the Orange River State, and counted on the success of a campaign of anti-British intrigue, maintained since 1881 in the Cape Colony, to carry the whole Dutch population of South Africa with them in the open breach with Britain which they had resolved to provoke. They began by a request for the abolition of the suzerainty, and with it of Britain's right of interference in the affairs of the Transvaal. Britain, on her part, demanded the observance of the convention by the grant of the electoral franchise to the industrial population. This demand was met by a practical refusal, and a counter-demand for the abolition of the suzerainty. The course of negotiation soon proved that no concession on the part of the Transvaalers was contemplated, and the patience of Britain was nearly exhausted when their government suddenly presented an insulting ultimatum, and the Boers of both states invaded and overran parts of Natal and the Cape Colony, proclaiming them to be annexed to the Transvaal. Unprepared as Britain was for the emergency—for the Boers had been credited with a desire to come to a peaceful arrangement—the substantial work of the contest which ensued was finished in a few months; and although a guerilla warfare was maintained for some time longer, the last year of the century saw the governments of the Boer republics extinguished, and their territories reannexed as colonies to the British Empire.

Among the most significant features of the Boer war was the spontaneous rally of the Colonies to support the parent country in maintaining the integrity of the Empire. From Canada, the Australian colonies, New Zealand, Ceylon, the Federated Malay States, and West Africa, offers of volunteer contingents for active service poured in as soon as war appeared to be impending; and the feudatory princes of India vied with the colonial governments in placing their military resources at Britain's disposition. Only from the self-governing colonies and Ceylon was assistance accepted; and many thousands of volunteers from distant parts of the Empire fought side by side with larger numbers raised in the Cape Colony, Natal, and Rhodesia, and with the regular and volunteer forces of the parent country, in repelling the Boer invasion. While the Canadian contingent excelled in completeness of organisation, Australasia

sent the largest numbers, New Zealand contributing
most largely in proportion to population; and all
distinguished themselves for discipline and efficiency.
Thus the war not only secured the Imperial position in
South Africa, but strengthened the Empire by drawing
its members more closely together.

The absorption of the Boer States into the Empire
has removed the chief obstacle to the formation of a
South African Union such as was contemplated by the
South Africa Act, 1877, passed by the Imperial Parliament immediately after the former annexation of the
Transvaal. Many years, however, must in any case pass
before the policy embodied in that Act could be
advantageously revived; nor is it clear that federation
on the lines there laid down, in substance identical with
those adopted in the case of the Canadian Dominion,
would be suitable to the very different circumstances of
South Africa. The difficulty does not arise from the
conditions existing in the newly added Boer colonies.
In the Transvaal, British population and British economic
interests have long preponderated, and this preponder-
ance is increasing. The people of the Orange River
Colony, who had no cause of quarrel with the Imperial
government, and were drawn into the recent war by
intriguing politicians, are likely to settle down with
little reluctance as loyal citizens of the Empire. Both
the Boer colonies might perhaps be safely entrusted, in
the course of a short time, with representative government. But British South Africa has so far outgrown
its former limits that the Cape Colony, Natal, the
Transvaal, and the Orange River Colony together now
cover less than half its area. The pacification of the

Zulus, the Basutos, the Bechuanas, and other native tribes has been secured by the guarantee of direct British protection. It is essential to the development of the vast territory of Rhodesia that the British South Africa Company should pursue its task unhampered by external complications. And as a South African Union worthy to rank beside Canada and Australia ought to include all Britannic territory from the Cape to Lake Tanganyika, it is evident that the necessary materials for constituting a federal union do not at present exist. It may, indeed, be doubted, especially in view of the strategic importance of South Africa, whether confederation is suitable to its conditions, and whether the general control over the governments of its various colonies and protectorates ought not to remain permanently vested, as it remains at present, in the British government.

In Australia, on the other hand, the last year of the nineteenth century saw the last obstacle to the work of federation removed, and the task of combining the five colonies of Australia and the island colony of Tasmania into a single Commonwealth finally achieved. On the first day of the twentieth century the Australian Commonwealth came into existence. The idea of federation had suggested itself when self-government was granted half a century before, but it was not until the Canadian Dominion had been successfully launched that it rose into prominence as a practical question, and a serious obstacle long obstructed its realisation. New South Wales, the oldest colony, had followed the fiscal policy of the parent country and adopted the principle of free imports. The younger colonies, following the example of Canada, imposed heavy protective duties on imports for the purpose of fostering native industries. The divergence thus established was persisted in, and effectually barred all prospect of union until successive annexations by foreign Powers in the Pacific, especially that of North-Eastern New Guinea by Germany in 1884, awakened a determination on the part of Australians to secure some united organisation which should formulate and give effect to a common policy for the Australian colonies; and after prolonged negotiation a basis of union was at length agreed on, and was sanctioned by the British Parliament in 1900. In entering into a federal union two of the principal colonies virtually consented to sacrifice rights which a majority of the people in each had considered to be conducive to their well-being—New South Wales, the right of maintaining its traditional policy of free imports, Queensland, that of employing coloured labour; for the mass of the Australian people were known to be in favour of fiscal protection and the exclusion of Asiatics and Polynesians. Among the first measures carried in by the Commonwealth Parliament were a protective tariff, and measures restricting alien immigration, prohibiting the introduction of Pacific Islanders, and compelling the deportation of those remaining in the Commonwealth after 1906.[1]

[1] Were it asked what fact throws the strongest light on the events here narrated, the answer would be—Britain's generosity; extended, in accordance with her traditions, alike to colonist and native, to friend and foe, and by the last always discounted and accepted in a spirit of ingratitude. Pervading all her dealings, it has been sometimes advantageous, sometimes injurious, to her interests, and has occasionally been carried so far as to place her imperial position in jeopardy. Nevertheless, "There is that scattereth, and yet increaseth."

CHAPTER III

STATISTICIANS calculate that the Britannic Empire is the wealthiest aggregate of communities in existence; that the only Power which rivals it in economic force and resource is the United States; and that the united wealth of the two Anglo-Saxon Powers probably exceeds the total wealth of the rest of the world. Russia competes with both in area and population, but is economically inferior to either; no other Power requires mention for purposes of comparison. Even if it be at the present moment an exaggeration to say that half the economic force of the world is controlled by the English-speaking nations, there can be little doubt, having regard to the undeveloped resources of each, that this ratio will shortly be reached. As between the two Powers, it is understood that while the British Empire maintains the lead, the States are not far in the rear, and are advancing at a greater rate. It would therefore not be surprising, under existing circumstances, if in the near future the Empire lost its economic primacy. Should the Empire fail to maintain the lead, it would probably recover it in the remoter future; for Canada, Australasia,

126

and South Africa, the great self-governing divisions of the Empire, to say nothing of the African protectorates, are young countries compared with the States, their aggregate resources exceed those of the States, and their development is likely to be proceeding when that of the States is substantially completed.

Next to the United Kingdom the great self-governing colonies constitute, from the economic point of view, the most important division of the Empire. Their prominence is of recent growth. At Queen Victoria's accession India was the most important part of the Empire beyond seas, and was reckoned more than thrice as wealthy as all the colonies together. The balance is now reversed : the total wealth of the Colonies exceeds that of India; the aggregate wealth of Canada, Australasia, and South Africa probably equals that of India, and is nearly thrice that of the rest of the colonies. Estimated by income, without reference to capital, the wealth of Canada, Australasia, and South Africa is supposed to be equal to one-third of that of the United Kingdom. While the three self-governing colonial groups take collectively the first place in the colonial section of the Empire, the first place among the three belongs, and has always belonged, to Canada. The British North American provinces were flourishing colonies when New South Wales and the Cape Colony were in their infancy. Their established position as a field for colonial enterprise, and their proximity to Europe and the United States, compensated to some extent for the superior attraction exercised over capital and immigration fifty years ago by the gold-fields and the boundless capacity for wool-production of Australasia; and since the construction of the Inter-Colonial and Canadian Pacific railways, and the opening of the North-Western Territory to settlement the primacy of the Dominion among the colonial constituents of the Empire has been confirmed. Australasia takes the second place, South Africa the third, in economic importance, among the self-governing colonial groups.

The economic position of the residue of the Colonial Empire, consisting of the Crown colonies and Protectorates, mostly situated within the tropics and chiefly peopled by coloured races, like the colonies of all other colonial Powers, is inferior to that of the self-governing groups. It is, however, conspicuously superior to that of the colonies of any other Power, and exhibits an immense advance on that of the colonies which remained to the British Crown after the separation of the United States. Geographically the Crown colonies and Protectorates fall into two main sections, an Eastern and a Western one, divided by a line drawn from north to south through the middle of the African continent. Of these, the Eastern is the more prominent, being at once the wealthier and the more widely distributed, and in closer contact with the great commercial routes of the globe. Mauritius, Ceylon, the Straits Settlements, and Hong-Kong stand prominently forth as the principal economic centres of this group—Mauritius as a producing colony, and the principal sugar-growing island in the Empire ; Ceylon as a producing colony, being the largest and richest among the tropical island colonies in the Empire, and possessing in the port of Colombo one of the great centres of the world's transit trade ; the Straits Settlements, with the Federated Malay States under

British protection, as a producing colony larger in area than Ceylon, and having in Singapore a commercial port of greater importance than Colombo ; Hong-Kong as the principal European port in the Farther East, and the centre of British trade with China and Japan. The outline of the Eastern group of Crown colonies and Protectorates is completed by adding Fiji and British Borneo, the Seychelles and other islands in the Indian Ocean, and the African Protectorates bordering on that ocean ; and its various members stand in more or less close relation with Egypt, India, Australasia, and South Africa.

Next in economic importance to the Eastern Crown colonies follows the West Indian group, consisting of the British West Indian Islands and the continental colonies of British Honduras and British Guiana. The principal units in this group, in order of economic importance, are Jamaica, British Guiana, Trinidad (with Tobago), and Barbados ; after which, in similar order, follow the Windward Islands, important colonies secured by Britain at the end of the struggle with France,—the smaller Leeward Islands, representing the original West Indian possessions of England with the addition of Dominica,—the Bahamas, and the Bermudas. The West Indian colonies are mainly seats of production, their commercial status being dependent on their exports of native produce and their imports of articles for local consumption from other countries. Remote from the greater channels of the world's commerce, they have little transit trade, except such as passes by way of Trinidad to and from Venezuela, and since the abolition of slavery have had little or no connection with the

K

African colonies on the opposite side of the Atlantic.
The West African colonies, acquired for the purpose of
procuring slaves for the West Indies, and afterwards
held as stations for the suppression of the traffic they
were designed to support, now form a separate group
of producing colonies, and at present take the third
rank in order of economic importance, after the Eastern
colonies and the West Indies.   Foremost among the West
African group stand Northern and Southern Nigeria,
forming together with the adjacent colony of Lagos a
single geographical area.   The Gold Coast Colony, with
the Ashanti Protectorate, takes the second place ; Sierra
Leone the third, and the Gambia colony the fourth and
last.   Although now occupying the lowest rank in the
list of colonial groups, the West African colonies and
protectorates have a larger population than any other
group, and it is anticipated that they will in the course
of a few years yield large supplies of raw material for
use in British industries, and become a valuable market
for British manufactures.   The small colonies of Ascension, which is merely a naval station in mid ocean ;
St. Helena, a port of call on the route to South Africa ;
and the Falkland Islands, in the south-western Atlantic,
belong to no geographical group, and are of little
economic importance.

The Colonies and Colonial Federations, to sum up
what has preceded, form in the aggregate the most
important section of the Empire after the United
Kingdom ; the self-governing Federations and Colonies
are the most important parts of the Colonial Empire ;
among these, Canada with Newfoundland takes the
first place ; Australia with New Zealand the second,

South Africa the third; and these have between them nearly three-fourths of the wealth of the British colonial system. The remainder belongs to the Crown colonies, arranged in geographical groups in the following order: the most important division is formed by the Eastern colonies from Eastern Africa to Hong-Kong; the West Indian section has the second place, West Africa the third. The order of economic importance above indicated, beginning with Canada and ending with West Africa, is also the order assumed by the six colonial groups when arranged with reference to the degree in which the European element enters into the population. Canada and Newfoundland, Australia and New Zealand, are entirely European in social structure and aspect; the aboriginal races, never very numerous, have not contributed to colonial development, and their surviving remnants, numbering about 100,000 in Canada, and 200,000 in Australia and New Zealand, are without economic importance. In South Africa the natives outnumber the white population by four to one, and are extensively employed as labourers; large sections of the country, moreover, are occupied by partially civilised native tribes, living by agriculture and pasturage. To supplement the industry of the natives, the great reserves of labour existing in Asia have been drawn upon. In the Cape Colony, chiefly in the neighbourhood of Cape Town, there are many thousands of Malays, besides other Asiatics; in Natal the immigrants from India, chiefly employed in the plantations, outnumber the European colonists. In the Eastern tropical colonies the white population numbers only a few thousands, most of the labouring population being of

Asiatic origin.   In Mauritius, where the white element
is still numerous, two-thirds of the population are East
Indians, originally imported as coolies for the sugar industry, many of whom have now become landowners ; the
residue consists of Chinese, Malays, and other Asiatics,
and of descendants of African slaves.   In Ceylon, out of a
population of three and a half millions, the Europeans
number less than 7000 ; nearly two-thirds of the inhabitants are native Sinhalese, and nearly a million
East Indians are employed in the plantations and mines ;
the residue consists of half-breeds and descendants of
Mohammadan settlers.   In the Straits Settlements and
the Federated Malay States the European residents are
still fewer, and the Chinese and East Indian settlers
greatly outnumber the natives.   In British Borneo,
Chinese and East Indian immigrants furnish the most
efficient source of labour.   In the West Indies the mass
of the population is descended from emancipated negroes,
but in Trinidad and British Guiana about one-third are
East Indian immigrants.   In the West African colonies
the white population numbers only a few hundreds.   In
the protectorates of British East Africa, British Central
Africa, and Uganda, the natives, who form the bulk of
the population, are not numerous relatively to the area,
and East Indians are settling in all these countries in
increasing numbers.

The British colonies, offering, as they do, undeveloped
resources of every description to the settler, are the
natural emigration-fields of the world.   Only the United
States and Argentina can compete with Canada, Australia, New Zealand, and South Africa as places of
destination for emigrants from temperate latitudes.

But the United States are rapidly assuming the character of a fully settled country; the best lands have been taken up, and Americans are now quitting the States in great numbers for Canada. Argentina is found to be unsuitable for settlers from Northern Europe, and draws its immigrants chiefly from Italy, Spain, and southern France. As resorts for emigrants from tropical and sub-tropical countries, the British Crown colonies and the Protectorates are altogether without rivals. Yet, with some exceptions in comparatively small areas, such as Malta, Barbados, and Bermuda, the Colonial Empire is still conspicuously under-peopled. In Canada, Australia, and South Africa vast expanses of fertile land, capable of growing grain and raising stock to an unlimited extent, still await the settler. These countries are still in their infancy. Canada has a population of some five and a half millions, the great majority of whom are Canadian born; Australia less than four millions, South Africa, reckoning white colonists only, and excluding the natives, scarcely more than a million. Adding another million for New Zealand and Newfoundland, the white population of the three great self-governing divisions of the Empire may amount to eleven and a half millions, or little more than one-quarter of the population of the parent country. The proportion of the population engaged in industries not directly connected with the natural resources of the soil is so small that it is within the mark to say that eleven millions of the colonial residents are engaged in developing these resources, and that the economic progress of these countries is mainly due to the capital and industry which have been thus employed. Under-population is observable, though in a less degree, in the tropical parts of the Empire.   Excluding, for the moment, the recently acquired African Protectorates, the tropical colonies have altogether a white population of less than a million, and a coloured population of about ten millions, all living on and more or less engaged in developing the resources of the soil.   Remarkable as the progress of the colonies has been, this state of under-population suggests at first sight that it has fallen short of what might reasonably have been anticipated.   Yet it would be easy to prove by figures that it compares advantageously with the progress of the United States and Argentina since the epoch of independence in each ; and although the rate of advance, under more favourable circumstances, might well have been greater still, it must not be forgotten that the colonies were long regarded with apathy by the parent country, which treated them as burdens rather than valuable assets, and interpreted such progress as they exhibited as a sign of impending severance.   In such circumstances it is not strange that the stream of surplus British capital, which might otherwise have been chiefly invested in developing their resources, should have been largely diverted from its natural channel, and spent in promoting the progress of foreign nations.   The stream of surplus population has been largely diverted in the same way.   While the continuous expansion of British industries has tended to diminish the number of emigrants, the colonies have, as a whole, taken little trouble to attract them.   Millions of citizens have been lost to the Empire, and gone to swell the population of the United States.

The economic machinery of the Colonial Empire

includes each of the three principal methods of wealth-production,—the development of natural resources by agriculture, pasturage, fisheries, forest-exploitation, and mining ; the transformation of natural products by manufacture ; and shipping enterprise, by which natural and manufactured produce are carried to foreign markets. In all colonies economic development begins with the first, and the second and third are usually long in making their appearance. Founded by adventurers in the natural course of maritime enterprise, colonies naturally send back their produce in the ships of the parent country. This produce is naturally exchanged for exports from the parent country ; and as the colony produces more and more of its own food-supply, its imports consist more and more of manufactures. Hence, in the absence of counteracting causes, a colony tends to remain in the first economic stage—the development of natural resources—until these resources are fully developed. Some forms of production, however, directly tend to the development of shipping. Such are the fisheries and timber-trade of British North America. As the colony grows, its internal and its export trade alike tend to the creation of large seaport and inland towns ; and in towns of a certain size the lower forms of manufacturing enterprise speedily make their appearance, although their progress is sure to be checked by the superior quality and cheapness of manufactured articles exported from the parent country. A more effectual check on the diversion of capital and labour to manufactures lies in the fact that so long as natural resources are imperfectly developed, the process of developing them is at once the most profitable form in which capital can be employed, and the most attractive to the capable immigrant.   But not even prohibition, which was enforced by the British Parliament against certain manufactures in the original American settlements, will keep the economic growth of a colony from taking its natural course; and in the long run manufacturing enterprise will become permanently established, and will follow, though at an unequal rate of progress, that development of the natural resources of the country in which the primary business of colonisation consists.

Situated in climates approximately corresponding to those of Europe, the great self-governing colonies and federations have an economic basis for the most part derived from, and nearly identical with, that of Europe. What distinguishes the colonies is that in them this basis has been transferred to virgin soils, freed from burdens which depress productive industry in the Old World, and developed in the quickening atmosphere of modern economic conditions.   The colonist owns the land he cultivates, pays no tithes and little taxation, and enjoys the advantages of co-operative organisation and cheap carriage for his produce in a higher degree than his European competitor.   Thus aided, and favoured by almost every circumstance, the agriculturist, the cattle farmer, and the flock-master raise large crops of cereals, herds of horned stock, and flocks of sheep, not only supplying local markets with grain, meat, dairy produce, and wool in abundance, but producing an ever-increasing surplus available for export.   For this surplus the parent country, with its ever-increasing industrial population and its limited agricultural resources, is an ever-ready

customer.   The ever-increasing capacity, in fact, of
Britain for taking the food and raw material produced
for export by the colonies has been the foundation of
colonial progress.   If this capacity were suddenly
checked, the check would be felt as a disaster in every
corner of the Empire.

Nor is the export of rural produce confined to the
ordinary objects of husbandry and pasturage.   The cultivation of orchard fruit is universal in the temperate
climates of the colonies : Canada and Tasmania, in particular, send large quantities of apples to the English
market.   The warm climates of Australia and South
Africa and the southernmost part of Canada (Ontario)
encourage the production of valuable crops unknown to
British agriculture.   Maize is one of the principal staples
of Southern Canada.   Maize and tobacco are largely
grown in Australia and South Africa ; the vine flourishes
in both, as well as in Southern Canada, and in the Cape
Colony wine-production is an industry of long standing.
But Australia, where wine-culture has been introduced
with the greatest success, is pre-eminently the vintage
country of the Empire.   South Australia, New South
Wales, and Victoria are the chief wine-producing States,
and from the first named there is a large and increasing
export of wine to the parent country.   Tobacco is one
of the most widely diffused products of the Empire, and
is largely grown for local consumption ; but the perfection of culture attained in the United States and Cuba
has hitherto prevented colonial tobacco from entering
largely into general commerce.   Jamaica, however, furnishes a small export of cigars, and the planters of British
Borneo now produce in considerable quantities cigars

of a quality scarcely inferior to those of the West Indies. The specific range of pastoral enterprise is but little extended in the warmer latitudes of the self-governing colonies ; the camel, however, has been introduced into Australia ; the Angora goat, which yields a fleece more valuable than wool, is bred in South Africa ; and the ostrich farms of the Cape Colony supply the rest of the world with ostrich-feathers.

The economic progress of all the great self-governing groups is largely due to the development, concurrently with agriculture and pasturage, of their valuable fisheries, forests, and mines. Here again British North America takes the first place ; its fisheries being at once the most widely distributed, the most valuable in their nature, and the best developed, its forests the most extensive, the richest in timber most in demand, and the most accessible to good markets, and its mineral wealth, though less developed than that of Australia and South Africa, probably not less ample. Canada's abundant stores of coal and iron and the boundless water-power of her rivers are rapidly raising her to the rank of a great manufacturing nation. The fisheries of Newfoundland, Eastern Canada, and British Columbia— furnishing, as they do, enormous yearly supplies of cod, herrings, salmon, lobsters, and seals—are the most important in the world. Those of New Zealand and Australia, especially around Tasmania, might be of great value, but are little worked ; all the South African coasts abound in excellent fish, and afford ample supplies for local consumption. Vast as is the wealth drawn by Canada from her seas, lakes, and rivers, it is far exceeded by that derived from her forests of pine, larch, and spruce, as well as of oak, elm, maple, birch, and other deciduous trees, which are largely exported to the United States, Britain, South Africa, and Australia. Timber is exported from New Zealand and Tasmania, and the vast forests of the hard woods called karri and jarrah, varieties of the eucalyptus or blue gum tree, have greatly contributed to the development of Western Australia. Queensland is well timbered, producing hundreds of kinds of useful woods, and some of its trees are 500 feet high. South Africa is not richly provided by nature with timber, but many foreign kinds thrive abundantly when planted. In Natal the bark of the Australian black wattle tree has become an important item of export.

Of all the natural riches yielded by the soil, minerals are, in an advanced stage of society, the most important ; and the mineral most eagerly sought is gold, the most valuable of the metals, and the only universal medium of exchange. New gold-fields quickly attract population and capital, and when successfully worked furnish a powerful stimulus to agriculture, general industry, and external commerce. The gold-fields of Australia and South Africa have largely contributed to the establishment of these countries on their present economic footing. Canada also is highly auriferous ; the mines of British Columbia secured the economic development of that important province ; new gold-fields have been opened in Ontario, and in the far north on the Yukon river. The gold-production of the Empire, including India, exceeds that of all the rest of the world together ; and there is reason to suppose that it will be considerably increased in the near future. The resources of Australia, the earliest to be developed, and of South Africa, at present the most productive, are still imperfectly explored; those of British America are probably in their infancy. Silver mines are worked in Canada and Australia; platinum ores exist, but apparently not in great abundance, in Canada. Nothing could more strikingly illustrate the power of a valuable mineral product as a factor in economic development than the diamond-mining industry in South Africa. Little more than thirty years ago Kimberley and Barkly West were an arid desert far in the interior, of difficult access, and known only to a few impoverished farmers. The town of Kimberley now has 28,000 inhabitants, and is the third largest town in South Africa. The diamond-mining industry has enabled the Cape Colony to bear the cost of self-government, has been the means of civilisation to many thousands of natives, and has furnished the capital by means of which Rhodesia was added to the Empire. New South Wales is rich in diamonds, which are found also in Queensland and Victoria; and miscellaneous gems of many kinds are found in all these States.

All the useful metals, except mercury and zinc, abound in the self-governing colonies. Iron, the most important, and the most widely distributed, exists in all parts of Canada, most parts of Australia, and many parts of South Africa. In Canada iron is extremely abundant, but is little worked, notwithstanding the bounty granted by government on the production of pig-iron; the chief workings at present are in Quebec Province, Nova Scotia, and British Columbia. In Australia and New Zealand excellent ironstones abound, but little progress has been made in working them. South Africa is even more backward in the development of her stores of iron (Cape Colony, Natal, Transvaal). In the more highly priced metals, copper and tin, the self-governing parts of the Empire are unusually rich. Very rich deposits of copper, covering large areas, are worked in Canada (Ontario, British Columbia, Alberta) and Newfoundland; those of New South Wales, South Australia, and Queensland are probably of greater commercial importance, and there are less extensive ones in Victoria, Tasmania, and Western Australia. The Namaqualand mines (Cape Colony) are the chief copper-mines in South Africa; but there is abundance of copper in the Transvaal. The distribution of tin is more limited, but this metal is extensively mined in Australia (New South Wales, Queensland, Victoria). Large quantities of plumbago exist in Canada.

Of all products of the mine the most important to a maritime empire is coal. The British Empire and the United States are the only Powers having ample supplies of the best bunker coal (South Wales, Tyne, New South Wales, Virginia). Abundance of coal is got in various parts of India, much of which, though comparatively poor in quality, is available for steam-raising. Coal is found in all parts of Canada, from the Atlantic to the Pacific. British Columbia, in particular, abounds in coals of every description; the coal-fields of the North-West Territories, covering an area half as large as the United Kingdom, contain vast deposits of steam coal. Nova Scotia (Sydney, near Cape Breton) is the chief coal-producing province on the Atlantic side of Canada; Newfoundland, also, has important coal-fields. Australia ranks next after Canada as a coal-producing country. Coal is found in abundance on the eastern coasts, as well as in Western Australia and Tasmania; the coal-fields of New South Wales are among the most extensive and valuable in the world; Victoria and Queensland are also amply provided, the latter state having a coal-field half as large as England. New Zealand has large coal-fields. In South Africa, the Cape Colony, Natal, and Transvaal have immense reserves of coal. A valuable supplement to the Empire's fuel resources is found in rock-oil or petroleum, of which abundant supplies exist in Canada, Newfoundland, and New Zealand. Petroleum, when refined, is largely employed as a substitute for coal in steam-raising, is in universal use as an illuminant, and some varieties are increasingly employed for lubricating machinery.

From what has preceded it will be seen that British North America, which represents about one-third of the entire wealth of the Colonial Empire, has a substantial foundation for its economic primacy. Its early start in the colonial race, its proximity to the United States and the parent country, its bracing climate, especially attractive to the hardy races of Northern Europe, its immense and fertile territory, its facilities for water-carriage, water-power, and the construction of roads, canals, and railways, its stores of iron and coal, have sufficed to secure its internal development; and its fisheries and forests provided it from the first with material at once of the greatest value for its economic expansion, and well adapted to become the foundation of a profitable external commerce. The trade with the parent country in agricultural food-products, which Canada has built on this foundation is shared with India, Australia, and New Zealand among the members of the Empire, and with the United States, Russia, and Argentina among foreign countries; but Canada is now devoting herself with characteristic energy to the business of supplying the parent country with food-stuffs as her primary source of wealth, and in so doing she has an obvious advantage in her geographical situation. The contribution of Canada to the food-supply of Britain is nearly double that of Australasia, and amounts, in wheat and flour, cattle and sheep, bacon and hams, fish and butter, to over fifteen millions sterling. In addition to food-stuffs Canada exports to Britain timber to the value of over five millions sterling, and has with the parent country a total export trade of over twenty-one millions, or rather more than half a total export trade of over forty millions. These figures are in excess, though not largely, of the corresponding ones for the Australian Commonwealth; when the exports of New Zealand are added to those of Australia, it appears that the exports of Australasia exceed those of Canada—a result produced by the very large exports of wool from Australia and New Zealand. In population, as in export trade, Canada heads the list of the colonies : a fact which partly explains why her import trade is less than that of Australasia. Canada has a million more people, and a larger proportion of the population is employed in manufacturing industries than in Australasia. Hence Canada's home trade is larger, and her external trade relatively smaller. Having inexhaustible supplies of iron and coal, Canada manufactures for herself, amongst other things, imple-

ments, machinery, and hardware, and exports pig-iron
to Britain; her local supply of raw leather is more
largely worked up in home manufactures than is the case
in Australasia; and she carries on manufactures (cotton
and tobacco) for which the raw material is imported.
Canada, it will be seen, more than any other colonial
community, approximates to the United States in self-
sufficiency.   She has an extensive mercantile marine,
largely engaged in trade with foreign countries, while
the maritime commerce of Australia and New Zealand
is mainly carried in European vessels, the shipping of
these colonies, large as it is, being chiefly employed in
Australasian waters.

Australia and New Zealand are pre-eminently pastoral
countries.   Their principal export is wool, which they
furnish to the rest of the world to the value of twenty-
one and a half millions sterling annually, being nearly
half their total export trade, and the largest item
attributable in the Empire's economy to a single
commodity.   Nearly two-thirds of this is sent to the
parent country, and supplies three-fourths of the
material of Britain's woollen manufacture.   Australasia
contributes largely, though to a less extent than Canada,
to Britain's food-supply.   Like Canada, Australia and
New Zealand export to Britain wheat, flour, and butter;
but their principal export to the parent country, next
to wool, is frozen mutton, which their immense flocks
of sheep, taken in connection with their large profits on
wool, enable them to sell at low prices.   A special
characteristic of Britain's trade with Australasia is the
proportionately large amount of the exports from the
parent country to the colonial markets.   Britain's

exports to Australia and New Zealand amount to over thirty-two millions sterling, or more than thrice the amount of her exports to Canada, and nearly as much as the value of her imports from the Australasian colonies. Although the manufacturing industries of Australasia are less developed than those of Canada, Sydney and Melbourne are important industrial centres, producing, mainly for local consumption, leather and leather goods, woollen cloth, furniture, pottery, paper, hardware, and ironwork. Next to wool the most important product of Australasia is gold, which is mined in all the Australian States and in New Zealand, the annual output amounting to fifteen millions, most of which is remitted to Britain in the course of trade, largely in payment of interest on capital advanced by British investors for the construction of railways and other public works.

The South African colonies are also pre-eminently pastoral countries, wool being their most valuable export next to diamonds and gold. Angora hair and ostrich feathers are exported from the Cape Colony to a value equal to the export of wool. The food-stuffs raised in South Africa are mostly consumed locally, and both corn and meat are largely imported. There is, however, a small export of fresh and dried fruits, and this industry might probably be extended. The manufactures of South Africa are of limited extent, the most important being concerned with the means of transport (waggons, carts, harness, and saddlery). South Africa has little shipping of its own, its rapidly increasing trade, both coasting and external, being mainly carried on in European vessels. The apparent backwardness of

South Africa in this respect is due to its exceptional position.   Canada and Australia, each situated at the termination of a main commercial highway, are also centres of radiation for minor and local commercial routes ; South Africa has developed around isolated ports of call.   On the whole, the local shipping of the colonies has of late years rapidly increased, and their aggregate purchases of new vessels from British shipbuilders in each year exceed those of any single foreign country. The registered tonnage of British North America alone falls little short of that of the United States, while that of British North America and Australasia together is only exceeded by that of the parent country and that of Germany.

Considerable areas in South Africa and Australia are situated within the tropics, and to these the European basis of economy is only partially applicable.   In South Africa the torrid area is less extensive than might appear from the map; for the interior tracts, owing to their elevation above sea-level, have a comparatively temperate climate, and only British Central Africa and part of Northern Rhodesia can be considered as completely subject to tropical conditions.   In Australia the area subject to those conditions is larger.   It includes a large part of Western Australia, the northern territory of South Australia, and half of Queensland ; and although much of these areas is available for cattle-raising, their natural economic basis is tropical rather than European.   The mining industry, however, in Western Australia and Queensland, draws with it an extension of the European basis wherever such an extension is possible, and as the existing law of the Commonwealth prohibits the

introduction of coloured labour, on which tropical agriculture mainly depends, .the natural course of tropical
development in Queensland is likely to be long delayed.
Having regard to the fact that the tropical colony of
British New Guinea has also become a territory of the
new Australian Commonwealth, the problems of tropical
development appear to demand more patient consideration than they have hitherto obtained in Australia.
For Britain these problems are a matter of greater
moment, for, having parted with the control of nearly
all her colonies in temperate climes, the tropical
colonies only remain to her as the immediate objects of
economic policy and administrative statesmanship.   For
the British citizen, therefore, these colonies possess a
special interest, and this interest is specially prominent
at the present time.

The results of colonial enterprise within the torrid
zone, as compared with parallel results in temperate
climes, show that the latter in general exceed the former.
A good illustration is furnished by a comparison of Brazil
with the United States; and having regard to the immense economic resources of Canada and Australasia it is
not strange that the British Crown colonies, as hitherto
developed, should represent little more than one-fourth
of the total economic force of the Colonial Empire.   Yet
in spite of the drawbacks attending on tropical enterprise, Britain's tropical colonies have since the
late Queen's accession made great economic progress.
Hong-Kong, then a nest of Chinese pirates, has become
the busiest emporium in the Empire outside Britain.
The ports of the Straits Settlements, then only rising
into notice, now have a commerce rivalling that of Hong-

Kong ; the Settlements themselves, with the Federated
Malay States, compete with Ceylon for the chief place
among the producing colonies.   Ceylon, which at present
stands first in the list, was in 1837 of less economic
importance than Malta.   Even the severely tried West
Indies have succeeded in holding their own ; Jamaica,
which once took the first place among the tropical
colonies, still ranks next after the great settlements
in the Eastern seas, while Trinidad has developed at
a rate which throws the progress of some self-governing colonies into the shade.   Starting at that date with
a population less than that of Tasmania, Trinidad now
supports half as many inhabitants again as the latter
island, and has a larger external trade.   Next to
Trinidad the most prominent example of colonial
progress in hot climates is British Guiana, which has
risen from a low rank to the next place in the list after
Jamaica.   The population and produce of Mauritius
have been quadrupled, notwithstanding the general
decline of the sugar industry, on which its prosperity
almost entirely depends.

In all these cases the means of increased prosperity
have been found partly in the extension of the economic
basis by the introduction of new staples, partly in the
systematic introduction of new supplies of labour from
India and China to replace the shrinkage consequent
upon the abolition of slavery, and partly in the establishment of improved means of transport, especially by
railway.   In the past half-century tropical enterprise has
suffered heavily through the vicissitudes of demand.
Cane-sugar has lost its monopoly of the market in
consequence of the extended cultivation of the beet in

Europe; indigo has been hard pressed by the production of dyes from coal tar; coffee has lost ground in competition with tea and cocoa. The change from old staples to new ones has involved planters in considerable losses; but the storm has been weathered, and with the help of organised immigration and railway transport the older tropical colonies have not only recovered their position, but have stimulated by their example the prosecution of tropical enterprise in new fields of vast extent and excellent promise.

Cattle-raising and sheep-farming are pursued in some of the tropical colonies, but to any considerable extent only in those exceptional localities, chiefly at considerable elevation above the sea-level, where there is good natural pasturage. The elevated tracts of tropical Queensland are among the finest pastoral regions of the world. Horses and horned cattle are abundantly produced in the mountain districts of Jamaica, and more land is retained for pasturage than is devoted to agriculture; some other West Indian islands are favourable for stock-breeding. Stock-farming is indicated as a promising industry in Ceylon, and, by a careful selection of suitable breeds, might probably be successfully pursued in other tropical colonies. But the chief economic resource of the tropical colonies lies in the rich soil of the lower levels, stimulated to a fertility unknown in temperate latitudes by a moist atmosphere and the forcing heat of the sun. The conditions of successful tropical agriculture, the botanical variation of old staple products and the discovery of new ones, have in recent times been the object of widespread investigation; and there is reason for believing that this will in the course of time lead to important economic developments, especially in the production of material for textile manufactures.

The agriculture of the tropical colonies, like that of the self-governing ones, is at present mainly concerned with the production of food-material. The local food-supplies largely consist of cheap grains, roots, and fruits, which with some exceptions in the latter class do not enter into commerce; and it is largely supplemented by food-stuffs imported from temperate countries. The farinaceous foods produced in the tropical colonies enter but little into colonial commerce. Rice is cultivated for local consumption in Ceylon, the Straits Settlements, British Borneo, and the West African colonies. Sago and tapioca are exported from the Straits Settlements; arrowroot is cultivated in the West Indies, large quantities of the finest sort being exported from St. Vincent. The commercially important produce of these colonies consists of four principal articles—cane-sugar, tea, cocoa, and coffee; after these follow fruits and spices; drugs, which now have but little economic importance, may be ranked in the same class. These products furnish more than half the exports of the tropical colonies, and sugar, the original basis of tropical colonisation, still holds the first place in tropical enterprise.

The cultivation of the cane remains the sole mainstay of the original English West Indian islands (Barbados, St. Kitts, Antigua, and Nevis), by far the most important one of Mauritius and Guiana, and is still an important industry in Trinidad and Jamaica, although in the latter island the enterprise of the planter is becoming mainly concentrated on fruit-production (bananas and oranges) and in the former on cocoa. The sugar-cane is largely grown in Australia, especially in Queensland, which ranks next after Mauritius in production, and New South Wales. In South Africa, Natal is important as a seat of sugar cultivation, having nearly as much land under the cane as Barbados, and the production of Fiji is nearly as great. In the West Indies a large proportion of the produce of the cane is exported in the form of rum and molasses : in Jamaica the cane has held its ground largely in consequence of the excellence and reputation of the rum produced on certain sugar estates. By the Sugar Convention of 1902 the bounties given by European Powers on the production of beet-sugar have been counteracted, and cane-sugar, it is anticipated, will henceforth be free from the unjust disadvantage to which it has long been subject, and recover its natural position in the world's markets.

Tea, cocoa, and coffee are now so largely produced on Britannic soil that the aggregate value of the crops annually produced is not much less than that of the sugar crop. Of the three, the production of tea is by far the largest, although in no colony is the industry of more than a few years' standing. The tea-tree, cocoa-tree, and coffee-tree thrive in the same climates ; in Ceylon patches of each may be seen flourishing side by side. The cultivation of the tea-tree is not confined to the East. It flourishes in Brazil and South Carolina, and has been introduced in Jamaica and St. Lucia. Possibly the West Indies, which produce coffee and cocoa of the finest descriptions, may be found to produce teas having qualities enabling them to secure a place in the market. The tea plantations of Ceylon, where experienced planters not long since ridiculed the idea of tea-cultivation, now rival those of China and British India, and more tea is exported from India and Ceylon than from all other countries in the world together. Tea has been success-fully grown in Natal, Tasmania, Fiji, and the Andaman Islands ; and the native Malay States, British Borneo, New Guinea, and East Africa are indicated as probable seats of the tea industry in the future.

Although cocoa and coffee are largely planted in both sections of the tropical colonies, the production of both together is far below that of tea. The cultivation of coffee has of late been declining, but that of cocoa has been increasing ; and no tropical product is more eagerly introduced wherever there is a prospect of success. While this increased production is largely due to an extended use of the cocoa bean as the material of a beverage, it is perhaps more largely due to the cheapness of sugar, and the facility thus afforded for employing cocoa as a compound in confectionery. Next to sugar, cocoa is the principal product of the West Indies. Trinidad, which produces cocoa only surpassed by that of Venezuela, exports more than all other West Indian colonies together ; but production is rapidly advancing in Jamaica and British Guiana, and extending in Mont-serrat, Dominica, Grenada, St. Vincent, and St. Lucia. The cocoa-tree is found to thrive in tropical Africa. There is already a large export from the Gold Coast ; Lagos and Southern Nigeria promise to become important sources of supply, and cultivation has begun in the Uganda Protectorate. Cocoa cultivation has of late advanced rapidly in Ceylon, and the produce, probably prepared with greater care for the market, has realised higher prices than the cocoa of the western hemisphere ; the tree has also been successfully introduced in the Seychelles and the Federated Malay States. No staple is more generally planted in the tropics than coffee ; and although its production for export has declined, not only in the British possessions but throughout the world, new fields of cultivation are constantly being opened, partly for local consumption, partly in the hope of producing a bean which cheapness and excellence may secure a place in the general market. Unfortunately for the coffee-planter, Britain stands low on the list of nations in its consumption of coffee per head of population ; and those which consume the most chiefly import the cheaper coffees of tropical America. The coffee of the Blue Mountains in Jamaica maintains the highest rank in the market, and cultivation is extending in Trinidad. In St. Lucia, Grenada, Dominica, Tobago, and some other West Indian islands coffee culture holds its ground with difficulty ; in Ceylon, which formerly exported large quantities to the English market, the coffee industry has been almost ruined by leaf disease and insect pests. Coffee has recently been introduced into British Honduras. Wider fields have been opened in Africa and Australasia. Native varieties of coffee are cultivated in Sierra Leone, the Gold Coast Colony, and Lagos, and planting might be largely developed in Northern Nigeria. Uganda and the highlands of British East Africa are probable seats of coffee culture in the near future ; in British Central Africa the industry has made considerable progress, and it is well established in Natal. In the East, coffee is exported from the Straits Settlements and Federated Malay States, and there are good prospects in British Borneo. In Australasia the coffee-producing colonies are British New Guinea, Fiji, and Queensland ; the tree flourishes also in the Pacific groups, and coffee is exported from the Tonga and Cook Islands.

Fruit has of late become an important item in the commerce of the tropical colonies. Since the decline of sugar the cultivation of oranges and bananas for the American and English markets has become a leading industry in the West Indies ; and more than half the exports of Jamaica now consist of these and other fruits. Besides oranges, the Bahamas export large quantities of fresh and preserved pine-apples ; and the culture and canning of this valuable fruit is largely carried on in Antigua. British Honduras produces oranges, and has a large export of bananas and plantains. The sweet lime is a special product of Dominica and Montserrat, which largely export lime-juice Tropical fruits of many kinds are planted in Grenada, and St. Lucia is well adapted for an extensive fruit culture. Cocoa-nuts, which are chiefly grown in the Eastern section of the tropical colonies as the material of oil and fibre, are largely grown as fruit in Trinidad and Tobago, in the low alluvial lands of Jamaica, and in other West Indian colonies. Almost every species of tropical fruit grows freely in British East and Central Africa, Ceylon, and the Malay Peninsula, but there is little or no production for export. The Fiji Islands are the fruit-gardens of Australia and New Zealand, as the West Indies are of North America and Britain ; and their export of bananas, pine-apples, oranges, and other fruits, both fresh and dried, is only exceeded in value by that of sugar.

Fruit culture has recently been extended in Queensland, and this colony not only competes with Fiji in supplying the rest of Australasia, but exports oranges to Europe.

Tropical condiments and spices, in quest of which Europeans first resorted to India and the Far East, are now so extensively produced within the Empire that there is none for which Britain is compelled to resort to foreign countries; and there are large areas—Fiji, amongst others—suitable for spice-growing, in which this profitable form of agriculture might be practised. Of Britain's annual import of condiments and spices, amounting to over a million sterling, more than half consists of the various kinds of pepper, the principal source of the supply being the Straits Settlements, with the Federated Malay States, and the protected Malay State of Johore. Pepper is among the rising exports of Ceylon. Cayenne or chilli pepper, the chief indigenous condiment of America, is cultivated in various parts of the West Indies and in British Guiana, and has been introduced into tropical Africa. Ginger has spread from the East to the West Indies, tropical Africa (Sierra Leone), and Australia; the finest description is grown in Jamaica. Vanilla, indigenous to America, is profitably grown in St. Lucia, but is more extensively cultivated in Mauritius and the Seychelles. The cheap and excellent condiment called pimento or allspice is peculiar to the West Indies, and is chiefly exported from Jamaica. Ceylon, the original home of cinnamon, still furnishes most of the supply of this finest of the spices; this island also exports cardamom seeds. The clove and nutmeg, once exclusively grown in the Dutch Spice Islands, have now spread to other lands. Most of the

world's supply of the clove is now yielded by Zanzibar
and Pemba; the nutmeg is grown in the Straits Settlements and the West Indies. In Grenada the nutmeg
ranks next to cocoa as a staple product, and both clove
and nutmeg have been successfully introduced in
Dominica. Grenada also produces cloves, vanilla, carda-
moms, and pepper, and has been called the "Spice Island
of the West." The stimulant African kola-nut, now
exported in large quantities from the Gold Coast and
Sierra Leone, was long since introduced into the West
Indies by negro slaves, and is cultivated in Jamaica, St.
Lucia, and Grenada. The areca or betel-nut, one of the
chief luxuries of the East, is largely produced in Ceylon,
and in Penang, which takes its name from the areca
palm; this palm also flourishes in British New Guinea.
Among vegetable drugs the first economic place belongs
to cinchona or quinine, successfully introduced into
India by Sir Clements Markham, and since largely
cultivated in Ceylon and Jamaica. Opium, an important
product of Southern Asia, is an export of British Borneo,
and is also produced in New South Wales. The camphor
tree is being extensively planted in Ceylon; British
Borneo also exports large quantities of camphor, chiefly
for the Chinese market. The valuable drug strophanthus,
first used by the natives as an arrow-poison, is an important export of British Central Africa. The medicinal
aloe is produced in the West Indies and Cape Colony;
the castor-oil plant grows wild in the Bahamas; sarsa-
parilla is cultivated in Jamaica, and is being planted in
British Honduras.

The vegetable oils in which Africa is especially rich,
originally valued as articles of food, are now largely

exported for industrial purposes. Among these the
first place belongs to palm-oil, obtained from the fruit
of the Guinea palm, and the staple product of the Gold
Coast, Lagos, and Southern Nigeria: a large trade in
kernels of this fruit, which yield palm-nut oil, the
residue being made into oil-cake, has sprung up in recent
years. Next to tallow, palm-oil and palm-nut oil are the
substances chiefly used in England for making soap and
candles; and the same purpose is served by cocoa-nut
oil, an important export of Ceylon and Mauritius, produced from the kernel of the cocoa-nut broken into small
pieces and dried in the sun (copra): the residue after
extraction furnishes a species of flour. While the
Guinea palm is confined to West Africa, the cocoa-nut
palm flourishes throughout the tropics; and copra is
exported in large quantities from the Straits Settlements,
British Borneo, New Guinea, Fiji, Tonga, and other
possessions in the Pacific. The ground-nut, largely
cultivated in the Gambia Colony, yields an alimentary
oil equal to that of the olive, and commonly blended
with the latter by oil-merchants; inferior sorts are used
in soap-making; this valuable nut thrives in British
Honduras, and might be profitably cultivated in many
parts of the West Indies.

Cotton, the world's cheapest and most popular
clothing material, exceeds even sugar in importance as
an agricultural product of tropical and subtropical
countries; and for Britain an adequate cotton supply is
a matter of the greatest moment. Next to agriculture,
the cotton manufacture is Britain's most important
industry. Probably one-fourth of her population
directly or indirectly depend upon it; to keep her mills

employed, cotton is imported to the value of more than forty millions sterling, being her largest import next to food-stuffs ; cotton manufactures are also her largest export (sixty millions sterling).   Little more than a century ago most of the supply came from the British West Indies.   As the British cotton manufacture progressed, the planters of the Southern United States were alone able to supply the increasing demand ; and at present the States furnish four-fifths of Britain's cotton supply, most of the remainder being supplied by India, Egypt, Turkey, and South America, and the contribution of the colonies (Queensland, Fiji, Lagos, the West Indies, and British New Guinea) being insignificant. The supply and price are subject to fluctuation, the former depending mainly on the season in the Southern United States, the latter on the operations of American speculators ; and local cotton manufactures are being developed in the principal producing countries (United States, India, and Brazil) at such a rate as must greatly diminish in the near future the quantity of raw material remaining for export.   Britain's chief manufacturing industry, therefore, stands in a critical position ; and vigorous efforts are now being made to extend the existing colonial production, especially in the West Indies and West Africa, and to introduce the cotton-plant into Ceylon and British Borneo.   Possibly the principal British cotton-growing districts in the near future may be those great African river-basins which have been recently brought under Britain's control. Cotton has been grown from remote times by the natives throughout the vast territory of Nigeria, and the cultivation might be greatly improved and extended.

The Anglo-Egyptian Sudan has an area suitable for cotton-growing ten times as large as Egypt, which country already provides much of Britain's cotton supply; and the completion of the railway from Berber to Suakin will shortly provide the Sudan grower with ample means of transport. Cotton might be largely grown in British East Africa, and has been found to thrive in British Central Africa and Southern Rhodesia; other parts of the Zambesi basin are also considered suitable for cotton-planting. There is thus a prospect of large additions being made, within the limits of the Empire, to the world's cotton-growing area; and, in view of the paramount importance of the object, British planters are not likely to be deterred by the fact that sufficient labour could scarcely be obtained without having recourse to organised immigration. The American planters, who might largely extend their area of production by resorting to districts capable of irrigation, would of course not relinquish without a struggle that control of the market which they have held for nearly a century. But the manufacturers of France, Germany, and Belgium are no less interested than those of Britain in becoming independent of the American supply; and strenuous efforts are being made, at their instance, to cultivate cotton in the African possessions of all these Powers. Experiments already made encourage the belief that European enterprise in this direction will be successful.

Although silk might be extensively produced in various tropical colonies by cultivating not only the mulberry but those tropical plants on which the silk-worm thrives, such as the castor-oil plant, there is

practically no production in any British colony except
Cyprus. The natives of Ceylon might probably be
induced to give attention to silk-worm rearing, if central
mills were provided to which the cocoons could be sold;
and this industry, so profitable in India, China, and
Japan, might be introduced elsewhere. The demand
for raw silk in Britain is at present but small, though
the silk manufactures of other countries are imported
to the amount of many millions sterling. Altered
circumstances might lead to a revival on a considerable
scale of what was once an important British industry;
and the cheap labour of the East, where the silk
manufacture originated, might be advantageously employed in producing the raw material on colonial soil.

Among the tropical plants yielding coarse hemp-like
fibres for textile purposes the first place belongs to the
palms, and among these to the widely distributed cocoa-
nut palm. Large quantities of the fibrous husk (coir) of
the cocoa-nut are imported into Britain for manufacture
into rope and matting, an industry also carried on in
India and Ceylon. The Brazilian piassava palm is
cultivated for its valuable fibre in Western Africa; and
the common oil-palm of the same district produces a
strong fibre of long staple which promises to become an
important export. Next to the palms comes the aloe
group, prominent in which is the plant yielding
" Mauritius hemp," largely cultivated in that island, and
also in British Central Africa and Sierra Leone. Fast-
growing and easily propagated, Mauritius hemp is well
suited for torrid and humid climates; while the Mexican
aloe, producing the fine white fibre called " sisal " or
" grass hemp," largely planted in the West Indies

(Bahamas, Barbuda, Anguilla), grows freely on poor soil in moderately hot countries. The African "bow-string hemp" is planted in Ceylon, and bids fair to become an important export of Uganda and British Central Africa. China grass or "ramie," a grass fibre of the Far East which demands little outlay and yields abundant returns, is largely planted in the Malay States, and has been introduced into Jamaica.

The natural dyestuffs of the tropics have, during the past half-century, lost much of their former prominence in commerce and planting enterprise, chemical dyes produced in Europe from coal-tar having largely taken their place ; and some minor dyeing products have been driven altogether from the field. Indigo, once among the chief industrial products of Jamaica and other islands, is no longer resorted to by the West Indian planter, though its cultivation is still extensively carried on in British India, and a hard struggle is maintained in its behalf against the artificial indigo of the chemist. Among the West Indian dyewoods, logwood and fustic hold their ground. The famous khaki brown dye of the Malay States, obtained from the catechu (cutch) tree, and commercially known as "gambier," keeps its place in commerce largely in virtue of its value as a tanning stuff; and its production is rapidly extending. Camwood, the material of a valuable dye, is an export of the West African colonies. The contest between natural and artificial colouring products is by no means at an end; probably improvements in the methods of production will enable many among the natural dyes of the tropics to hold their ground, even at such reduced prices as may be necessary to

M

enable them to compete with the chemical dyes of Europe.

The solidified juices of certain tropical trees are products which recent industrial progress has brought into unusual prominence. Gums and resins of tropical origin have entered into commerce from the earliest times. The gum-arabic, copal resin, and other gums and resins of tropical Africa are largely in demand, and an extension of cultivation with a view to their production is anticipated as the Anglo-Egyptian Sudan is opened to planting enterprise. Cashew gum is produced in Jamaica, and the hard resin called " dammar " is an important product of British Borneo. Far more important commercially than gums and resins, are the elastic but tenacious and durable substances known as indiarubber and gutta-percha, produced from juices yielded by the bark of a few tropical forest trees and climbing plants. The demand for rubber and gutta for use in the manufacture of various kinds of machinery, as well as for wheel-tyres, piping, and waterproof fabrics, has of late increased to such an extent that they are perhaps the most valuable, weight for weight, among the products of the tropics ; and the forest lands of every tropical country are eagerly traversed in quest of them. All the British possessions in tropical Africa, including Uganda and the Sudan, are prominent as rubber-yielding districts ; and as the natural supplies diminish each of them is likely to become the seat of extensive rubber cultivation. For this purpose the rubber trees of the New World are preferred, although the Lagos rubber has been successfully planted. The Para and Ceara rubbers from Brazil, and the rubber of Central America, are especially suitable for cultivation. Large plantations of the Para tree, which yields the best rubber of commerce, and is ready for tapping in six or seven years, have already been formed in the Malay States; this tree has also been introduced in Trinidad and Tobago, St. Lucia, and other West Indian islands. British Honduras and British Guiana are indicated as suitable for rubber-planting; and by selecting trees specially suited to each locality there is probably no tropical colony in which this profitable form of enterprise might not be successfully carried on. The Belgians in the Congo State, the Dutch in the East Indian islands, and the Germans in East Africa are devoting much attention to rubber cultivation.

Gutta-percha is found within a more limited area than rubber. The trees producing it are confined to the Malay Peninsula and the adjacent large islands, the Straits Settlements furnishing the bulk of the export; but increasing quantities are being sent from the Federated States and British Borneo. Balata, a substance closely resembling gutta-percha, and largely used as a substitute, is the produce of a forest tree indigenous to Trinidad and British Guiana. Like gutta-percha, balata is obtained from the natural forest; and, unlike gutta-percha, it is still obtainable in quantities only limited by the supply of labour for collecting. In the case of gutta-percha, the trees have been extensively destroyed, and plantation on a large scale must be resorted to if the supply is to be maintained. Preparations are being made for cultivating the most valuable species; experiments have also been made in planting the balata tree, which is considered suitable for cultivation in the African tropical colonies.

Besides forest trees, such as those above mentioned, valued for their products, the tropical colonies contain vast reserves of such as are valued for their timber. British Honduras is famous for its inexhaustible stores of the finest mahogany and cedar; these timbers, together with rosewood, and other fine cabinet woods, exist abundantly in the remaining forests of the West Indian islands. Most of British Guiana is still covered with virgin forest, including timbers of special value in shipbuilding, and timbering is an important industry. The fine timber called Gambia mahogany has recently become a prominent export of the West African colonies. Cedar and ebony abound in Sierra Leone; from the Gold Coast, where the back country is densely wooded, there is a large export of mahogany, cedar, and other timbers, and as railways are pushed into the interior the production will be greatly extended. Timber is now exported in increasing quantities from Lagos and Southern Nigeria. Ebony, satin-wood, and other fine cabinet timbers abound in Ceylon and British Borneo, and there is a large export of timbers of this class from the Straits Settlements. Fiji has excellent indigenous timbers, and by systematic planting might produce in perfection almost every tropical species of timber known to commerce. Cedar, mahogany, and ebony abound in British Central Africa, lignum vitæ and other fine timbers in British East Africa. The plantation of the more valuable timber trees in the tropical colonies is expected to yield large returns, and tropical forestry, at present in its infancy, is engaging much attention.

Although the shores of the British tropical possessions abound in excellent fish, and the fisheries of the West

Indies, especially Jamaica, might be valuable, little marine produce is now exported from them except a few articles of luxury, such as the turtles of the Bahamas and other West Indian islands, and the sharks' fins and trepang of Ceylon, the Straits Settlements, and British Borneo. The tropical coast-waters and lakes support the minor industries of salt-raking and sponge-gathering in the Bahamas and Turks Islands. Diving for the pearl oyster and its shell is carried on throughout the Eastern possessions, from the Bahrein Islands in the Persian Gulf in the west to British New Guinea and the Pacific Islands in the east; and this industry is actively pursued on the tropical coasts of Western Australia and Queensland. The most valuable pearl fisheries are those of Ceylon. Pearl oysters have been found on the Sierra Leone coast, which is regarded as a probable seat of the pearling industry.

The mineral resources of the tropical colonies and protectorates are but imperfectly known. Gold has in recent years been largely mined in several districts of British Guiana, and the royalty upon its production is an important item in the colonial revenue; diamonds have also been found in large numbers in the auriferous districts. Gold abounds in the Gold Coast Colony, where many mines are being energetically worked; and it is known to exist in the back country of other West African colonies. Gold is very widely distributed in Southern Rhodesia, and mining is actively pursued in several districts. In the Eastern section the Malay Protectorates, British Borneo, and British New Guinea are gold-producing colonies. Auriferous quartz has been recently found in Ceylon. Silver and platinum are

obtained in British Borneo.   Gems are largely mined in
Ceylon, where sapphires, rubies, and other valuable
stones are washed down by the rivers, and hundreds of
quarries are in working which yield emeralds, moon-
stones, cinnamon-stones, and garnets.   The plumbago
production of Ceylon has in recent times been rapidly
extended, now employing 100,000 labourers and a large
amount of capital; this valuable mineral has also been
found in British Central Africa.   At the present time
the most important mining district of the tropical
colonies is the Malay Peninsula, which yields the greater
part of the world's supply of tin, and an export duty on
the produce furnishes a considerable revenue.   A new
source of tin has recently been opened in Northern
Nigeria.   The mineral wealth of the West Indian
islands, which is known to be very great, is at present
imperfectly explored.   Gold, silver, and platinum,
besides lead, tin, zinc, and other metals, are believed to
be abundant in Jamaica.   British Central Africa and
Uganda are rich in iron ore, and Ceylon contains ores
of high quality which may one day be worked.

Rhodesia, British Central Africa, and British Borneo
are abundantly supplied with coal, and the latter colony
exports large quantities from the mines of Labuan.
Borneo is also extremely rich in petroleum; and a large
fleet of steamers, some of which use only petroleum as
fuel, are engaged in carrying it as their principal cargo.
Petroleum is found in the West Indies, and the wells of
Trinidad yield a product having a large percentage of
illuminating oil.   The petroleum of the Gold Coast, of
inferior quality, is chiefly valuable for lubricating purposes.   The asphalt of Trinidad, mainly produced from

a single large lake, is so valuable that the government royalty levied on it suffices to pay the interest on the colony's public debt; mineral asphalt exists in Barbados, and has recently been found in the island of Bahrein. The mica and the porcelain-clay of Ceylon, and the phosphate deposits of some islands in the West and East Indies and off South Africa, also deserve mention among the mineral products of the tropical colonies.

The chief products of tropical agriculture demand a considerable degree of preparation for the market by highly specialised processes. Sugar production, indeed, is half as much a manufacturing as an agricultural industry;[1] the cane must be crushed in the mill, and the juice boiled and crystallised by evaporation, before the product becomes merchantable in its lowest form, raw or muscovado sugar. In this state it is most commonly exported from the colony, and undergoes the process of refining elsewhere; but some West Indian colonies export refined sugars (crystals). In some colonies the processes of cultivation and manufacture tend to separate, the former being carried on by the coloured peasantry, and the cane sold to the mill-owner; in others the owners of large estates combine to maintain large mills, furnished with improved machinery. Tea-growing tends to become more and more a factory industry, the curing and rolling processes being now largely done by machinery; the cocoa bean must be fermented and dried, the coffee-berry pulped, dried, and shelled. Analogous processes, of a simple kind, are required in the preparation of spices, drugs, and dye-stuffs; but in no case does the labour intervening

---

[1] Eight months are spent in field work, four in indoor work.

between cultivation and marketing amount to what is commonly meant by "manufacture." Ceylon is the only tropical colony in which manufactures, in the usual sense of the word, have been developed to any noteworthy extent; these are chiefly connected with the extraction of oil and manufacture of coir derived from the local staple, the cocoa-nut. There are also sugar-mills, and it is possible that the cotton manufacture, which is rapidly growing in India, may be extended to Ceylon. Hong-Kong has a few sugar-mills, besides rope-works and other manufactures chiefly connected with shipping; both here and at Singapore a large amount of labour is employed in the docks and warehouses, and in foundries and engineers' and carpenters' shops connected with the shipping industry. The sago and tapioca produced in the Malay Peninsula and its neighbourhood are extensively milled at the last-named place for export to Europe. In the tropical colonies generally the hand-to-mouth industries — tobacco and cigar manufacture, pottery, tanning, brewing, ice and mineral-water manufacture, and the like—are pursued to supply local needs, but contribute little, or not at all, to their commerce with distant countries.

The commerce of the tropical colonies is mainly carried in vessels belonging to the European, Asiatic, or American countries with which they exchange commodities; but most of them have a maritime trade, principally local, carried on in shipping of their own. As might be anticipated, local shipping is less developed in the tropical than in the self-governing colonies. It is best represented in the eastern hemisphere : the registered tonnage of the Straits Settlements alone exceeds that of the West Indies, British Guiana, and British Honduras together, and consists to the extent of three-fourths of steamships, while in the West Indian section sailing vessels largely predominate. The local steam tonnage of Hong-Kong nearly equals that of the Straits Settlements. Ceylon and Mauritius have a local marine chiefly consisting of sailing vessels. Bermuda, British Honduras, and British Guiana have more local shipping in proportion to the amount of their trade than the West Indian islands; and among these Bermuda, with its brisk trade to the United States and Canada in fruit and garden vegetables, has the largest amount of tonnage.

The trade of the colonies with the parent country and other nations has increased tenfold since the late Queen's accession; a far larger increase than has taken place during the same period in the external commerce of the United Kingdom itself. Even more remarkable is the fact that the external commerce of the Colonies and Colonial Federations now amounts to three times the entire external commerce of the United Kingdom itself at the late Queen's accession. It is not far below that of France, the world's fourth commercial power; and the proportion which it bears to the population and wealth of the communities engaged in it exceeds the corresponding ratios in France, Germany, and the United States. It is highest in the eastern hemisphere; in the Australasian colonies the ratio of external trade to population probably exceeds the corresponding ratio in the United Kingdom. It is lower in Canada, where a larger population gives greater scope to internal consumption; but even in Canada the

ratio has doubled since 1837, and is double the ratio of
external trade to population in the United States. Even
the external commerce of the Crown colonies, where
the ratio is lowest, and the actual increase of external
trade is least, is five times as much as at Queen Victoria's
accession. As traders with the rest of the world the
Colonies and Colonial Federations stand with the parent
country in the first rank, strongly contrasting with
British India, which in this respect ranks below Russia,
the most self-contained among the world's great nations.
Their total external commerce, omitting bullion and
specie, amounts to considerably more than three
hundred millions sterling, of which more than half
represents imports into the colonies. The greater part
of this trade is intra-imperial, being carried on either
with the parent country, or with other British possessions. The residue, representing more than two-fifths
of the colonial imports, and nearly two-fifths of the
colonial exports, is transacted with foreign countries.
In particular cases these general proportions are greatly
varied, some colonies having a largely preponderant
trade with foreign countries. Such is the case with the
trade of such colonies as Hong-Kong, established for
the special purpose of facilitating commerce with China,
and Singapore, a natural centre of trade with Siam,
Cochin-China, the Dutch Indies, and the Pacific ports of
the United States; while the commerce of Ceylon and
Mauritius, both situated in the midst of the eastern
section of the Empire, is predominantly intra-imperial.
The West Indian colonies, with the exception of St.
Vincent and Grenada, trade more largely with the
United States and the countries of South America than

with the parent country or its offshoots, although they
have a considerable commerce with Canada ; but most
of the West Indian islands, like the West African
colonies, while sending the larger part of their exports
to foreign countries, receive the larger part of their
imports from the parent country and British possessions.
The reverse is the case with Canada, which disposes of
most of its exports in Britain and British colonies, while
taking most of its imports from foreign countries,
the United States standing first on the list.

Among the great self-governing colonies those of
South Africa and Australasia have the largest intra-
imperial trade, and rank as the "best customers" of the
parent country.   Each New Zealander takes British
manufactures to the value of £8 : 8s., and each Australian
to the value of £6 : 14s. ; textiles and apparel, railway
plant, hardware and machinery, and paper, stationery,
and books, being prominent items.   In South Africa,
having regard to its mixed population and the economic
disturbance caused by recent events, such an estimate is
not easily made ; but the white colonists are certainly
consumers of British goods to an equal extent with
Australians.   In the western hemisphere Jamaica,
British Guiana, and the Windward Islands are Britain's
best   customers; Newfoundland   receives   from   the
United States imports to a larger amount than from the
parent country, and from Canada to an amount still
larger.   Canada's exceptionally large imports from the
United States consist, to a great extent, of articles of
food and of raw or partially manufactured industrial
material destined for use in her own manufactures.   In
finished manufactures the British exporter to Canada

encounters the competition not only of the States, France, Germany, and Belgium, but of the steadily growing industries of the Dominion. By way of counteracting the competition of foreign countries Canada in 1897 granted to British goods a reduction of 25 per cent on the duties levied on importation; and this preference has lately been increased to 33⅓ per cent. British exports to Canada have been doubled since this policy was adopted; and Canada's example has been followed by the South African colonies and New Zealand. The Cape Colony and Natal have granted British imports a remission of duties equivalent to 25 per cent on the general tariff; New Zealand has consented to a reduction of 10 per cent, and it is anticipated that a similar preference will be granted by the Australian Commonwealth. Nor has the movement in favour of preference been confined to the self-governing colonies. British Guiana has agreed to a reduction of 10 per cent, and other Crown colonies are likely to follow her example. Such reductions would probably be increased if Britain, on her part, would meet them by returning to the system of preferential treatment for colonial produce in her own markets which largely, though not universally, prevailed before self-government was granted to the principal colonies; and without some step being taken in this direction it is scarcely probable that they will be maintained.

In some colonies preferential treatment has been given to the parent country not by reducing existing import duties in her favour, but by increasing them against the foreigner. In either case preference represents substantial sacrifices on the part of the colonial tax-payer. Most colonies, taking them all round, raise the greater part of their public revenue by customs duties. The external trade of all colonies being greater, in proportion to their population and resources, than is the case in fully developed countries, it is natural that it should bear the main burden of taxation. Where the standard of comfort is high, and moderate prosperity is generally diffused, no tax is more nearly equal in its incidence, or less felt by the tax-payer, than a duty on imports; none is more easily and cheaply collected; none commends itself more strongly to the manufacturing section of the population, who see in it a protection to their own industries; no other, except a duty on exports, raises the fascinating suggestion that some part, perhaps the greater part, of the tax is ultimately paid by outsiders. Most of the revenue thus raised falls on articles of necessity or convenience— textile fabrics, iron, iron wares, and machinery, leather and leather manufactures, earthenware, porcelain and glass, oils, soap, coal, candles, and articles of food and drink, being among the chief items. Alcoholic liquors and tobacco are also important sources of revenue; and these are taxed on import even in the case of Gibraltar, which is for all other commodities a free port. In the Federated Malay States there are duties on tobacco, spirits, and opium. In the Straits Settlements there are import duties on alcoholic liquors, but taxation of this description is chiefly levied by an excise on spirits and opium, and there are no custom-houses. In Hong-Kong, which is a free port, the sale of opium is a government monopoly.

In many cases it is found convenient to raise revenue

by a tax on the produce of the colony, usually in the form of an export duty.   If the colony imposing such a duty had a monopoly of the article so taxed, such a duty would fall ultimately on the foreign purchaser ; and it might obviously be imposed wherever the colony enjoys special advantages in the production of the article in question.   Export duties on cultivated produce were formerly universal in the West Indies, but have been abolished in Jamaica, St. Lucia, Antigua, and Montserrat, and in other islands have in general been reduced.   In Dominica a small export duty is levied on bananas, oranges, limes, and lime-juice, as well as on cocoa and coffee ; the latter articles are also subject to export duties in Trinidad and St. Vincent.   In Ceylon a small export duty is levied on tea, coffee, cocoa, and cinchona. Natural products, of which the supply is exhaustible, are more proper subjects for taxation than cultivated crops ; export duties, for example, are levied on the logwood and mahogany of British Honduras, the plumbago of Ceylon, the diamonds of the Cape Colony, the asphalt of Trinidad, the coals of Labuan and British Columbia, and the phosphate deposits of the Bahamas, St. Helena, the Seychelles, and Queensland.   The ground-nuts of the Gambia are still capable of bearing an export duty, but no similar duties now exist in any other West African colony.   An export duty has recently been imposed in New Zealand on its white pine and kauri timber.   The duty on pine-apple plants exported from the Bahamas is of a protective nature ; but the only example of effective protection in this form appears in the duties of £100 each on the export of live ostriches, and £5 on ostrich eggs, levied in the Cape Colony.   In

the Protectorates, which have a large trade in natural
produce, export duties are largely resorted to as a means
of raising revenue ; special exports raised by cultivation
are also found capable of bearing a heavy duty.   Thus
cloves in Zanzibar pay 25 per cent *ad valorem* on
exportation, and in British East Africa 30 per cent.
The rest of the public revenue of the Colonies is derived
from such internal sources as the sale and rent of public
lands, land taxes, excise duties, income tax, stamp and
licence duties, mining and pasturage licences, post office
and telegraphs, government railways and other public
works, and royalties on minerals.   In Ceylon, as in
India, the government has a monopoly of salt.

In Australasia and South Africa the apparent amount
of the revenue is considerably augmented by taking into
account the gross receipts from the government railways
and other public works.   Of the 40,000 miles of railways in the Colonies more than half are government
property ; and of the sixty-six millions sterling received
as public revenue in the colonial section of the Empire
more than a third represents gross income from railways,
one of the other thirds roughly representing revenue
from customs duties, the remaining third miscellaneous
sources of income.   In Canada, on the contrary, the
greater part of the railway mileage belongs to private
companies, the entire income of the Dominion government from public works being less than a million
sterling, while the income from railways alone credited
to the colonial governments in Australasia amounts to
thirteen millions.   Of this gross railway income about
two-thirds is absorbed in working expenses, leaving one-
third net income, applicable in payment of interest on

the borrowed capital expended on them. The railway mileage in the tropical colonies is at present comparatively small, Ceylon, with 297 miles, heading the list, and Jamaica, Mauritius, British Guiana, Trinidad, and Barbados following in order. In Lagos, Sierra Leone, and the Gold Coast railway extension is proceeding, though less rapidly than could be wished in the interest of the economic development of these colonies and their adjacent protectorates.

Interest on the public debt is often a considerable item in the expenditure of a colony. Most of the colonies have contracted public debts, and in the case of some self-governing ones these form a heavy charge on the public revenue. But colonial public debts represent, as a rule, money expended in public works, which remain available as public assets of increasing value. The original public property of a colony lies in its forests, mineral tracts, and improvable land. In order to render these accessible to emigrants, the interior country must be surveyed, railways, roads, and bridges must be made, sites chosen for townships and farms, and the lots laid out for purchasers. Post-office and telegraph services must be provided. Docks, harbour works, and lighthouses must be constructed. Nor can a colonial government withdraw its hand at the point where in old countries the work of local government usually begins. It must give a start to municipalities by establishing waterworks, gasworks, cemeteries, lunatic asylums, prisons, and penitentiaries. In general it is supposed that the extraordinary public expenditure necessary in developing a colony is twice as much as the ordinary expenditure. The most costly public

works yield an income to be set against the interest on
the capital expended on them ; and as the prosperity of
the colony increases, the returns from its public works
increase also. In those colonies where the expenditure
on public works has been largest, the time is anticipated
when the profit yielded by them will pay a very large
part, if not the whole, of the expenses of government.
The only colonial group in which public borrowings
have been heavy relatively to the population, is the
Australasian. The debts of the Australasian colonies
amount together to 250 millions sterling, as against 76
millions in the more populous British North American
group ; but of this a very large proportion (83 per cent
in New South Wales) is represented by railways and
other income-yielding public works, and the whole
represents no more than seven years' public income, or
about the same proportion as in British North America.

Besides interest on the public debt, the expenditure
of a colony chiefly consists of the balance of the cost of
public works in excess of the income derived from them,
and payments in respect of the civil service, education,
and constabulary and defence services. The last named,
in European countries a heavy item, and conspicuously
so in the case of Britain, is in the Colonies a comparatively
light one. The protection of the seaborne commerce of
the Colonies—the main source of their prosperity—falls
practically on the British tax-payer ; and although most
colonies, as will appear in the next chapter, make some
provision for their local defences and in some cases
contribute in a small degree to the cost of the Imperial
navy, their expenditure on these accounts is moderate
relatively to what they have at stake in the world—to

their realised property, their undeveloped resources, and their internal and external commerce. The benefit of the diplomatic and consular services maintained by the parent country in all foreign parts of the world is also enjoyed by all the colonies free of expense. It has been sometimes urged that the Colonies ought to contribute, each in proportion to its means, to the interest on and extinction of the Imperial debt, on the ground that this was chiefly incurred in prosecuting to a successful termination the prolonged and costly wars which, at various stages of history, preceded and made possible their establishment.

The economic condition of the Colonies as a whole is universally recognised as sound, and their prospects as favourable. With some exceptions of little importance, chiefly among the Protectorates, they cost the parent country nothing, and they afford outlets of evergrowing importance for British manufactures. The colonial trade of Britain grows in an increasing ratio, while her foreign trade, where it is growing at all, grows in a diminishing ratio. Meanwhile Britain's competitors in her main business, that of manufacturing for the world's markets, are ever acquiring a larger and larger share in the trade of her colonies. Even in Australasia and South Africa, Britain's best colonial markets, the manufactures of the United States, Germany, France, and Belgium have been gaining ground; a fact largely attributable to the systematic development of foreign shipping, and to subsidies and bounties granted by foreign governments on its employment in competing for British-Colonial trade. Hitherto little attention has been bestowed on the systematic organisation of the maritime communications

of the Empire.   An authority who commands general
attention has recently formulated a proposal for supplying this defect.[1]   Sir George Clarke suggests that a duty
of 1 per cent should be imposed as a surcharge upon all
foreign goods discharged at Imperial ports.   Such a tax,
which would probably be borne by the exporter rather
than the importer or the consumer, and, however borne,
would scarcely be felt, would yield an annual income of
about £4,600,000.   This sum, it is suggested, should be
placed at the disposition of an Imperial Maritime
Council, composed of about fifteen members, of whom
four would represent the parent country, two India, two
Canada, one the Cape Colony, one Natal, two Australia,
one New Zealand, and two the Crown colonies.   Sit-
ting annually for the transaction of business, the Maritime
Council would hold its meetings in every fourth year
at each of the chief centres of Imperial commerce—
Montreal, Cape Town, Bombay, and Sydney.   It would
dispose of its fund by way of subsidies, bounties, or loans
at low interest, subject to conditions of speed, tonnage,
periodicity, accommodation, and employment of British
subjects.   In the course of its proceedings it would
inquire into the possibilities of further commercial
development, bring governors and ministers, colonists,
planters, merchants, and shipowners into personal
communication, and ascertain the nature of business
interests at first hand from business men.   It would
form an Imperial board connecting local Chambers of
Commerce, and promoting their formation where they
do not exist.   Among its functions would be the provision and supervision of adequate coaling accommodation

[1] *Nineteenth Century*, May 1904.

for the mercantile marine, and in this way the Maritime Council might become auxiliary to the Admiralty. Nor need the efforts of such a Council be confined to the promotion of commercial traffic. What is urgently required in the interests of the Empire, is an extended system of passenger traffic, which should induce and enable the grown-up youth, the working-man and the tradesman, whether of the colonies or the parent country, to cross the ocean as a visitor. For the masses of the people on either side, the conception of the Empire at present chiefly rests on the exercise of the imagination. Visits of a few days might easily be organised, in the course of which the Canadian would behold some of the great cities and the historic sights of Britain, and the British citizen those of the Dominion. A cheap imperial tourist service would do much to make the Empire a substantive reality for the most intelligent section of the masses of its citizens. For the youth of the Empire—the citizens of the future—the educational value of such facilities cannot be overestimated. Arrangements might easily be made by which a portion of the holidays given in technical schools and colleges should be spent on the other side of the water. Organisation and co-operation, the great needs of the Empire in all its aspects, are alone wanted.

The greater degree of unification which must result from increasing facilities of transport and communication cannot fail to promote a conception of it in the public mind as an economic whole, and perhaps in the end to awaken throughout the length and breadth of the Empire a sense of the nature of the economic forces which are ever visibly altering the aspect of its component parts,

and controlling the direction taken by the elements which
give it economic vitality. Nothing is at the present
moment more striking than the unanimity with which
the leading countries of the world are preparing to
develop colonial enterprise in their tropical territories.
The nature of tropical products of every description,
the geology and climatology of the tropics in their
relation to planting and irrigation, forestry and mining,
the means of procuring labour, whether by training
local natives or by drawing on the reserves waiting for
profitable employment in other countries, are assiduously
studied in America, Germany, France, Holland, and
Belgium, as well as in Britain and her colonies ; and it
is often remarked that in the "Colonial Science," to
use an expression established in continental usage, other
countries are in advance of us. Yet no nation possesses
a share in the rich heritage of the tropics comparable for
a moment to that of Britain and her colonies. Unfortunately one of the fairest parts of this heritage—
tropical Australia—remains for the present practically
closed to the means of development by the policy of the
Commonwealth electorate. No one outside Australia
can believe that such a policy can be long maintained.
To shut the door of progress in one half of Australia in
the supposed interests of the labouring population in the
other half is to attempt a fruitless resistance to the laws
of nature. Long before the living generation has passed
away Australia must fall into line with the rest of the
world. Meanwhile, Australia's loss is likely to prove
Africa's gain. Less indefensible on general grounds, and
probably less likely, in the long run, to retard economic
progress, are the much - criticised labour laws of the

Australasian colonies.   Compulsory arbitration or conciliation in industrial disputes, limitation of the hours
of labour, exclusion of immigrants under contract for employment and old-age pensions out of government funds,
need from the economic point of view arouse no serious
apprehension.   They are the outcome of a period of
transition—a period when the voting strength of the
population was mainly concentrated in towns, and the
predominance of the labour vote enabled those who
wielded it to pass with little difficulty legislative measures
deemed essential to its interests.   The future of Australia
depends upon the development of the natural resources
of the soil.   The control of its destiny must pass, and
probably is gradually passing, into the hands of those to
whom labour laws are a matter of indifference—to the
ever-increasing freeholders of its rural districts, who are
engaged in raising corn and meat, in dairying, wine-
making, and fruit-growing for outside markets : a class
recruited from the best of its redundant urban population,
and substantially forming the same political element which
predominates in other countries which are at once democratic and conservative, and are models of excellence in
their internal economy — in France, Switzerland, and
Canada.

   The fact that Britain and her colonies constitute a
natural economic whole, and that this arises out of
the very circumstances under which the Empire has
taken shape, cannot be too strongly insisted on.   It may
be an exaggeration to say that were the globe, as yet
unpenetrated by human enterprise, placed at the disposal
of an economist endowed with intuitive knowledge of
its resources and possibilities, and of man's capacity

for developing them, he would straightway lay out the Britannic Empire on its existing lines as the most effectual system for bringing such development about. The exaggeration would be greatly diminished if the Empire's offshoot, the United States, with its natural commercial connections, were added. It would almost vanish if France, the chief colonial power of continental Europe, were added also. Britain, the States, and France form a natural triumvirate of Powers holding jointly in their hands the economic development of the globe. Upon their co-operation on the basis of permanent mutual good understanding the future of that development depends. But in order that such a co-operation may be effectual the economic consolidation of the Britannic Empire is absolutely necessary. How that consolidation may be best effected it is for Britain and her great self-governing Colonies and Colonial Federations to decide. It is strongly urged upon public opinion, by economists and statesmen, that now is the critical moment when that decision must be taken, if it is to be taken at all.

The most obvious mode of consolidation would be to return, in some form and degree, to the old system of mutual commercial preference between the parent country and the Colonies. The Colonies have shown decisively their willingness to take such a step, and controversy is at the present time fiercely raging over the question how Britain should respond to their offers. "Reason," it has been truly said, "predominates at the end of every crisis, but her voice is drowned at the commencement." It is not sufficiently understood in this country that the crisis, so far as concerns our

principal colony, is of long standing, and that only the
intelligence, the patience, and the patriotism of Canada
have hitherto prevented it from coming to a deplorable
termination.   The very state of things upon which the
case for preference is now based by British economists
was accurately predicted by a Canadian writer more
than thirty years ago; and instead of any original
discussion of a matter on which it is impossible in this
volume to remain altogether silent, a short review of a
portion of his long-forgotten volume may here be
profitably introduced.[1]   Behind the question of cutting
the colonies adrift, a policy then favourably regarded
by many in the parent country, there lay, urged the
colonist, another question.   How far was it safe for
England to rely on being able to retain that commercial
supremacy in virtue of which she was able to permit
the unrestricted importation of foreign manufactured
goods? If she lost the command of the world's markets,
how would she fare without the colonies to fall back upon?

"That such a contingency is possible is beyond doubt.
For, without entering into the question of the balance
of trade, it is undeniable that to import goods without
being able to pay for them by exports is impossible ;
and a nation can find a sale for its exports only so long
as it can furnish them as cheaply as others in the same
market.   England now exports manufactured goods
cheaper than other nations ; is she sure of being able to
continue to do so ?"

In thickly populated countries like England, the
colonist of 1872 argues, unrestricted importation is

---

[1] *A Colonist on the Colonial Question.*   By Jehu Mathews, of
Toronto, Canada.   London : Longmans, Green and Co.   1872.

possible under peculiar circumstances only.   England
imports food and raw material for her manufactures,
and pays for them by exporting her manufactures,
buying, of course, in the cheapest markets, and selling
in the dearest.

"But supposing that foreign markets should become
the cheapest for manufactured goods as well as for
bread-stuffs—how would the case then stand?   Supposing that Belgium could supply hardware, France cotton
goods, and Germany woollen goods, cheaper than they
could be manufactured in England, would it suit her
then to abandon the manufacture of these goods and
follow the policy of buying in the cheapest market and
selling in the dearest by importing manufactured goods
as well as bread-stuffs?"

Therefore, it is argued, in the event of foreign
markets becoming cheaper than English ones for
manufactured goods, England must either close her
ports against free importation of foreign manufactures,
or else see her people not only without the means of
purchasing food, but without food to purchase.

"But even a less improvement in the arts of manufacturing on the part of foreigners than that requisite to
enable them to undersell English manufactures at home
would suffice to destroy free trade in England.   Let
them improve only so much as to enable them to
dispense with English imports, and free trade is ruined.
For although they might be willing to export to England
the goods which she now imports from them, and she
willing to receive their exports, she would be unable to
do so, because to buy anything we must be able to pay
for it.   If foreigners could buy cheaper at home those

goods which they now import from England, they would not buy from her; and England, having lost the means of paying for the goods which she now imports from foreigners, would be unable to obtain them.

"In either of these cases the only manner in which England could procure a supply of those goods which are essential to her · existence—bread-stuffs and raw material for manufacturing purposes—would be by entering into treaties with other countries, granting them an advantage in her markets on condition of receiving a like advantage in their own.   This she might do with the colonies, and with them only : since it is only young countries that can import their manufactured goods and yet find employment for all their people ; and their extent and the variety of their produce would enable them to supply the diversified goods which she would require."

It might be answered, says the colonist, that the argument would be a practical one were there any prospect of such a contingency arising ; but that as there is no such prospect, it is worthless.   The course of events during thirty years has removed a doubt that may then fairly have been entertained.   The thing has happened. The contingency which was then at the most only possible, but which the diminished rate of increase in British commerce between 1866 and 1872 thus early rendered probable, has become an established fact. That the colonial trade of Britain has been increasing while her foreign trade has been diminishing affords ample testimony to the wisdom of the counsel which in 1872 bade her keep in her hands the means of securing a trade which would always maintain her in the position

of a great commercial Power. What the colonist then
brought forward as a suggestion has now been enacted
by the principal colonies as a substantive concession on
their parts. It remains for the parent country to make
concessions which, however slight to begin with, shall
re-establish the principle of mutual advantage in intra-
imperial trade. Whatever objections may be advanced
against proposals for imposing under existing conditions
substantial duties on foreign imports into the parent
country, it is difficult to see what valid objection could
be raised to the duty of 1 per cent suggested by Sir
George Clarke as a means of counteracting the subsidies
and bounties to foreign trade with Britain and the
colonies.[1] Such a duty would at once admit the principle,
and establish in outline a working system, of mutual
preference within the Empire ; and it would be easy
to develop the system in various directions, and in
different degrees, as expediency might require.[2]

---

[1] How can a state of things continue under which the whole of the
trade, for instance, of British Borneo has been captured by the heavily
subsidised North-German Lloyd ?

[2] The question of the day, so far as concerns the Colonies, lies in
a nutshell. The mutual preferences which existed before the change
to free imports, estimated proportionally to the then distribution of
wealth, represented a large gain to the Colonies, and a small loss to
Britain. The abolition of these preferences represented a large loss to
the Colonies, a small gain to Britain, and a larger gain to foreign
nations. This last has lately increased by leaps and bounds. Foreigners,
of course, are unwilling to lose it ; but neither Britain nor the Colonies
can any longer afford to let them enjoy it. The Colonies think that,
for obvious reasons, what gain can be made out of them ought, as far
as possible, to accrue to Britain. It is demonstrably Britain's interest
that what gain can be made out of her should, as far as possible, accrue
to the Colonies, in whose pockets it will not only be no loss to her,
but will become a productive investment for her and them alike. It
is idle to suppose that Britain's economic generosity to foreigners, who
scoff at the mere suggestion of reciprocity, can go on much longer.
Britain and the Colonies must consult their mutual interests, and act
on the principle that " charity begins at home."

CHAPTER IV

It is not easy to say, off-hand, how many governments the Colonial Empire includes. From one point of view there may be said to be only seven—the four self-governing colonies, the two self-governing Federations, and the government of the United Kingdom; for the Imperial government retains the ultimate control, and to a large extent influences the actual conduct of affairs in all the rest. To estimate the number of governments thus subject to the ultimate control and continuous influence of the Imperial government involves the exercise of some discretion. The Empire includes aggregated governments and governments within governments. The Governor of the Colony of the Straits Settlements, for example, is High Commissioner for the four Federated Malay States, which have separate legislatures presided over by their Sultans; he is, however, practically the responsible ruler of the Protectorate as well as the colony, and devotes twice as much of his time to the former as to the latter. He is also High Commissioner for three separate governments in the island of Borneo, each of entirely different constitution, and all under British protection, in different senses of

188

the term ; but in respect of these his responsibility is lighter. The three Windward Islands are under a single Governor, but each has its separate Executive Council and Legislative Council. Ought the States of Australia, under present conditions of transition, to be considered for the purpose of enumeration as constituting a single government, as may properly be done in the case of Canada? Disposing of occasional difficulties of this and other descriptions according to the circumstances of each case, the total number of colonial governments may, for practical purposes, be reckoned at fifty : any reasonable computation results either in this number, or one slightly below it, or one not greatly in excess of it.

Nor is it easy to reduce these fifty governments into groups with reference to their constitution. Whatever classification may be adopted will be found to require some exception or qualification, to involve some cross division, or to be liable to the objection that the assignment of a particular dependency to a particular group results from some circumstance of minor importance. Without wholly losing sight of the principle of grouping, we shall endeavour to arrange them as nearly as possible in the order of the progressive complexity of their political organisation, beginning with those in which the conduct of affairs is vested in governors, administrators, or other officers directly commissioned by the Crown or indirectly appointed by its authority, and is subject to the ultimate control of the Imperial government, and ending with those in which the substantial control is vested in local ministries commanding majorities in the local representative assemblies. Such an enumeration

naturally begins with a few isolated maritime stations
—passes from these to the Protectorates, from the
Protectorates to the Crown colonies, in which the
Governor is assisted by a Council composed of officials
and government nominees; thence to colonies having
a popular representative element in the Council; thence
to those having a separate legislative body, although
substantially controlled by the Governor in Council, all
of which last-named groups may be comprehensively
called Council-governed colonies—and concludes with
the self-governing colonies and the great self-governing
Federations of Canada and Australia. This progressive
enumeration is adopted for convenience only, and does
not represent anything in the nature of "evolution" in
colonial government. So far as any process of evolution
has taken place, the Council-governed colony represents
the rudimentary form.[1] By dropping the formal Council
this has become the Protectorate, by increasing the
power and developing the functions of the Council, the
self-governing colony.

The simplest form of administration occurs in a few
isolated maritime stations, mostly taken for naval
purposes, and, unlike the majority of such stations,
forming no part of larger colonial territories. Such are
Gibraltar, Ascension, and St. Helena. Gibraltar, a
rocky peninsula only two square miles in extent, occupied
by a first class fortress, is practically under military
government. The Commander-in-Chief of the fortress is
also the civil Governor; all executive and legislative
functions are vested in him, and military discipline is

[1] Bacon, *Essay of Plantations*: "For government, let it be in the
hands of one, assisted with some counsel."

everywhere maintained. Gibraltar is a considerable commercial port, and is ranked as a colony; there is a permanent staff of civil officers, such as a Colonial Treasurer, a Colonial Secretary, a Chief-Justice, and an Attorney-General. Such officials in most other colonies form an executive council for the Governor's assistance. In Gibraltar, however, they have no voice in the administration, which is conducted by the Governor alone, subject to the control of the Imperial government.

The case of Ascension is even simpler than that of Gibraltar. This barren island, used exclusively for naval purposes, being a victualling and refitting and coaling depôt, and a sanatorium for H.M. ships on the West African Station, is under the government of the Board of Admiralty, and is said to be rated in the Admiralty books as a man-of-war. The naval officer in charge is the sole administrator, and the Naval Discipline Act is the practical law of the island. Ascension is not regarded as a colony, and is exempt from the control of the Colonial Office. It has no commerce, public revenue, expenditure, or debt, and its population consists of naval officers and their families, seamen, marines, and a few West African negroes employed as boatmen.

Compared with Ascension, the little island of St. Helena—about one-third of the size of the Isle of Wight—is fertile and populous, and its inhabitants formerly carried on a flourishing commerce by supplying fresh provisions to passing vessels bound for the Cape of Good Hope. Since the opening of the Suez Canal this commerce has almost ceased, and St. Helena now derives all its importance from its use as a forti- fied coaling station for the navy, and its occasional

employment as a military prison. It has the smallest
population of any colony except the Falkland Islands,
and is the only true colony possessing no legislative
body. St. Helena is administered under the Colonial
Office by a civil Governor, who also acts as Chief-Justice
and Colonial Secretary.   He is assisted by an Executive
Council consisting of the Bishop, the officer commanding
the troops, and two residents. Power of legislating
by Order in Council is retained by the Imperial
government. Tristan da Cunha, the largest island in
a small group taken into possession by Britain in 1816
as a precaution against any attempt at the rescue of
Napoleon from St. Helena, furnishes subsistence to a
small population, usually about a hundred, of British
nationality, who are patriarchally governed by the
oldest inhabitant, and are said practically to enjoy their
possessions in common.   The younger generation usually
migrates to the Cape of Good Hope as it grows up.
There is an English chaplain, and a man-of-war annually
visits the island. Pitcairn Island, in the Pacific, is a
British possession of much the same kind.[1]

From these isolated stations in mid-ocean we pass to
two others—Aden and Wei-hai-wei—one at either extremity of the populous continent of Asia, in each of
which the maritime station is the centre of a protectorate. The government of Aden includes the island of
Perim, lying in the strait connecting the Red Sea with
the Indian Ocean, and an important military, commercial,
and coaling station.   Aden is one of the most frequented
ports in the Empire, and a strongly fortified coaling
station.   The government includes several towns and

---

[1] Pitcairn is the subject of R. Whiteing's classic romance *The Island*.

villages. Aden, with Perim, is considered as part of British India, and is attached to the Presidency of Bombay. The government is controlled by the Secretary of State for India, and is exercised by the officer in command of the troops, who also holds the civil office of Political Resident. Attached to the government of Aden is an extensive protectorate on the southern coast of Arabia, where the local sultans or chiefs are subsidised by Britain; and the large island of Sokotra, at some distance, is included in the protectorate. The Kuria Muria Islands, near the eastern extremity of the protected shore, are annexed to the British dominions.

Wei - hai - wei, formerly a fortified Chinese port, is occupied by a garrison, but the commander of the troops exercises no authority beyond the military station; the territory, 285 square miles in extent, with a sphere of influence comprising 1500 miles more, is administered as a protectorate by a civil Commissioner under the Colonial Office. The local administration in the villages remains with Chinese officials. Wei-hai-wei, chiefly used as a drill and exercise ground for crews on the China Station, was taken on "lease" from China in 1898 by the British government for a term to last as long as Russia's occupation of the opposite peninsula of Liau-tung and fortress of Port Arthur. It was intended to fortify it anew at the expense of four millions, and the intended works were begun, but have for the present been suspended. Russia's occupation of Port Arthur will probably be soon terminated; but should it pass into the hands of some other Power, or revert to the Chinese Empire, the British right of occupying Wei-hai-wei will doubtless be retained.

The protected territories attached to the military stations of Aden and Wei-hai-wei mark the transition to the Protectorates generally : a species of dependency strikingly prominent in the existing aspect of the Colonial Empire.   Some protectorates are administered through the Foreign Office, the nominal sovereignty remaining vested in native kings or chiefs ; others directly through the Colonial Office ; others under the Colonial Office through chartered companies responsible for their administration and development, or through the governments of previously existing colonies adjacent to them, to which they are attached ; and some protected districts inhabited exclusively or chiefly by native populations have become merged for government purposes in the colonies to which they adjoin.   The general mark of protectorates is that they have no Executive or Legislative Councils, that subsisting native political and social organisations worth preserving are utilised, as far as possible, for government purposes, and that these are controlled and supplemented by a British administrative staff.   In its simplest form, the protectorate is rather of a negative than a positive character ; what is prescribed is not so much what the native population shall do, as what they shall not do.   The importation of arms, ammunition, and intoxicants is prohibited.   They are forbidden to treat or intrigue with any foreign Power, to engage in inter-tribal war, or to change the existing state of society otherwise than by dropping institutions or practices condemned as inhuman or barbarous, and adopting others recognised by the protecting authority.   There are in Arabian waters two protectorates of this simple description, both closely connected with Aden and British India, but both under the control of the Foreign Office. These are Somaliland and Bahrein.

Somaliland is governed by a Commissioner and Consul-General. The control exercised over the Somalis, who are nomadic Mohammadans, is practically limited to the three ports, and is chiefly intended to secure free communication with the port of Aden, which has a large commerce with Somaliland, and draws from it most of its food supplies. The sheikhs of the coast tracts have for the most part acquiesced in the British protectorate, but Imperial authority is far from being established throughout the protected territory. The island of Bahrein, the largest of the group bearing this name, is under the sovereignty of a native sheikh, who is maintained in authority by British influence, and is subject to the supervision of a British Political Agent, subordinate to the British Political Resident stationed at the Persian port of Bushire, on the opposite or northern side of the Persian Gulf. The protectorate is chiefly maintained for safe-guarding an increasing trade with British India, and for enforcing the maritime truce established by treaties with various chiefs on the adjacent Arabian mainland for the prevention of piracy and the slave-trade. Many British-Indian merchants are resident on the island.

Like Somaliland, the rest of the protectorates lying in North-Eastern Africa are administered under the Foreign Office, but in these more important dependencies British control assumes a more determinate form. The southernmost is the Sultanate of Zanzibar. The British Protectorate of Zanzibar consists of the islands of

Zanzibar and Pemba, the former nominal dominions of the Sultan on the mainland being now included in British East Africa and German East Africa. The Sultan is practically a British pensioner, a fixed annual sum being assigned to him as a Civil List, and the rest of the revenue being applied to the expenses of government. The administration is directed by the Sultan's British prime minister, and there is a resident British Agent and Consul-General, whose sanction is necessary to all government expenditure. The British Agent administers justice in all cases in which a British subject is concerned, and the army, including the police, is commanded by a British officer. The British Agent at Zanzibar is also at the head of the administration of British East Africa, with the title of Commissioner and Consul-General. The protectorate is subdivided into seven provinces administered by the Commissioner with the aid of sub-commissioners ; but there are large tracts of country which have not been yet brought within the scope of government, although treaties have been entered into with most of the native chiefs. The Commissioner is Commander-in-Chief of the forces. The former Protectorate of Witu, nominally subject to its own Sultan, now forms part of Tanaland, one of the provinces of British East Africa. Mombasa, the capital of the protectorate, is connected by the Uganda railway with the Protectorate of Uganda. The kingdom of Uganda, the nucleus of the protectorate of the same name, is nominally subject to a native king. The present king being an infant, there is a regency of native chiefs ; there is also a native Assembly. The control is exercised by British officials, under a Commissioner and Consul-General, who is also Commander-in-Chief of the forces. Zanzibar, British East Africa, and Uganda are manifestly approaching the stage of development in which they might be properly transferred from the control of the Foreign Office to that of the Colonial Office; and probably Somaliland will in due time be transferred to that department also.

The Anglo-Egyptian Protectorate of the Sudan is jointly administered under the Egyptian and British governments; the Sirdar, or Commander-in-Chief of the Egyptian army, being also Governor-General of the Sudan, and possessing as such the power of legislating for the protectorate by proclamation. The seven provincial governments are administered by British military officers, and the entire administration is in the hands of British officials. Britain has here undertaken the task of substantially creating and providing for the development of a new African state, extending from the border between the former Equatorial Province and Uganda in the south to Wady Halfa in the north. The Sudan is practically British territory, and its international relations are conducted in all respects on this footing.

From the North African Protectorates, all of which are controlled through other State departments, we pass to those which are administered under the Colonial Office, either directly or through other authorities subject to its ultimate control. All those of the former class are situated in Western and South Africa. The largest and most populous, consisting of the lower valley and delta of the Niger, is divided into the two Protectorates of Southern Nigeria, formerly known as the Oil Rivers Protectorate, and Northern Nigeria, formerly the field of operations of the Royal Niger Company. Southern Nigeria is administered by a High Commissioner, who is also Governor of Lagos, and is invested with the power of legislation, the various districts being under Divisional Commissioners. The civil service includes a Treasurer, judges, and an Attorney-General. The larger Protectorate of Northern Nigeria, which includes several native kingdoms, is divided for administrative purposes into sixteen provinces. It is governed by a High Commissioner, who has the power of legislation, and directs a completely organised administrative service consisting of British officials. In both protectorates there are local forces commanded by British officers.

British Central Africa is a protectorate administered under the Colonial Office by a Commissioner resident at Zomba, in the highlands of the upper Shiré river. There are twelve administrative districts, each under one or more resident officials; and this promising country is rapidly assuming the aspect of a thriving colony. Liberated from the native slave-raider and the Arab slave-trader, and educated by energetic missionaries, the native population is increasing, and to a large extent settling down under the direction of British planters to agricultural pursuits; and British-Indian immigrants have been introduced. A considerable revenue is raised, but the Imperial government contributes a grant-in-aid. The north-western portion of the original Central African Protectorate has been severed from it, and now forms part of North-Eastern Rhodesia: a fact not to be forgotten when the recent statistics of the protectorate are compared with the figures of former years.

The Bechuanaland Protectorate and Basutoland are native protectorates administered under the direction of the High Commissioner for South Africa, in whom the legislative authority is vested. The nominal authority in each remains with the chiefs, but the principal functions of government are exercised by Resident Commissioners representing the High Commissioner, with assistants in the various districts into which each protectorate is divided. Both protectorates are included in the South African Customs Union. Basutoland cannot be considered as having the character of a colony, for Europeans are not allowed to acquire land for purposes of settlement, and the limited white population consists only of government officers, missionaries, and traders who have obtained special permits of residence. Unlike the Bechuanas, the Basutos are a restless and warlike race, and their attitude is always a cause of some anxiety. The Bechuanaland Protectorate, the eastern part of which is traversed by the railway from the Cape Colony to Rhodesia, is likely in due time to become Europeanised.

The territories ceded by chiefs and sultans to commercial companies such as the British South Africa Company and the British North Borneo Company, are protected states rather than protectorates, and may be regarded as inchoate colonies. Two similar companies —the Royal Niger Company and the Imperial British East Africa Company—have resigned their charters into the hands of the British government, and their territories, after a period of administration under the Foreign Office, have now passed under the control of the Colonial Office ; and probably Rhodesia and British North Borneo will in due time be absorbed into the colonial section of the Empire in a similar way. Meanwhile these territories are administered under the Companies which acquired them, both having their offices in London. In most respects their administration approximates to the colony rather than the protectorate. Of the three districts into which Rhodesia is divided, the southern is the most advanced in development. Southern Rhodesia is governed by an Administrator appointed by the British South Africa Company, who is assisted by a Resident Commissioner nominated by the Secretary of State for the Colonies, and by an Executive Council. There is also a Legislative Council, consisting of fourteen members besides the Administrator and the Resident Commissioner, seven members being nominated by the Company, and seven elected for a term of three years by the constituencies into which the district is divided. The assent of the Imperial High Commissioner for South Africa is required to all ordinances passed by the Legislative Council, and these may be disallowed by the Secretary of State for the Colonies. Rhodesia north of the Zambesi, consisting of the districts of North-Eastern and North-Western Rhodesia, remains under the direct control of the Company. In each district there is a resident Administrator.

The territories which have been brought under British administration or protection in the island of Borneo consist of three districts: (1) the kingdom of Sarawak, under its English Rajah; (2) the State of British North Borneo, to which the British Colony of Labuan has now been united, under the administration of the British North Borneo Company; and (3) the

native Sultanate of Brunei, the parent state both of
Sarawak and of British North Borneo. All three are
under British protection, but only Brunei resembles a
protectorate in its political conditions. The administration, as in Foreign Office protectorates, remains under
the control of the Sultan, who is assisted by a Council
of native chiefs, Britain being locally represented by a
consul, subject to the Governor of the Straits Settlements
as High Commissioner. Sarawak is governed by its
Rajah, the British government being represented by the
High Commissioner at Singapore; the local administration consists of British officials. British North Borneo
is a State under British protection, governed by the
British North Borneo Company. The Company appoints
the Governor, subject to approval by the Secretary of
State for the Colonies; he is also Governor of the
Colony of Labuan, which is now united for administrative purposes with the State of British North Borneo.
There is, as in Southern Rhodesia, a Legislative Council,
which indicates the government as of colonial character :
it is here, however, as in Crown colonies, entirely
selected by nomination from the principal residents.

Next in order to the Protectorates and Protected States
above enumerated come protected districts which have
been organised, under the name of Protectorates, in
proximity to colonies previously established, and are
administered in connection with the colonial governments. These may for the most part be regarded as
destined to be incorporated in due time with the colonies
to which they are adjacent. Protectorates of this description are attached to each of the West African
colonies, and to that of the Straits Settlements. The

existing arrangements for the administration of these Protectorates will be briefly described on another page in connection with the colonies themselves.

The distinction between those Protectorates and Protected States which are open to general enterprise, on the one hand, and Council-governed colonies having a considerable native element in the population on the other, is not very sharply drawn. The general outward marks of a colony are that it is administered by a Governor, assisted by an advisory body called the Executive Council, which includes the official heads of the principal departments, and that the power of legislation is vested in a separate Legislative Council. In most colonies the members of the Legislative Council either serve in virtue of their offices, or are nominated by the Governor. In a few Council-governed colonies the nomination of a limited number of members is entrusted to public bodies; in others there are representative members, elected in local constituencies by electors having a prescribed qualification. Three Council-governed colonies have a nominated Legislative Council, and a separate Representative Assembly—a system which once prevailed more extensively, but has in all other cases been voluntarily surrendered as less suitable to the needs of the colony than that of a single legislative body. In some cases representation has been surrendered altogether, and colonies which once elected their own legislature have accepted government by a Legislative Council wholly consisting of official and nominated unofficial members. Only governments having a Legislative Council of this description are in the proper sense of the term "Crown colonies"; but all

Council-governed colonies, as distinguished from self-governing colonies, are described in popular usage as Crown colonies.

While Southern Rhodesia and British North Borneo are protectorates having substantially the character of colonies, British New Guinea and Fiji are colonies having the aspect of protectorates. British New Guinea was originally occupied in 1884 as a protectorate, and placed under the direction of a Special Commissioner. In 1888 it was annexed as a British possession, and in 1889 was organised as a colony, under a Lieutenant-Governor, subordinate to the Governor of Queensland, with an Executive Council and a small Legislative Council. There are Resident Magistrates in the various districts, and a native constabulary is organised under a British Commandant. The colony does not yet pay its expenses, and the cost of administration, which is guaranteed by the Australian Commonwealth, is practically shared between the Australian and the Imperial governments. Colonial enterprise is at present in its infancy, and the colony has the general aspect of a protectorate, the main object of government being the suppression of savage habits of life. Intoxicants and arms and ammunition are rigorously excluded, missionary work is promoted, and agricultural industry encouraged.

Fiji, although organised as a colony on the annexation of the islands in 1874, and largely developed on colonial lines by the introduction of British-Indian labourers, has in its administration much of the character of a protectorate. The native system of village and district councils has been retained, and the Governor presides

over an annual assembly of the principal chiefs and native
representatives from each of the fourteen provinces.
There are Executive and Legislative Councils, the former
consisting of the principal government officials, the latter
of ten official and eight unofficial members, three of
the latter being elected by the British colonists.   The
Legislative Council fixes the amount of taxation to be
imposed on the natives; this is paid by them in kind,
and sold by the government, the surplus, if any, being
returned to them.   Regulations enacted in the native
councils must be approved by the Legislative Council
before coming into force.

The Governor of Fiji is also High Commissioner for
the Western Pacific, and as such has the charge of various
groups of islands which have either been annexed to the
Empire or taken under British protection.   The British
Solomon Islands, to which the Santa Cruz group and
some other islands have been added, form a single
protectorate, under the direction of a Resident Commissioner.   The Gilbert and Ellice Islands, near the
equator, form another protectorate, also under the
direction of a Resident Commissioner.   The Tonga
Islands, where the sovereignty of the native king is
acknowledged, are under the direction of a British Agent
and Consul.   For the New Hebrides there is a Deputy
Commissioner.   After prolonged disputes between
Britain and France, the New Hebrides are now under
the joint protection of both powers, exercised by a
mixed commission of officers serving on the British and
French Pacific Naval Stations.

The simplest instances of the Council-governed colony,
free from the complication of a native element, are

afforded by the isolated groups of the Falkland Islands and the Seychelles. The Falkland Islands, of which Britain obtained vacant possession in 1883 for the purpose of protecting the whale fishery, are a purely European colony, now largely owing its prosperity to the Falkland Islands Company, a commercial body engaged in sheep-farming and miscellaneous trade. The Governor is assisted by a small Executive Council, and there is a nominated Legislative Council including two unofficial members. The Seychelles, a group of small islands formerly attached to the government of Mauritius, but constituted a separate colony in 1903, have a government of the same type. The white population of these romantic and productive islands is mainly of French origin. Port Victoria, the seat of government, in the island of Mahé, the largest of the group, is an Admiralty coaling station of great importance on account of its central situation.

British Honduras was in its early days a self-governed colony. The only authority recognised by the logwood-cutters who formed the settlement was vested in one of their number chosen by them to be their "king." Later they elected annually a board of "magistrates," who administered justice and levied taxation. Subsequently a superintendent was appointed by the Imperial government, and in 1853 a Legislative Assembly was established, the majority of members being elected. In 1862 the settlement became a colony subordinate to Jamaica, under its own Lieutenant-Governor; but in 1870 the Assembly was abolished, and a nominated Legislative Council substituted. In 1884 the connection with Jamaica was dissolved, and British Honduras became a

separate Crown colony under its own Governor. Both
Executive and Legislative Councils consist of the principal officials with the addition of a few unofficial
members. Belize, the seat of government, is the natural
port not only of British Honduras but, of Southern
Mexico and Northern Guatemala, and a railway connecting it with the latter country would greatly conduce
to the prosperity of the colony.

The three comparatively small colonies above mentioned represent the Crown colony in its simple form.
We now pass to instances in which Crown colonies are
either combined with others in a single government, or
are connected with adjacent protectorates, or exhibit the
rudiments of popular representation. Of the first description are the Windward Islands and Trinidad-Tobago.
The three Windward Islands — Grenada, St. Lucia,
and St. Vincent—are, in fact, three separate colonies
under a single Governor resident at Grenada. Each
has its separate Executive and Legislative Councils, each
consisting of official and nominated unofficial members,
and its own tariff and treasury; the Governor, when
absent from St. Lucia and St. Vincent, is represented
by a resident Administrator, who is also the Colonial
Secretary. Grenada and St. Vincent are among the
islands which once possessed a separate Legislative
Assembly. Trinidad and Tobago, the latter being about
18 miles distant from Trinidad, have since 1889 formed
a single colony. In that year the two Governments
were united, Tobago being assigned to a separate
Commissioner and Financial Board; but in 1899 this
arrangement ceased, and Tobago became a district of
the united colony. The Executive Council consists of

seven official members, the Legislative Council of nine official and eleven unofficial members, each of the latter being appointed to represent one of the districts into which the islands are divided. Trinidad thus possesses a local representation, but on a non-elective basis. The Immigration Department is an important branch of the public service, and the Protector of Immigrants is a member of the Legislative Council. Most of the immigrants are British-Indians, who are engaged through a permanent agent at Calcutta.

The four West African colonies—Lagos, the Gold Coast Colony, Sierra Leone, and the Gambia—offer little to distinguish them from the ordinary type of the Crown colony, except that each has a protectorate attached to its government. In each the Executive Council consists of the Colonial Secretary and the heads of the principal government departments ; unofficial members are added to these to form the Legislative Council. Connected with the Gold Coast Colony are the two separate Protectorates of Ashanti and the Northern Territories. The former kingdom of Ashanti now forms part of the British dominions, the Governor of the Gold Coast Colony being also Governor of Ashanti ; at Kumasi, the former capital, there is a British Resident. The Northern Territories are controlled by a separate Commissioner. The protectorate attached to the colony of Lagos consists of the interior country as far as the French possessions on the Middle Niger, including several small native kingdoms, which are occasionally visited by Travelling Commissioners. Southern Nigeria will shortly be incorporated with this colony. The Sierra Leone Protectorate, inhabited by several native nations, is divided into districts, each of which is assigned to a District Commissioner. Protected territories of small extent, visited from time to time by Travelling Commissioners, are attached to the Gambia Colony. As the resources of the protected territories are developed, the colonial organisations will be extended, and the protectorates will ultimately become merged in the colonies.

In the three great Eastern colonies—Ceylon, the Straits Settlements, and Hong-Kong—the principle of representation on the Legislative Council is admitted, although it is effected, as in Trinidad, on a non-elective basis. Of the eighteen members of the Legislative Council of Ceylon, one is nominated as the representative of the Kandyan Sinhalese, and one represents the Mohammadan element, the so-called "Moormen." In this prosperous colony local government by Municipalities, Road Committees, and Boards of Health is highly developed on a popular basis. The Maldive Islands, under their native Sultan, who sends an annual embassy to the Governor at Colombo, have always been a dependency of Ceylon.

The Straits Settlements consist of three separate districts combined in a single colony—Singapore, the seat of Government; Penang, in which are included Province Wellesley and the Dindings; and Malacca. The Governor is assisted by an Executive Council, of which the Resident Councillors stationed at Penang and Malacca are members. These are also members of the Legislative Council, which consists of eight official and seven unofficial members, two of the latter being nominated by the Chambers of Commerce of Singapore and Malacca. Attached to the colony of the Straits Settlements is the important Protectorate of the Federated Malay States — Perak, Selangor, the Negri Sembilan (Nine Towns), and Pahang. Each of these is governed by a native Sultan, the legislative authority being vested in a State Council composed of landowners and traders, over which the Sultan presides. In each State there is a British Resident, who is a member of the State Council. The Governor of the Straits Settlements also holds the office of High Commissioner for the Federated States, and there is at Selangor a British Resident-General, who directs the affairs of all the States, assisted by a Federal Staff consisting of the civil, judicial, and military officers at the head of the various departments of the Federal government. The Malay State of Johore, governed by its own Sultan, though not included in the Federation, is under British protection, and its foreign relations are controlled by Britain.

The Crown colony of Hong-Kong requires to be considered in two aspects. It is, in the first place, a military and naval station of the highest importance, being the headquarters of the Imperial troops in the Far East, as well as of the large squadron of men-of-war maintained on the China Station, and a first-class Admiralty dockyard. Although there is a strong Imperial garrison, to the cost of which the colony contributes, the Governor is not, as in Gibraltar, Malta, and Bermuda, a military officer. The officer commanding the troops is, however, an important member of the Executive Council. The commercial aspect of the colony, with its vast maritime trade, docks, and harbour works, is of equal importance. The Harbour Master and the Director of Public Works are members of the

P

Legislative Council, and the expenditure connected with their departments is unusually large. The Legislative Council of Hong-Kong also includes a member nominated by the local Chamber of Commerce, another nominated by the Justices of the Peace, and a Chinese resident, nominated by the Government to represent the numerous Chinese population.

The Transvaal and Orange River colonies are at present constituted under a single Governor, who is also the Imperial High Commissioner for South Africa, and in this latter capacity supervises the administrations of the Bechuanaland Protectorate and Basutoland. Swaziland, annexed by the former Transvaal Republic in 1894, remains under its native queen as a protectorate, included in the present colony. The Transvaal and Orange River colonies have each its own Lieutenant-Governor, Executive Council, and Legislative Council, the members of both Councils being nominated by the Crown. Elected members representing constituencies, consisting of members having a prescribed qualification, will probably be in due time added to the Legislative Council of each colony. An Inter-Colonial Council meets for the transaction of financial business common to the two colonies, chiefly concerned with the construction and management of the railways, and both colonies are included in the South African Customs Union.

The remaining Council-governed colonies,—Malta, Cyprus, Mauritius, British Guiana, and the five older West Indian colonies—the Leeward Islands, Jamaica, Bermuda, the Bahamas, and Barbados—have in their Councils a measure of popular representation on an elective basis. In Malta, Cyprus, Mauritius, British

Guiana, the Leeward Islands, and Jamaica elected representatives sit on or with the Legislative Council; in Bermuda, the Bahamas, and Barbados the elected representatives constitute a separate Assembly. In Malta the Legislative Council is termed the Council of Government, and consists of ten official members and eight representatives, one for each of the districts into which the colony is divided. Representation, originally less limited in its extent, was granted in 1849. Malta being an Imperial naval and military station of the first importance, the Commander-in-Chief of the fortress is always, as in Gibraltar and Bermuda, the Governor of the colony.

Cyprus is divided into three electoral districts, each returning to the Legislative Council one Mohammadan and three Christian members. The electoral franchise is a liberal one, every tax-payer having a vote. The Governor has the title of High Commissioner. For administrative purposes the island is divided into six districts, each under a subordinate Commissioner. Although Cyprus still forms part of the Turkish dominions, and is not likely to be utilised as an Imperial "place-of-arms,"—the purpose for which it was stated to be acquired,—Britain has made considerable grants-in-aid to the administration, and loans have been raised on British credit, and expended on railways, harbours, and irrigation works.

The Executive Council of Mauritius consists of five official and two elected members. The Legislative Council consists of eight official members, nine appointed by nomination, and ten elected by constituencies—two for Port Louis, the capital, and one for each of the eight districts into which the island is divided. The elective

element was introduced so recently as 1885, in somewhat tardy fulfilment of a promise made on the cession
of the island, which had enjoyed representative institutions under its last French government. Next to
Ceylon and the Straits Settlements, Mauritius is the
principal immigration colony in the tropics, and the
Protector of Immigrants, who is in charge of the
Immigration Department, has a seat in the Legislative
Council. The French of Mauritius are republican in
sentiment, and greatly value their political privileges.
Port Louis, the capital, has an elected municipal corporation. The island of Rodrigues, where there is a
resident magistrate, the four islands forming the Chagos
group, and some minor islands, are dependencies of
Mauritius. Diego Garcia, the chief island of the Chagos
group, is an important coaling station on the direct route
from the Red Sea to Australia.

The government of British Guiana, which is founded,
with some modifications, on the original Dutch government of the colony, presents peculiar features. Originally
the only Colonial Council was that called the Court of
Policy, which discharged under the Governor executive
as well as legislative functions. In 1892 the work of
administration was transferred to a separate Executive
Council, consisting of six official members, and three
unofficial members appointed by nomination. The Court
of Policy, as at present constituted, consists of five
official members and eight elected members, and dis-
charges the usual functions of a Legislative Council, with
the exception of levying taxation. For financial purposes
there is a " Combined Court," consisting of the members
of the Court of Policy, and six " Financial Representa-

tives," elected by the people. Most of the electors are coloured people, and coloured men are found among the representatives. The Immigration Agent-General is a member of the Court of Policy, and immigration is conducted through an agent stationed at Calcutta.

In Trinidad, Mauritius, and British Guiana the immigration system is gradually transforming the aspect of the colony; and its effects are seen to a less degree in Jamaica. After serving under contract a term of five years on a sugar estate, under regulations which ensure to him fair and even generous treatment on the part of his employer, the immigrant is entitled, if he so pleases, to his passage back to India, whither he often returns with his savings. In the majority of cases he either remains in the colony or returns to it, becoming either a free labourer, a shopkeeper, or a cultivator of hired or purchased land. His children, who have been educated at the public expense, grow up as colonists, and a new class of citizens is thus gradually being created, which in Mauritius numbers, together with the contract labourers on the estates, two-thirds, and in British Guiana and Trinidad one-third, of the entire population—a class more industrious and thrifty than the negroes, and destined in the end, to judge from the case of Mauritius, to become small landed proprietors.

The last group of Council-governed colonies includes the original English colonies in the West Indies—the Leeward Islands, to which the formerly French island of Dominica has been added; Jamaica, with the Turks and Caicos Islands; Bermuda; the Bahamas; and Barbados. All the original English West Indian colonies once possessed separate Councils and Representative

Assemblies, the Virgin Islands, and, as at present, the
Bahamas, counting each as a single colony, and Anguilla
being regarded as a district of St. Kitts ; each had its
own Governor and government staff, but for defence
purposes the Leeward Islands were included in a single
command, the Governor of Antigua being Captain-General
of the forces.   This arrangement has now been extended
to the civil administration, each island retaining, nevertheless, a limited measure of home government.   Hence
the constitution of the colony of the Leeward Islands is
somewhat complicated.   It consists of five Presidencies :
(1) Antigua, with Barbuda and Redonda ; (2) St. Kitts
and Nevis, with Anguilla ; (3) Dominica ; (4) Montserrat;
and (5) the Virgin Islands.   There is a single Governor,
resident at Antigua, a General Executive Council, and a
General Legislative Council.   The chief administrative
officer in each of the subordinate governments—called
in Antigua the President, in St. Kitts and Dominica the
Administrator, in Montserrat and the Virgin Islands the
Commissioner—presides in each over a local Executive
Council, and, excepting in the Virgin Islands, a local
Legislative Council.   The General Legislative Council
alone contains an elective element.   It consists of eight
official members, and eight elected by the constituencies.
The Councils of the subordinate governments are composed of nominees.   Each Presidency has its own tariff and
treasury.   The Danish West Indian islands—St. Thomas,
Ste. Croix, and St. John—and the island of St. Martin,
which is Dutch, except a small portion belonging to
France, form geographically part of the Virgin Islands
group.

In Jamaica the Executive Council retains its old

title of Privy Council. The Legislative Council consists of twenty-four members, ten of whom are officials,
or unofficial members appointed by nomination : the
remaining fourteen are elected by the inhabitants, one
for each of the parishes into which the island is divided.
The present constitution dates from 1866, when the
separate Representative Assembly, after an existence of
more than two centuries, was abolished. The Turks
and Caicos Islands, geographically belonging to the
Bahamas, were in 1873 annexed to the government of
Jamaica, and are now administered by a resident Commissioner, subordinate to the Governor of Jamaica.
These islands have a Legislative Board, which controls
local finance and enacts local ordinances, subject, however, to a concurrent power of legislation vested in the
Legislative Council of Jamaica. There is at Port Royal
a naval station and dockyard, and at Kingston an Imperial garrison, the officer in command having a seat on
the Legislative Council. Immigration from British India
is encouraged, and there is a Protector of Immigrants,
but without a seat on the Council.

The only Council-governed colonies now possessing
separate Representative Assemblies are Bermuda, the
Bahamas, and Barbados. In Bermuda the Executive
Council, as in Jamaica, is called the Privy Council.
Both the Privy Council and the Legislative Council
consist of official members and unofficial nominated
members. The House of Assembly consists of thirty-
six members, four being elected for each of the nine
parishes into which the islands are divided, eight of
these being in the Main Island. In Bermuda, which is
dependent on external supplies for its corn and meat,

the character of a fortress predominates over that of a colony; and the Commander-in-Chief of the forces is also the Governor. One of the islands—Ireland Island —is entirely given up to the naval dockyard and other naval establishments.

The Bahamas have Executive and Legislative Councils constituted in the usual forms, and the Representative Assembly consists of twenty-nine members representing the fourteen districts into which the islands are divided. About thirty of these fertile islands are inhabited, and twelve have resident officials. Nassau, the seat of government, is in the island of New Providence. Although little developed, the Bahamas are a colony of great economic promise, and production is being rapidly extended by the aid of government Agricultural Boards. The aggregate area of the islands is equal to that of Jamaica, and most of it lies outside the tropical line. About a fourth of the population is of European descent, and the islands, which are in almost all respects unlike the rest of the West Indies, offer excellent prospects for resident British enterprise.

In Barbados, where the proportion of white inhabitants is remarkably high, being 12 per cent of the whole, and the negro and coloured population are unusually prosperous and intelligent, the franchise is a liberal one, and the constitution secures to the Assembly a greater degree of influence over the Executive than is found elsewhere in the tropical colonies. As in other Council-governed colonies, there is an Executive Council, consisting of official and unofficial nominated members; there is a nominated Legislative Council : there is also, as in the Bahamas and Bermuda, a Legislative Assembly, annually elected. What is peculiar to Barbados is the "Executive Committee," which consists of the members of the Executive Council, one member of the Legislative Council, and four members of the House of Assembly, nominated by the Governor. The Committee thus constituted prepares the colonial estimates, introduces votes of supply, and initiates all government measures. Barbados is the headquarters of the Imperial forces in the West Indies, and the officer in command is a member of the Executive Council. The command extends to all the British West Indies except Jamaica, and includes British Guiana.

In passing from the Council-governed colonies to the self-governing ones we turn to a class of governments of a fundamentally different character; and something should here be said of the advantages conferred on the former by the species of administration they enjoy. The principal of these cannot be better stated than in the words of an American observer : "The administration is entirely in the hands of trained officials, free from local prejudice, absolutely forbidden to engage in any trade, or to be in any way connected with any commercial undertaking, and unhampered by the constant antagonism of local elected assemblies. . . . It is to the manifest interest of the officials to govern well, for the better they govern the more likely are they to obtain promotion; and the Secretary of State for the Colonies is well informed as to the work of candidates for promotion in the service, since the Governor of each colony is required to send home each year a confidential report of the work of his officers." [1]   Such an adminis-

---

[1] Alleyne Ireland, *Tropical Colonisation*, p. 69.

tration is especially qualified to hold an even balance
between the ever-conflicting interests of land and capital
on the one hand, and labour on the other, and between
differing capitalist interests, such as mining, planting, and
general commerce : to give the policy of the colony that
continuity which alone gains the permanent confidence
of investors, and to enable every colony to profit by the
experience gained in others.   The Councils of colonies
of this description are not dominated by numerical
majorities.   Every element represented obtains a hear-
ing, deference is always paid to local experience and
economic knowledge, and in raising public revenue
suggestions made by the elected members are usually
carried into effect.   Self-governing colonies, on the
other hand, are liable to all the evils which inevitably
result from party government.   Scattered as their
inhabitants are over much larger areas than is the case
in Council-governed colonies, they are less amenable to
the personal influences best qualified to guide them ;
the best men often shrink from the toils and annoyances
of political life ; and the conduct of affairs tends to fall
into the hands of organisations formed for promoting
sectional interests, and to be largely directed by one-
sided and irresponsible newspapers.   The best way,
perhaps, of obviating these dangers, to which the smaller
self-governing colonies are the least exposed—is to
give stability to the legislature by keeping one of its
branches free from the disadvantages incident to popular
elections.   This is done in Newfoundland, Natal, the
Cape Colony, and Canada.   In Australia both branches
of the legislature are popularly elected ; New Zealand
occupies in this respect a middle position between

the four governments above mentioned and that of
Australia.

The constitution of Newfoundland has scarcely been
changed in its general outline by the grant of responsible government in 1855.   There is an Executive
Council, consisting, besides the Governor, of four
ministers at the heads of departments (the Colonial
Secretary, the Minister of Justice, the Minister of
Finance and Customs, and the Minister of Agriculture
and Mines), and four other members.   The members
of Legislative Council, not more than fifteen in number,
are appointed for life by the Governor in Council.   The
House of Assembly consists of thirty-six members,
elected for eighteen districts, by all the male population
of full age.   The House is elected for four years.   The
Atlantic coast of the peninsula of Labrador, sparsely
occupied by a fishing population, is included in the
colony.   The Imperial government organises and maintains in Newfoundland a branch of the Imperial Naval
Reserve.   The long-agitated question of French fishing
rights has in the present year been settled on terms
entirely satisfactory to the people of the colony.   The
question whether Newfoundland should join the
Dominion of Canada is still occasionally mooted, but
cannot be considered as at present within the scope of
practical politics.

The government of Natal is largely modelled on
that of the Cape Colony, presently described.   In Natal
the Executive Council, which is in fact a Cabinet formed
by the Prime Minister, consists of five heads of departments, the Treasurer, the Colonial Secretary, the
Minister of Justice and Education, the Minister of

Lands and Works, the Secretary for Native Affairs, and the Minister of Agriculture. The Legislative Council consists of twelve members nominated by the Governor in Council to serve for ten years, one-half retiring every five years. The Legislative Assembly consists of forty-three members representing fifteen districts, and elected for a term of four years by electors possessing a property qualification. The natives, who greatly outnumber the white population, live chiefly in tribes upon sections reserved for them by government, but partly on lands held by missionary bodies, partly as squatters, paying a quit-rent, on Crown lands, and partly as labourers on the lands of colonists. The tribal organisation has been superseded; there is a separate Native High Court with its own judge, and a British magistrate resides in each tribal area. Zululand, formerly a separate British protectorate, was in 1897 incorporated with the colony of Natal, and is represented by one member in the Legislative Council, and two in the Legislative Assembly.

In the Cape Colony the Upper House, or Legislative Council, consists of twenty-three members elected for seven years, who represent a division of the colony into eight provinces; the Lower House, or House of Assembly, of ninety-five members elected every five years, and representing a large number of urban constituencies. The same voters, who must possess a property qualification, elect to both houses; and there is a property qualification for membership of the Upper House. The Ministry, or Cabinet, consists of five members: the Treasurer, the Colonial Secretary, the Commissioner of Works, the Secretary for Agriculture, and the Attorney-General. Colonists of Dutch descent predominate in the western part of the Colony, while the eastern is mainly British. Natives are found everywhere; but the Transkei, Tembuland, East Griqualand, and Pondoland, all in the extreme east, bordering on Basutoland and Natal, are the chief native districts. The native tribes are controlled through their chiefs by officials under the Cape government. The anti-British party in the colony, created and maintained by the intrigues of the Transvaal and Orange River Boers, is fast losing ground, and it is anticipated that in a few years the mutual animosity of the English and Dutch colonists, engendered by events which culminated in the recent war, will cease. There is an Imperial garrison at Cape Town, independent of the Cape government; the Governor, who is also Commander-in-Chief, having a military secretary and staff. At the neighbouring naval station of Simon's Bay, the headquarters of the Cape and West Africa squadron, there is a first-class dockyard. The port of Walfish Bay, situated within the tropic on the coast of Damaraland, and surrounded on other sides by the German protectorate, forms part of the Cape Colony, and there is here a resident magistrate.

In New Zealand, as in Newfoundland, the Legislative Council, consisting of forty-six members, is nominated by the Governor in Council; the members, as in Newfoundland, formerly held their seats for life, but their tenure of office is now limited to seven years. The House of Representatives consists of eighty members elected for three years. The Executive Council is a Cabinet nominated by the Prime Minister, consisting of the heads of the chief departments. A Maori chief serves on the Executive Council; there are also two Maoris on the Legislative Council, and four members of the House of Representatives are Maoris returned by the voters of the four native districts. Of the nine provinces into which the Colony is divided four are in the North Island and five in the South Island; but local government is founded on a division into counties. The Cook Islands, forming a federation nominally subject to the native queen of Raratonga, are included in the colony of New Zealand, and are administered under the Governor by a British Resident stationed at Raratonga. In the "Fortunate Islands of the South," as New Zealand has been called, the currents of social and political life run smoothly. Every species of interest is in a thriving condition; labour is well paid and contented, and the apprehensions aroused by the Industrial Conciliation and Arbitration Act, which took effect in 1895, have not been realised. So far from capital having been withdrawn from the colony, the amount invested in industrial undertakings has since that date increased by one-half, and is still increasing.

The federal constitutions of Canada and Australia are framed on the principle, already illustrated in the cases of the Windward and Leeward Islands, of uniting several colonies under a single government for certain purposes. Prominent among these purposes are the establishment of a single fiscal area by the abolition of internal customs duties; the organisation of general post-office and telegraph services, and of a common system of local defence; and there are other matters in which uniformity of legislation and unity of adminis-

tration are manifestly desirable. In Canada and
Australia federal union has been approached from a
different standpoint. In Canada full legislative powers
on the most important matters have been conferred on
the Federal Government, other specified matters being
reserved to the provinces. In Australia, as in the
United States, the general control of legislation remains
with the original colonies, power being conferred on
the Federal Government to legislate in certain matters
and assume the control of certain administrative departments. While the functions of the Central Government
cover nearly the same ground, that of Canada has more
extensive powers than that of Australia. In Canada,
for example, only the Governor-General is appointed
by the Imperial Government, the Lieutenant-Governors
who preside over the Provincial Governments being
appointed by the Governor-General in Council; the
Governors of the States in Australia are appointed by,
and remain in direct communication with, the Imperial
Government. The Federal Government of Canada has
the power of disallowing within a year laws passed by
the Provincial Legislatures ; this power, which is seldom
exercised, is unknown to the Australian constitution.
In Australia the transfer of authority and responsibility
from the States to the Commonwealth is far from completed, at present only the customs and excise, and the
postal and defence services being controlled by the
Federal Government ; the central administration of the
Dominion covers a more extensive field. In Canada the
greater part of the public debt—much smaller than the
aggregate of the public debts of Australia—has been
transferred to the Federal Government ; in Australia

each State remains responsible for its own public liabilities. In Canada the whole of the customs and excise revenue is collected and retained by the Federal Government, the fixed subsidies paid to the Provincial Governments amounting to only a fraction of the national income derived from these sources; in Australia three-fourths of the corresponding revenue is handed over to the State Governments. The State Governments are more prominent in Australia, the Federal Government in Canada.

The distinction above indicated corresponds in some degree with a dissimilarity of geographical conditions. Canada is enclosed within natural or political boundaries on all sides, excepting the comparatively narrow sea-boards at its eastern and western extremities, and its development naturally proceeds by steps on internal lines. With one of the great Powers on its principal flank, and the others, including the parent country, within a few days' steam, it stands in the midst of the world's affairs. Such circumstances point to the necessity of a strong Central Government as a means of pushing on internal development, and consolidating the Dominion as rapidly as possible into a self-balanced and self-acting whole. Australia, on the other hand, at the antipodes of Europe and North America, but easily accessible in all parts to the outside world, can only be developed from the several States established on its coasts as independent centres of movement. Without much danger to its position in the world, it can take its own time in the process of unification, can carry this process as far as it chooses, can indulge in experimental legislation, and leave problems for posterity to solve which Canada has deemed it necessary to grapple with at once.

The greater importance retained by the Legislatures of the Australian States, as compared with those of the Canadian provinces, is illustrated by the fact that the former without exception adhere to the British precedent of a double legislative chamber, while the latter, with the exceptions of Quebec and Nova Scotia, have abandoned it. In each of the Australian States there is a Legislative Council and a Legislative Assembly, the latter having about twice the numerical strength of the former, and limited in every State to a duration not exceeding three years. The numbers vary from 38 in Tasmania to 125 in New South Wales. All male citizens of full age are entitled to vote, and in South Australia, as in New Zealand, the electoral franchise has been extended to women. The Legislative Councils vary in their constitution. In New South Wales and Queensland the members are nominated by the Provincial Governor in Council, and hold their seats for life. In the other provinces they are elective, a property qualification being required for both members and electors. In Victoria, Western Australia, and Tasmania the Council has a duration of six years. In South Australia one-third of the members, twenty-four in all, retire every three years. The Executive Council in each case consists of the Ministers in charge of the chief administrative departments, who vary in number from four in South Australia to eleven in New South Wales, with the addition in most cases of one or more members without portfolio. Members of this Council must be members of one of the chambers, or must become so within a limited time;

they may speak in either chamber, but may only vote in that to which they belong. Norfolk Island, a dependency of New South Wales, 1250 miles distant from Sydney, has a Resident Magistrate and a local elective Council.

The Commonwealth Parliament consists of a Senate and a House of Representatives, the latter having about twice the numerical strength of the former. Each State elects six senators, who hold office for six years, the elections being so arranged that half the number retire every three years. Everywhere except in Queensland all the electors vote for senators as a single constituency. The electorates in each State return to the House of Representatives a number of members proportionate to the State population, with a minimum number of five. At present New South Wales and Victoria together return nearly two-thirds of the whole number, having twenty-six and twenty-three members respectively; Queensland returns nine, South Australia seven, Western Australia and Tasmania five each. The House of Representatives has a maximum duration of three years. Prolonged conflict of opinion between the House of Representatives and the Senate is obviated by a provision that in such a case the Senate may be dissolved, and a new Senate elected. The Executive Council of the Commonwealth consists of seven Ministers—the Minister for External Affairs, the Attorney-General, the Minister for Home Affairs, the Treasurer, the Minister for Trade and Customs, the Minister for Defence, and the Postmaster-General.

The federal system of Canada differs conspicuously from that of Australia in the constitution of the Senate.

The senators are appointed for life by the Governor-General in Council. Instead of an equal representation for each of the provinces, as in Australia, the number of senators appointed to represent each province is proportionate to the population of the province, more than half the members in each being assigned to Ontario and Quebec. Senators must possess a property qualification. In the House of Commons the populous provinces of Ontario and Quebec predominate in a still greater proportion, returning nearly two-thirds of the members. The executive power is vested in the King's Privy Council, which consists of fourteen Ministers at the head of government departments, and two Ministers without portfolio.

The Provincial Governments of Canada are eight in number—Ontario, Quebec, Nova Scotia, New Brunswick, Prince Edward Island, British Columbia, Manitoba, and the North-West Territories. Out of the vast tract comprised under the last-named denomination the provisional districts of Assiniboia, Alberta, Saskatchewan, Athabasca, and Keewatin have been organised for electoral purposes, and will in due time be constituted as provinces. The unorganised portion of the territories to the northward has also been divided into four districts, named Ungaya, Franklin, Yukon, and Mackenzie. At no distant date Canada will therefore consist of sixteen provinces. All the existing provinces excepting Quebec and Nova Scotia are organised on the principle of a single chamber. The Legislative Assembly of Ontario consists of ninety-two members, representing ninety-one electorates, and has a maximum duration of four years. The Executive Council consists, besides the Lieutenant-

Governor, of seven heads of the provincial departments, chosen by the Prime Minister from the members of the Assembly.   Toronto, the chief city of the province, is the seat of the Provincial Government.   The Provincial Governments of New Brunswick (capital Fredericton), Manitoba (capital Winnipeg), the North-West Territories (capital Regina, in the district of Assiniboia), and British Columbia (capital Victoria) are similarly constituted, the number of members being roughly proportionate to the population.   Quebec and Nova Scotia have provincial constitutions organised on the principle of a double chamber.   There is in each, besides the popularly-elected Assembly, a Legislative Council of twenty-four members in Quebec, of twenty-one in Nova Scotia, who are appointed in the name of the Crown by the Lieutenant-Governor in Council, and hold office for life. Members of the Executive Council, which consists of the heads of departments, with one or more members without portfolio, may be selected from either chamber.

The Party system—the succession to power of the "ins" and the "outs," of a responsible government and a vigilant opposition—prevails in the self-governing colonies in varying degrees, and is organised in each on different lines.   Both in Canada and Australia there existed, previously to the grant of self-government, an anti-British party bent on severing the connection with the parent country in its then existing form.   By the grant of self-government this party lost its footing, and questions of local policy, most of which have now been settled, continued for some years to divide the electorates in each.   In general, parties are now organised on lines similar to those in the United

Kingdom, under the labels "liberal" and "conservative," but are chiefly dependent for cohesion on the
influence of individual politicians, who have earned
public confidence by parliamentary and administrative
ability.   In Canada the "liberal" party is now in
power, having ousted the liberalised "conservative"
ministry in 1896.   In the Commonwealth, where
ministries have for some time held office by the support
of the independent "labour" party, this party has been
installed in office, largely, however, in consequence
of the apathy of the electorate, the majority of whom
could probably not be counted on to support it on a
future appeal to the constituencies.   In the Cape
Colony an ostensibly loyal ministry, relying for support
on the Dutch vote, has recently given place to a "progressive" ministry formed on liberal imperial lines.

It remains to show how the colonies and federations
are politically connected with the Imperial Government.
The strongest bond of union between the parent country
and its offshoots is doubtless that sense of a common
patriotism to be exercised, and of a common destiny to
be wrought out under varying conditions, which comes
of descent from the same stock, and of free institutions
derived from the same source, and enjoyed by the same
title.   The common economic interests of the various
members of the Empire are links of a more tangible
kind, and they are capable of being strengthened and
multiplied.   Political ties are more varied in their nature,
and more complicated in their operation ; and they are
felt in different degrees in different sections of the
Empire.   A colony so closely connected with the
Imperial government as Gibraltar or Bermuda is for

practical purposes as much a part of the parent country as the Isle of Man or the Channel Islands. In the Council-governed colonies generally there is a strong feeling of attachment, especially on the part of the labouring population, to the monarchy and the Sovereign's personality—a feeling closely connected with a sense of the protection afforded by the British connection; in the capitalist class this feeling is equally marked, and is reinforced by experience of the attention paid by the home government to the nation's colonial interests. In the self-governing colonies and the Federations the sense of political connection may tend to become dormant, in the ordinary course of affairs, during times of peace. But it everywhere subsists and is vigorously awakened, with a tendency to develop into a sense of co-ordination and alliance, whenever war, or the menace of war, darkens the horizon; nor are circumstances of urgency necessary to prove its vitality whenever Imperial interests are in any way affected or called in question. First among the visible links which unite the Empire stands that of common allegiance to the Sovereign. Associated in the highest degree with splendour of national achievement, wealth of national resource, and permanence assured from age to age, the British Crown is in every respect a fitting exponent of Imperial dominion. In the Sovereign's name every colonial governor receives his commission, every legislative Act is passed and colonial legislature is convoked, every colonial court of justice issues its writ. The currency bears his image and superscription; every festal assembly unites in singing the anthem, "God save the King." The 24th of May, being the birthday of the late Queen, has been observed as a national holiday, under the name of " Empire Day," in the schools of five out of the six self-governing colonies and federations, and of a large proportion of the others. The celebration has been extensively introduced in the elementary schools of the United Kingdom, and will doubtless become universal throughout the Empire. In Canada, " Empire Day " has been accepted as a general festival, preliminary to the celebration of Dominion Day (July 1) ; and it is emphatically marked as such by the adjournment of the Dominion Parliament. The day has been happily chosen, for no period in Imperial history could be fraught with events more momentous, be marked by progress more brilliant and more uniform, or give rise to auspices more propitious, than the reign of Queen Victoria.

In each colony the Sovereign is represented by the Governor, in Canada and Australia by the Governor-General. Colonial governors constitute an important class of British officials, for on their tact and judgment the preservation of harmonious relations between the parent country and the colonies in a great measure depends. The most important governorships are usually filled by eminent peers of the realm, or by distinguished officers in the British army or navy. Many capable governors have risen from subordinate positions in the Colonial service ; in exceptional cases appointments have been made from the official staff of the Colonial Department in London. Governors are appointed by letters-patent under the Great Seal, and hold office during the pleasure of the Crown ; but it is understood that their tenure shall not, as a rule, extend beyond six years from the assumption of their duties. Although the Governor

is the Crown's vicegerent in the colony, he does not
possess general sovereign power, his authority being
limited by his commission, by the laws of the colony,
and by the general regulations of the Home Government ;
and he is liable, like any other subject, to be sued in
the courts of the colony.   Though usually invested with
the title of Captain-General or Commander-in-Chief, he
does not actually command the forces, unless specially
commissioned in that behalf.   It is his duty to repel
aggression and to suppress piracy, but he has no power of
declaring war against any foreign State, or against the
subjects of any foreign State.   As the head of the civil
government he issues writs for the election of legislative
councils and representative assemblies, convokes and pro-
rogues the legislative bodies, and dissolves, when such a
measure is proper, those which are subject to dissolution.
He withholds, or grants, as the case may be, the assent of
the Crown to Bills passed by the legislative bodies ; this
power, however, is limited by his instructions, which
direct him to reserve certain Bills—usually such as deal
with the currency, the army and navy, differential duties,
the effect of foreign treaties, and matters affecting the
parent country, for the direct assent of the Crown at home,
or to assent to such Bills only with a clause suspending
their operation until they have been confirmed at home.
He issues warrants for the expenditure of public moneys,
grants pardons, respites, and remissions of fines and
penalties, and appoints and suspends public officers.
It is his duty to send regularly to the Home Government
the " Annual Blue Book " of the colony, containing
returns of the colonial revenue and expenditure, and
copies of all laws passed by the Colonial Legislature.

In most matters pertaining to his office the Governor acts in session with the Executive Council. Here a broad line of demarcation separates the Council-governed colonies from the self-governing colonies. In the former the councillors are only a consultative body; and although in some colonies it is held as constitutional doctrine that the Governor can do no official act without their concurrence, he has the power of overruling them, and acting on his own judgment, relying for his justification on the support of the Home Government. In such cases dissentient members usually record their adverse opinions for transmission home. The Governor has the power of suspending councillors, but the Crown alone, acting through the Home Government, can dismiss them from their office. In ordinary circumstances the Governor, having usually had less experience of the affairs of the colony than the majority of the Council, defers to their opinion. In the self-governing colonies and federations the Governor or Governor-General has no such overruling power. The Executive Council being practically a committee of the Legislature, formed under the direction of a Prime Minister supported by parliamentary majorities in the chambers, the Governor is little more than an instrument of the Council, and the practical control of affairs rests with the Prime Minister and his colleagues. Although deprived of the initiative in legislative and administrative matters, the Governor may, as the representative of the Crown, the Home Government, and the parent country generally, exercise by his personality, social bearing, and public utterances a powerful and salutary influence on colonial opinion, as well as on the policy of the Ministry. The acquisition and

maintenance of such an influence is the true test of a
Governor's success.

The devotion of the self-governing colonies and
federations to those free political institutions—identical
in object, and almost identical in substance, with her own
—which Britain has implanted in her offshoots beyond
sea, ranks even before identity of economic interests
as a bond of Imperial union.   These are the "similar
privileges" which a statesman of the past, in memorable
words, described as "ties which, though light as air,
are strong as links of iron.   Let the colonists," he
continued, "always keep the idea of their civil rights
associated with your government—they will cling and
grapple to you, and no force under heaven will be of
power to tear them from their allegiance."   Burke's
prophecy has been fulfilled, in a broader sense, in other
colonies than those intended by him.   " . . . The spirit
of the English constitution, infused through the mighty
mass, pervades, feeds, unites, invigorates, vivifies every
part of the Empire, even down to the minutest member.
. . . Slavery they can have anywhere.   It is a weed
that grows in every soil.   They may have it from Spain,
they may have it from Prussia.   Freedom they can have
from none but you.   This is the commodity of price of
which you have the monopoly."[1]   Britain has been
called the "mother of Parliaments": no other nation
can claim a similar title.   In their Parliaments the
colonies possess a heritage with associations only less
ancient, not less splendid and imperishable, and more
closely interwoven with their daily life, than those
connected with the Crown itself.   Inspired with this

[1] *Speech on Conciliation with America.*

feeling, the free colonists of Barbados called their island
"Little England." Those of Canada and Australia are
making each of those countries a greater England.
But their work, if performed in the spirit of their calling,
and we doubt not that it will be so performed, must
embrace the whole Empire as its sphere. The public
man who wins the confidence and influences the policy
of a colonial assembly knows himself to be doing something more than attending to the business of his colony.
He is carrying on the work of the British statesmen
who in bygone centuries founded, enlarged, or secured
the Empire of which that colony forms part. He
knows that he may in due time be called on to meet
their successors in personal conference, to co-operate
with these in solving Imperial problems, and to carry
on in concert with them the never-ceasing work of
Imperial policy. The Britannic Empire is the first
school—to all appearance the only school destined ever
to exist—of co-operative statesmanship on a world-wide
scale.

Closely connected with the attachment of the colonists
to their political institutions is their attachment to the
varied laws under which they live—laws mainly based
on the law of England, and in all cases brought to their
existing form by continuous modification and addition
according to English precedents, in response to local
needs and aspirations. Subject only to necessary safe-
guards, each of the fifty or more colonial governments
has a free hand in modifying and developing its local
law, whether derived, as in colonies originally British,
from the common and statute law of England, or, as in
colonies obtained by cession or conquest, from the

jurisprudence of other countries.   Among legal systems
of foreign origin found in the colonies the most conspicuous is the Roman Dutch law, long superseded in
the Netherlands, but still forming the "common law,"
or basis of existing law, in the Cape Colony, Natal, the
Orange River Colony, the Transvaal, the Bechuanaland
Protectorate, and Rhodesia, as well as in British Guiana
and Ceylon—that is, over a total area more than half the
size of the Roman empire at its greatest extent.   The
old French law, according to the custom of Paris, is the
nucleus of the civil law in Quebec Province and St.
Lucia; the modern French Civil Code, in Mauritius and
the Seychelles; the old Spanish law, in Trinidad; the
old Sicilian feudal law, modified by ordinances of the
Order of St. John, in Malta, once a fief of the kingdom
of Sicily.   Colonial legislators, whether in the Council
or the Assembly, have built on existing foundations
with the freedom that might be expected of an age
penetrated with the spirit of Bentham, and in some
instances may be thought to have pushed the principle
of the greatest happiness of the greatest number to the
verge of imprudence.   In Australia, it must be conceded,
the interests of Britannic citizens outside the Commonwealth have not been treated with much consideration.
Elsewhere, perhaps, the coloured immigrant and the
native have been regarded with a too-partial eye.
Colonial legislation responds readily to the necessities,
real or fancied, of the day—a circumstance which goes
far to disarm criticism, for its underlying policy is
thereby deprived of the character of finality.

The bond of union above indicated is widely and
deeply rooted in those subordinate departments of local

public activity, which fill a larger space in the daily life
of the Britannic citizen than politics in the ordinary
sense of the term.   The familiar elements of British
local government have been introduced in the colonies
wherever and to such an extent as circumstances admit.
The county, the municipality, and the parish or town-
ship, with their boards and committees of various
descriptions, afford the same sort of training to the
colonial citizen as the corresponding institutions of the
parent country afford to the British citizen at home.
This training, again, which has the advantage of being
economic rather than political, is rooted in the admirable
educational systems, varied in many ways, but all
framed on British models, which exist in every colony,
from the largest to the least; and in the larger ones
fill every grade of civic requirement, from the village
day-school to the technical college and the State
university.   Every colonial child is brought up, by the
mere necessity of the situation, to be a citizen of the
Empire.   The day must come—it is distant as yet—
when the same can be said of every British child.   But
Britain is Anglicising half the world—not the colonies
and protectorates alone, but the populous nations of the
Far East—and the people of Britain are scarcely aware
of the fact.   Somebody has said that the most probable
dissolvent of the Britannic Empire in the future is
ignorance.   Much ignorance there undoubtedly is; and
it must be admitted that although British educators are
at length waking up, the Empire, its nature, history,
resources, peoples, and prospects are less understood in
the parent country than in the colonies.

Largely as a consequence of the causes above indicated,

there lives and works throughout the Empire that principle of integral cohesion which is the recognised condition of all political stability. It may be that in others of the world's great states this principle operates in equally full measure ; but nowhere does it operate quite in the same way, or at all on the same scale. Its peculiar action in the Empire may perhaps be connected with the action of a similar principle in the parent country—an aggregate of remarkable stability, though composed of two ancient and once bitterly hostile kingdoms, an imperfectly assimilated principality, and an insular dependency conquered and colonised in comparatively recent times. "The Empire" has been by some denounced or derided as a misleading abstraction.   There are others who, having approached the subject from this point of view, have ended in the conviction that, with all the defects of its existing organisation—and these are many—it is as much a substantive reality as the composite United Kingdom from which it springs. In both there is the same pervading sense of the possession of a common and rather peculiar civilisation, and the same conviction that this civilisation is worth preserving, and worth keeping intact.   It is a civilisation which, like many other things, is most easily described in terms of what it is not.   It is not aristocratic nor democratic ; it might be called aristodemocratic.   It is not the civilisation of a dry-rotten bureaucracy, out of all sympathy with the people, and as obsolete at bottom as that of China itself.   It is not a brain-cram and jack-boot civilisation.   It is not a dollar-for-its-own-sake civilisation.   Be it what it may be, it is something which no country outside the Empire has got. Impersonal in its operation, it is something founded on the average personality of the Britannic citizen. It is something which respects and is disposed to be satisfied with what exists, is not prone to imitation, and adapts itself slowly to the state of facts, the course of events, and the changeful character of circumstances, but possesses, nevertheless, initiative as well as staying power; which can distribute itself with ease by many channels, and increase its original energy in each; which develops the man all round, and applies itself equally to business, to local government, and to politics; which is interested in science, and in charitable and philanthropic work, likes society and club-life, loves sport and miscellaneous reading, and is devoted to country pursuits, after-dinner speeches, and travel by land and sea; which thinks life worthless unless based on fair play and straight dealing, and incomplete unless equally developed in the home, the local district, the state, and, we will add with confidence, the Empire.

From those connecting links between the parent country and the colonies which exist in colonial institutions we turn to the elements and agencies in the parent country which link it with its colonial offshoots. Here, again, we begin with the Crown. The personality of the Sovereign counts for more, as an element of substantial connection between the heart of the Empire and its distant members, than those who have not visited the colonies would readily believe. Constitutionally, the Sovereign is merged in the Imperial Parliament, of which he is the hereditary head. In the Imperial Parliament the colonies are specially represented by the Secretary of State for the Colonial Department, who is a member of the Cabinet, and by a parliamentary under-secretary attached to the same department. Distinguished colonists have been created peers, while others represent constituencies in the House of Commons; some members of both Houses have served the Crown in the colonies as governors or minor officials, and some others, not immediately connected with the colonies, are distinguished for knowledge of colonial affairs, often obtained by personal observation.

According to the strict canon of constitutional law the Imperial Parliament retains authority over the whole of the Empire, and has even power to revoke or alter the constitutions of the self-governing colonies. This power has never been exercised, and its application could only be justified as a last resource, when all prospect of the satisfactory working of existing institutions had vanished. A recent crisis in the Cape Colony, when anti-imperial feeling among the Dutch ran high at the conclusion of the Boer War, was thought at the time to call for its exercise. Happily, the crisis passed without any necessity for interference. The power of revoking the constitution of Natal was reserved to the Crown by the Act authorising responsible government. A less drastic remedy against ill-considered action on the part of colonial legislatures is the power of withholding the Crown's assent to their Bills. Occasionally there has been some difference of opinion between the Imperial government and the legislature of a self-governing colony as to the propriety of particular measures, or of the form in which they have been passed, but the difference has been adjusted by negotiation, and direct conflict of authority avoided.

Of all the bonds between Britain and her Colonies the most prominent and effective is their common system of defence, in which the first place belongs to the Imperial navy. An empire distributed along all the world's great maritime highways necessarily rests on naval power, and in the case of Britain and her chief Colonies the navy is of unique importance to national and Imperial life. No nation in the world is so dependent as Britain on importation for its food supply. No countries are more dependent on a single market —that of Britain—for their general prosperity, than are Canada, Australia, and New Zealand. Hence, the oceanic supremacy of the Imperial navy, the existence of Britain as a nation, and the prosperity of the chief Colonies, are correlative facts; were the first lost, the rest must follow. It is idle to imagine that in such a case the Colonies, in their existing stage of under-population and imperfect development, could survive as political units. They must pass into the hands of the Power or Powers that had driven the Imperial navy from the seas. Such Powers as could aspire to perform, or rather to assist in performing, this feat already possess colonial dependencies; and these they would naturally, and indeed must necessarily, seek to augment by annexing the Colonies of Britain. For no Power derives from its colonial possessions any strategic advantages comparable for a moment with those which her widely distributed Empire confers on Britain.

The question where, from the political and strategic points of view, the strength and the weakness of the Empire chiefly lie recalls an ancient fable. We are reminded of

R

> . . . the Gardens fair
> Of Hesperus, and his Daughters Three,
> That sing about the Golden Tree.

The ocean gardens of Hesperus were guarded by a single dragon. Defenceless in themselves, their safety from spoliation depended solely on the swiftness of the dragon's wings, and the sharpness and strength of his beak and talons. The fable is a perfect allegory of Imperial defence. In the effective conduct of its operations the navy, like the dragon, is an indivisible unit; centralised in mechanism and intelligence, it is universal in vigilance and organisation. The question on what part of the Empire the wolf's eye is chiefly cast is really an idle one. Whichever colony may be the prize fought for, the blow that could secure it, and the blow which must defend it, must alike be struck wherever the main fighting strength of the enemy happens to be, and would probably be struck within the patrol of the Channel Fleet, whose Station extends from Gibraltar to the coasts of Norway and Scotland. Yet the Empire, as we have pointed out,[1] has its weak side—the Australasian colonies, the farthest removed from the Imperial centre and strategic base in the northern hemisphere.

Australasians, who are well aware of the weakness of their position, believe that the wolf's eye is cast more favourably on their colonies than on any other. The robber's hand, it is urged, could not be laid on Canada; for although neither on the part of the Empire nor of the Dominion are her defences adequately organised, she holds a strong position against European attack, and

[1] Pp. 25-27.

the States and the Monroe Doctrine rise threateningly
in the background.   In South Africa also, the would-be
intruder, had he not already burned his fingers, must
for other reasons be content to "let 'I dare not' wait
upon 'I would.'"   There remains, as the spoil of a blow
to be successfully aimed at Britain, Australasia ; in the
opinion of many the "pick" of the Empire, if not of
the globe ; inhabited by well-to-do, comfortably-living,
pleasure-loving people, none too numerous, and prone
to imagine, and to imagine very vainly, that their
Golden Gardens can be maintained against invasion and
rapine by their own coast and internal defences.

It is notorious that only in the recently founded
German Empire have aspirations avowedly based on
the prospective spoliation of the Britannic Empire
been cherished in recent times.   Probably German
ideas on the subject have been modified by the events
of the past twenty years ; but there is no doubt that
during a longer period such aspirations have been
seriously entertained.   They arose to some extent out of
a misunderstanding for which the blame rests largely
with British politicians.   Before 1880 it seemed probable
that the national reaction against that policy of indifference, and even hostility, to the Colonies, which had
come in with Free Trade, would be maintained.   When,
in 1880, Mr. Gladstone was reinstated in power by large
electoral majorities, it seemed as though this reaction
had failed : a conclusion apparently confirmed by the
acts of the new ministry and the utterances of its sup-
porters.   Especially misleading was a pamphlet, entitled
"British Colonial Policy," issued among the manifestoes
of the "National Liberal Federation."   Printed in large

type, and extensively circulated, this remarkable production was accepted abroad as Britain's authorised
national programme in colonial matters.   It was declared to be the interest of Britain to get rid of colonial
connections, to abstain from further extension, and, so
far from obstructing similar designs on the part of
foreign Powers, to encourage them, on the Machiavellian
principle that their resources and energies would thus
be squandered, and that any colonies founded by them
would become hostages for good behaviour to a Power
whose navy commanded the ocean.   Deaf to the warning,
Germany snapped at the bait, and is now writhing upon
the hook.   Aspirations, hitherto vague, took definite
shape, and the flood-gates of a reckless expenditure on
the foundation of colonies, and subsequently on the construction of a "battle-fleet" destined to increase their
number, were opened.   Germany was prospering, and
this luxury was one which she could afford.

It could be shown by inference from events, even were
it not known as a fact, that these aspirations took the
form of a regular scheme for the construction of a brand-
new "world-empire," and that the intended ecumenic
dominion stretched out towards, and was intended to
include and culminate in, the British colonies of
Australasia.   Hatched from the brain of a Prussian
pedagogue, this scheme readily commended itself to
German statesmen.   The intended empire was to move
in the concentric orbits of an Inner and an Outer Circle.
Both were to be approached by an entirely new "world-
route," leading from central Europe, through Asia
Minor and the Euphrates valley, to the Persian Gulf.
The Inner Circle consisted of the African coasts generally,

the main positions being Zanzibar, Nigeria, and Morocco ;
Damaraland was suggested by the events of 1881. The
Outer Circle was reached by prolonging the new "world-
route" from the Persian Gulf to the Dutch Indies ;
drawn on a map according to Mercator's projection,
this route takes an almost straight line from the Danube
to the Java Sea. The Dutch Indies—a portion of the
"Dutch heritage" almost as valuable as the Netherlands
—were to be the keystone of an arch resting on
Australasia in the south, and China in the north, as its
two substantial abutments and foundations.[1] Pending
favourable opportunities for bolder strokes, Germany
began by picking up unconsidered trifles in the Pacific,
between China and Australasia—the Pelew, Ladrone,
Caroline, and Marshall groups. None of these were of
importance to Britain. The annexation of New Britain
with New Ireland and the adjacent islands, and of
north-eastern New Guinea, and the claim advanced to
the Solomon Islands, were steps of other significance.
Here Germany, by a masterly negligence on the part of
British statesmen, was allowed to bestride the direct route
from Sydney and Brisbane to Hong-Kong, Shanghai,
and Japan. France had avoided this pitfall, but Germany fell into it with open eyes. The names " New
Britain " and " New Ireland "—the former conferred on

[1] As to China, the seizure of Kiau-chau, the Germanisation of
Shan-tung, and an undisguised ambition for further extension are
evidence enough. As to Australasia, the annexation of Northern New
Guinea—the question once asked by Bismarck of the British
Government, What parts of the Australian continent were claimed
by Britain ?—the suggestion that Australia forms part of the " Dutch
heritage " by its association historically with such names as Carpentier
and Tasman, surviving in existing local nomenclature, and the
existence of 10,000 Germans and Scandinavians in the colony of
South Australia alone—are significant indications.

the principal island by Dampier, its discoverer—were
ostentatiously abolished, and the whole group was de-
nominated "the Bismarck Archipelago."

For the accomplishment of her scheme Germany
counted not only on the abandonment by Britain of her
Imperial policy, but on the weakness of France, the
prostration of Spain and China, and the indifference of
America and Japan. The events of 1894 and 1898 led
to consequences which took her completely by surprise.
Largely as a result of the China-Japan and Spanish-
American wars, an iron barrier has now been drawn
round the embryo "world-empire." No extension is
possible northwards and westwards into Chinese waters,
for the States are established in the Philippines, Japan
in Formosa and Loo-choo. To the southward a boundary line between the Britannic Empire and Germany
has been drawn through New Guinea and the Solomon
Islands; beyond these lie British Melanesia and Fiji,
Australia and New Zealand, British Polynesia and the
French colony of New Caledonia. The Samoa group,
which includes the most valuable of the German Pacific
Islands, is surrounded by British possessions, and the
eastern islands of the group belong to the United States.
Guam, the largest of the Ladrone Islands, also belongs
to the States.

But our survey of the new "world-empire" is not yet
complete. Following the Outer Circle by the homeward
route eastward by way of New Zealand, the first place
touched at after rounding Cape Horn is the British
colony of the Falkland Islands—already more frequented
by German than by British shipping, and an excellent
base, if in German hands, for naval operations against

Argentina and Uruguay, in each of which republics there are many thousand German colonists. Beyond Uruguay, in the southernmost of the United States of Brazil—Santa Catharina and Rio Grande do Sul—there reside about 400,000 colonists of German descent. The republican government of Brazil being none of the strongest, Germany might begin operations here by claiming a protectorate over her expatriated sons; and a similar process might take place in Venezuela and Mexico. In the neighbourhood of Venezuela the "Dutch heritage" again comes conveniently in. Dutch Guiana and the Dutch West Indian Islands—Margarita, Curaçao, and St. Martin—are already almost within Germany's grasp; while St. Thomas, the commercial centre of the West Indies, and some other of the Virgin Islands, are Danish. Unfortunately for all these aspirations, the United States points to the Monroe Doctrine and bars the way. Taking the Inner and Outer Circles together, it will be seen that the proposed "world-empire" represents designs against the world's peace on too great a scale to have much chance of success; for Germany has succeeded in arraying against her, not merely Britain and the States, but France, Holland, Denmark, Belgium, Portugal, Spain, Japan, and every Power in South America worth considering, except Chile.

The British navy stands first among the world's peace-keeping forces. Its main strength is necessarily retained in home waters, forming two squadrons—the Home Fleet and the Channel Fleet. For the purpose of operations elsewhere the world's waters are divided into eight sections or "Stations," each corresponding to some portion, large or small, of the Colonial Empire.

Adjoining home waters on the west are those of the
North American and West Indian Station; on the
south the Mediterranean and Red Sea Station.   In each
of these the navy rests as its bases of distant action on
two first-class fortresses—Halifax and Bermuda in the
west, and Gibraltar and Malta in the south.   Beyond
the Mediterranean and Red Sea Station stretches to the
southward the field of operations defined as the Cape
and West African Station, and to the eastward the
East Indian Station.   Beyond the last lie the China
Station on the north, the Australasian on the south ; and
beyond these, again, the vast expanse of waters forming
the Pacific Station.   West of the Cape and West African
Station is the South Atlantic Station.   Each of these
Stations forms the field of operations of a squadron
under a flag officer.   The strength of the squadrons varies
from time to time according to the exigencies of the
service ; those posted at either end of the great maritime
highway of the Old World—the Mediterranean and Red
Sea squadron in the west, and the China squadron, in
the Far East—are by necessity the strongest next to
the Home and Channel squadrons.   No others include
battleships, and all the battleships on these Stations are
of the first class.   These two extreme Stations are linked
by the field of the East Indian squadron.

For the purpose of maintaining the fleet in efficiency,
the Imperial government maintains dockyards, victualling yards, and coaling stations on colonial soil in all
parts of the Empire.   The chief dockyards outside the
United Kingdom are at Malta and Gibraltar, Hong-
Kong, Simon's Bay, Sydney, Bermuda, Halifax, Jamaica
(Port Royal), and Esquimalt ; there are minor ones at

Ascension and Trincomalee; the Admiralty also provides dock accommodation at Antigua, Bonny (Southern Nigeria), St. Helena, and Port Said. The construction of naval works will probably be soon resumed at Wei-hai-wei. The Indian government maintains dockyards at Bombay and Calcutta. Attached to the principal dock-yards are victualling yards and medical establishments, and every dockyard contains coal stores on a large scale. Among the coaling stations the most important are at Aden, Labuan, Fiji, Sierra Leone, and St. Lucia, Port Stanley (E. Falkland), Colombo, Diego Garcia, Mahé, Mauritius, and Zanzibar. The principal ports of Australia and New Zealand are also coaling stations. There are Imperial garrisons at the principal naval bases, in some cases supplemented by colonial forces, and partially paid for out of colonial revenues. Con-siderable sums have been expended by the Imperial and Colonial governments in fortifying ports, dockyards, and coaling stations ; but expert opinion is adverse to an extension of such a policy, the only real defence being command of the sea.

In all the Colonies except the self-governing ones of Australasia, the direction of naval defence is undertaken by the Imperial government. The colonial navies of the Commonwealth and New Zealand consist of small flotillas of torpedo boats and gunboats, manned by local naval brigades; and Victoria and Queensland possess each a coast defence vessel. There is a small volunteer naval corps in Natal, and others are shortly to be formed in Canada and elsewhere. The main defence, however, of all the Colonies lies in the strength of the Imperial fleet, maintained in readiness for action in close proximity to the sources of foreign war-power within certain limited areas in the northern hemisphere. In view of this, all the self-governing colonies except Canada follow the example of British India in making appropriations out of revenue in aid of Imperial naval expenditure. The Commonwealth contributes £200,000, New Zealand £40,000, the Cape Colony £50,000, Natal £35,000, and Newfoundland £3000, making a total colonial contribution of £328,000, or less than a hundredth part of the cost of the navy to the parent country. It is generally felt throughout the Colonies that this contribution is disproportionate to their aggregate wealth and the magnitude of their sea-borne trade; and, thanks largely to the energy of the British Navy League, the propriety of gradually increasing it is being more and more recognised by colonial opinion.

Of the local military forces maintained by the self-governing colonies, that of Canada is the most perfectly developed. The "active militia" of Canada, together with the small body of "permanent militia" or regular force which supplies technical training to the active militia, numbers about 40,000 men, besides a large reserve. The force is completely organised in every branch, including infantry, cavalry, mounted rifles, field and garrison artillery, engineers, and subsidiary services, and the Dominion government maintains an efficient military college. The military forces of the Commonwealth, distributed in the various States, and of the Cape Colony and Natal are largely composed of volunteers. The colony of the Straits Settlements maintains a large local force of armed police, and there are volunteer corps at Penang and Singapore, as well as in Ceylon and Hong-Kong. These colonies also contribute to the cost of the Imperial army in respect of the garrisons of their ports. Ceylon makes a contribution of £130,000, the Straits Settlements £117,500, Hong-Kong £76,400. Other colonies making contributions in the same respect are Mauritius £26,200, Canada (for Esquimalt only, the more costly garrison of Halifax being entirely paid for by Britain) £22,100, the West African Colonies £5000, exclusive of the cost of military expeditions; Malta £5000, and Natal £4000. Native military forces are employed in special circumstances. The West India Regiment, battalions of which are stationed in Jamaica, Sierra Leone, and Bermuda, consists of negroes; the native forces of the Gold Coast and Lagos are excellent soldiers; and a Chinese regiment, now disbanded, was formed for service at Wei-hai-wei.

The Imperial system of defence cannot be said to be at present equal to the needs of the day, much less to larger demands impending in the future. The potential resources of Britain and her Colonies are probably adequate to any contingency; but the existing machinery of the Empire is incapable of promptly calling them forth, and employing them effectively as a single fighting machine. The maritime superiority of Britain was attained in the course of international rivalries which mainly affected home waters, and the Atlantic and Indian oceans. The past half-century has made the Far East the seat of international jealousies and conflicting interests more dangerous in their character, and doubtful in their issues, than any hitherto known. The entire strength of all other Powers claiming a voice in the settlement of these issues is capable of being exercised by undivided authority ; nor is there any reason why that of Britain and her Colonies, which have no conflicting interests, should not be so organised as to be capable of similar action, by the constitution of a permanent Imperial board of defence.   What remains to be done has often been pointed out. The self-governing colonies require to be represented on the existing Defence Committee of the Imperial Cabinet, by the periodical attendance, for purposes of consultation, either of their Defence Ministers, or of one or more deputies specially com- missioned to represent such Ministers.   The Imperial Defence Committee has already summoned the Canadian Defence Minister to its assistance, and a beginning has thus been made which should lead to an effective organisation of defence for the whole Empire.

It unfortunately happens that the exigencies of the public service sometimes conflict with the interests of political parties.   Recent occurrences in Canada, in relation to the dismissal of the late Commander-in- Chief of the Militia, will occur to the reader.   They are here mentioned because of the fundamental connection of this matter with another urged by the writer at an earlier stage in this volume — the completion of the Trans-Canada railway.   That undertaking, of equal importance economically and strategically, was in 1903 practically brought to a standstill by the present Dominion Parliament at the instance of influential capitalists interested in the Grand Trunk Pacific scheme —a scheme which, if carried out, must weaken the strategic position, and could not for a moment compete with the Trans-Canada as a means of developing Canadian resources over the widest possible area.   The

Conservative party recognise that if successful at the elections which are now impending, one of their first measures ought to be the annulment of the powers conferred on the Grand Trunk, and the grant of greater facilities for prosecuting an enterprise which has long contended with difficulties, but is gaining ground, and from a national point of view is an indispensable one. In such circumstances, apart from the incidents above alluded to, those who regard the security and economic progress of Canada as a matter of greater importance than the return to office of a particular group of politicians, will readily decide which side shall have their sympathy and assistance in the coming struggle.

We have exceeded our limits, and must be content barely to mention the organisations and functionaries constituting the administrative and auxiliary machinery of the Empire in London: (1) the Colonial Office, of late years increased in importance by the development of the tropical colonies and the establishment of the African protectorates, and controlled by Ministers who have approached their task in another spirit, and with other qualifications, than predecessors who could publicly deride the inefficiency and narrowness of a public department which they had been paid to direct, and which it was their duty to have reformed; [1] who could serve their terms of official life, and quit office in ignorance of cardinal facts affecting the very existence of colonies of the first importance; [2] and who could meet appeals on the

[1] Who amongst other things publicly repeated the wretched jest of " Mr. Mother-Country "—the clerk who, having directed the affairs of the Colonial Empire from a closet in Downing Street, went home to dinner on the top of the Clapham omnibus.

[2] The late Lord Cardwell, for instance, believed that all the Dutch in South Africa had migrated to the " Free States," and that the Cape

part of inchoate protectorates destined to become, under
other auspices, valuable members of the Empire, with the
parrot cry—"The Queen has black subjects enough";[1]
(2) the Agents-General maintained in London by
the self-governing colonies, among whom the High
Commissioner for Canada, raised to the peerage for
public services, stands first,[2] and the incorporated Crown
Agents for the Colonies, who transact the financial and
other business of the lesser colonies in London, and
pass through their hands annually funds to the amount
of nearly a hundred millions sterling; (3) the Judicial
Committee of the Privy Council, which decides final
appeals not only from certain courts of the United
Kingdom, but from those of India, and from the fifty
judiciaries of the Colonies,[3] each administering its
own body of laws—a task demanding a versatile and
discriminative ability which no other bench in the
world, perhaps, could provide; and (4) the Order of
St. Michael and St. George, established in 1818 for
recognising military and naval services rendered in

Colony was entirely English (Froude, *Oceana*, chap. iii.). The disastrous mistakes committed under Lord Kimberley and Lord Carnarvon
are partially attributable to ignorance, but in the case of the former
chiefly to the influence of Mr. Gladstone, who was at the head of the
government.

[1] The late Lord Derby, following the policy embodied in a resolution
passed by a former House of Commons.

[2] Nova Scotia and New Brunswick employ separate Agents-General.
The Australian Dominion is not specially represented, each State maintaining its own Agent-General. New Zealand, Cape Colony, and Natal
have each its own Agent-General; Newfoundland, alone among the
self-governing colonies, has none, and transacts its business through
the Crown Agents for the Colonies.

[3] Appeals are permitted to be brought from the Supreme Court of
Canada and that of Australia only by special leave. The Australian constitution, unlike the Canadian, excludes from the jurisdiction of the
Privy Council disputed matters arising under the constitution between
the States.

defending the recently extended Empire, and now
numbering many hundreds of distinguished knights and
companions.[1] Nor ought we to forget the numerous
societies, clubs, leagues, and other voluntary institutions established for promoting intra-imperial union and
communication, many of which have done and are still
doing valuable service.[2]

[1] The Order was intended to commemorate the incorporation of
Malta with the Empire, and to replace the disestablished Maltese
Order of St. John ; it also referred to the protectorate assumed over
the Ionian Islands. Distinguished residents of both were eligible as
recipients of the honour. The scope of the Order has long been enlarged
to include the whole Empire, and members of the Colonial service and
others are now admitted to it. AUSPICIUM MELIORIS AEVI was adopted
as the motto of the Order. The archangel Michael was the celestial
protagonist in the wars of heaven and hell (Apocalypse of John, chap.
xii. v. 7 : compare Epistle of Jude, v. 9, and Book of Daniel, chaps.
x., xii.). A French Order of St. Michael, having for its motto the
phrase IMMENSI TERROR OCEANI, had been established in 1469. Its
principal seat was Mont St. Michel, Normandy.

[2] Among these (apart from missionary and emigration societies)
the useful and flourishing society called the Royal Colonial
Institute (established 1868) was, it is believed, the first. Soon
afterwards came the Imperial Federation League, dissolved in 1893,
when the British Empire League was established to succeed it as an
organisation for furthering its main objects, while avoiding the
fallacies with which it had been associated. The cry of "Imperial
Federation " was useful in its day, but its day was soon over. The
argument in favour of a new Imperial federal government, empowered
to control the existing governments of the United Kingdom and the
Colonies, rested on a fallacy which seems to have entirely escaped
the observation of the many worthy persons who advocated it.
"Where there is a Federation," it was said (we copy from a very good
book on the subject), "there must of necessity be a Federal government."
What would be thought of a writer on Statics who laid down that
where there was composition of forces there must of necessity be a
new force to control the forces compounded ? The natural sense of
" Federation " is " alliance," a better word. The true note was
struck in the preface to the *Times*' collection of its Annual Summaries
from 1851 to 1875, by a distinguished writer, who described the
principal Colonies as having, during that period, "risen to the rank
of free States and valuable allies."

INDEX

257   S

THE END

Printed by R. & R. CLARK, LIMITED, *Edinburgh.*

𝔗𝔥𝔢 𝔈𝔫𝔤𝔩𝔦𝔰𝔥 ℭ𝔦𝔱𝔦𝔷𝔢𝔫:

A SERIES OF SHORT BOOKS ON

HIS RIGHTS AND RESPONSIBILITIES

EDITED BY SIR HENRY CRAIK, K.C.B., M.A. (OXON), LL.D. (GLASGOW).

Crown 8vo.

THIS series is intended to meet the demand for accessible information on the ordinary conditions and the current terms of our political life.

The series deals with the details of the machinery whereby our Constitution works and the broad lines upon which it has been constructed.

The books are not intended to interpret disputed points in Acts of Parliament, nor to refer in detail to clauses or sections of those Acts; but to select and sum up the salient features of any branch of legislation, so as to place the ordinary citizen in possession of the main points of the law.

THE ENGLISH CITIZEN SERIES.